Instructor's Guide

College Algebra

Fifth Edition

James Stewart
McMaster University

Lothar Redlin
The Pennsylvania State University

Saleem Watson
California State University, Long Beach

Prepared by

Douglas Shaw
University of Northern Iowa

BROOKS/COLE
CENGAGE Learning

Australia • Brazil • Japan • Korea • Mexico • Singapore • Spain • United Kingdom • United States

ISBN-13: 978-0-495-56527-7
ISBN-10: 0-495-56527-X

Brooks/Cole
10 Davis Drive
Belmont, CA 94002-3098
USA

Cengage Learning is a leading provider of customized learning solutions with office locations around the globe, including Singapore, the United Kingdom, Australia, Mexico, Brazil, and Japan. Locate your local office at: **international.cengage.com/region**

Cengage Learning products are represented in Canada by Nelson Education, Ltd.

For your course and learning solutions, visit **academic.cengage.com**

Purchase any of our products at your local college store or at our preferred online store **www.ichapters.com**

For product information and technology assistance, contact us at **Cengage Learning Customer & Sales Support, 1-800-354-9706**

For permission to use material from this text or product, submit all requests online at **www.cengage.com/permissions**
Further permissions questions can be emailed to **permissionrequest@cengage.com**

READ IMPORTANT LICENSE INFORMATION

Printed in the United States of America
1 2 3 4 5 6 7 11 10 09 08

Preface

The purpose of this *Instructor's Guide* is to save you time while helping you to teach a nice, honest, interesting, student-centered course. For each section, there are suggested additions to your lecture that can supplement (but not replace) things like the factoring of $x^2 + 3x + 2$ or the simplification of $2\sin x \cos x$. Lecturing is not your only option, of course. This guide provides group activities, ready for reproducing, that will allow your students to discover and explore the concepts of algebra. You may find that your classes become more "fun", but I assure you that this unfortunate by-product of an engaged student population can't always be avoided.

This guide was designed to be used with *College Algebra, Fifth Edition* as a source of both supplementary and complementary material. Depending on your preference, you can either occasionally glance through the *Guide* for content ideas and alternate approaches, or you can use it as a major component in planning your day-to-day classes. In addition to lecture materials and group activities, each section has examples, sample homework assignments, and reading quizzes.

For many students, college algebra is the class where they decide whether or not they are good at math, and whether or not they like it. Among those students who do go on to take calculus, one major stumbling block for many is trigonometry. Therefore, teaching college algebra and trigonometry is an important and noble task. It is my hope that this book will make that task a little easier.

This guide could not have been completed without the help of many people. For giving me this opportunity, I thank Jim Stewart, Lothar Redlin, Saleem Watson, Bob Pirtle, and Gary Whalen. Natasha Coats has been a great editor who has brought together many different documents on very short notice whenever I asked for anything; I appreciate her work. Thanks to Job Evers, Ken Doss, and especially Melissa Pfohl for their proofreading and suggestions for previous editions of this guide. Kate Degner gave this edition a very thorough read, and many excellent changes came as a result of her ideas. My wife Laurel's support and love throughout this and all of my projects have been key to their completion. In addition, she did the research for the exponent group work, and proofread many others. If you like the way this book looks, if you admire the clarity of the graphics and the smoothness of its design, join me in thanking Andy Bulman-Fleming, one of the best typesetters in the business.

This book is dedicated to my brother Gordon. In honor of his advancing age, I now admit three things in print that I've never admitted to him in person. First, he is much better at chess than I am. I used to study for weeks before every "casual" Thanksgiving game. Secondly, he is a half-inch taller than I am. Every time we went back-to-back as youths I would cheat and put improvised lifts in the back of my shoes. Lastly, he does *not* have a peanut head. I invented that slander in sixth grade out of whole cloth, and it became a habit.

You are an awesome guy, G.A., and I'm glad you are my brother.

Douglas Shaw
University of Northern Iowa

Contents

P | Prerequisites 1

1 | Equations and Inequalities 45

2 | Coordinates and Graphs 77

How to Use the Instructor's Guide

For each section of *College Algebra, Fifth Edition*, this *Instructor's Guide* provides information on the items listed below.

1. **Suggested Time and Emphasis**   These suggestions assume that the class is fifty minutes long. They also advise whether or not the material is essential to the rest of the course. If a section is labeled "optional", the time range given is the amount of time for the material in the event that it is covered.

2. **Points to Stress**   This is a short summary of the big ideas to be covered.

3. **Sample Questions**   Some instructors have reported that they like to open or close class by handing out a single question, either as a quiz or to start a discussion. Two types are included:

   • **Text Question:** This question is designed for students who have done the reading, but haven't yet seen the material in class. These questions can be used to help ensure that the students are reading the textbook carefully.

   • **Drill Question:** These questions are designed to be straightforward "right down the middle" questions for students who have tried, but not necessarily mastered, the material.

4. **In-Class Materials**   These suggestions are meant to work along with the text to create a classroom atmosphere of experimentation and inquiry.

5. **Examples**   These are routine examples with all the computations worked out, designed to save a bit of time in class preparation.

6. **Group Work**   One of the main difficulties instructors have in presenting group work to their classes is that of choosing an appropriate group task. Suggestions for implementation and answers to the group activities are provided first, followed by photocopy-ready handouts on separate pages. This guide's main philosophy of group work is that there should be a solid introduction to each exercise ("What are we supposed to do?") and good closure before class is dismissed ("Why did we just do that?")

7. **Homework Problems**   For each section, a set of essential **Core Exercises** (a bare minimum set of homework problems) is provided. Using this core set as a base, a **Sample Assignment** is suggested.

Tips on In-Class Group Work

This *Instructor's Guide* gives classroom-tested group work activities for every section of *College Algebra, Fifth Edition*. One reason for the recent surge in popularity of in-class group work is that *it is effective*. When students are engaged in doing mathematics, and talking about mathematics with others, they tend to learn better and retain the material longer. Think back to your own career: didn't you learn a lot of mathematics when you began teaching it to other people? Many skeptics experiment by trying group work for one semester, and then they get hooked. Pick a group activity from the guide that you like, make some photocopies, and dive in!

1. Mechanics

Books and seminars on in-class group work abound. I have conducted many such seminars myself. What follows are some tips to give you a good start:

(a) **Do it on the first day.**

The sources all agree on this one. If you want your students to believe that group work is an important part of the course, you have to start them on the first day. My rule of thumb is "at least three times the first week, and then at least once a week thereafter." I mention this first because it is the most important.

(b) **Make them move.**

Ideally, students should be eye-to-eye and knee-to-knee. If this isn't possible, do the best you can. But it is important to have them move. If your groups are randomly selected, then they will have to get up and sit in a different chair. If your groups are organized by where they are seated in the classroom, make them move their chairs so they face each other. There needs to be a "break" between sitting-and-writing mode and talking-to-colleagues mode.

(c) **Use the ideal group size.**

Research has shown that the ideal group size is three students, with four-student groups next. I like to use groups of four: if one of them is absent (physically or otherwise), the group still has three participating members.

(d) **Fixed versus random groups.**

There is a lot of disagreement here. Fixed groups allow each student to find her or his niche, and allow you to be thoughtful when you assign groups or reassign them after exams. Random groups allow students to have the experience of working with a variety of people. I believe the best thing to do is to try both methods, and see which works best for you and your students.

(e) **Should students hand in their work?**

The advantage of handing in group works is accountability. My philosophy is that I want the group work to have obvious, intrinsic benefit. I try to make the experience such that it is obvious to the student that they get a lot out of participating, so I don't need the threat of "I'm grading this" to get them to focus. I sometimes have the students hand in the group work, but only as a last resort.

2. Closure

As stated above, I want my students to understand the value of working together actively in their groups. Once you win this battle, you will find that a lot of motivation and discipline problems simply go away. I've found the best way to ensure that the students understand why they've done an activity is to tell them. The students should leave the room having seen the solutions and knowing why they did that particular activity. You can have the students present answers or present them yourself, whatever suits your teaching style. I've had success with having groups write their results on transparencies and present them to the class (after I've checked their accuracy).

Here is another way to think about closure: Once in a while, give a future homework problem out as a group work. When the students realize that participating fully in the group work helps them in the homework, they get a very solid feeling about the whole process.

3. Introduction

The most important part of a group activity, in my opinion, is closure. The second most important is the introduction. A big killer of group work is that awful time between you telling your students they can start, and the first move of pencil on paper—the "what on earth do we do now?" moment. A good introduction should be focused on getting them past that moment. You don't want to give too much away, but you also don't want to throw them into the deep end of the swimming pool. In some classes, you will have to say very little, and in some you may have to do the first problem with them. Experiment with your introductions, but never neglect them.

4. Help when you are needed

Some group work methods involve giving absolutely no help when the students are working. Again, you will have to find what is best for you. If you give help too freely, the students have no incentive to talk to each other. If you are too stingy, the students can wind up frustrated. When a student asks me for help, I first ask the group what they think, and if it is clear they are all stuck at the same point, I give a hint.

5. Make understanding a goal in itself

Convey to the students (again, directness is a virtue here) that their goal is not just to get the answer written down, but to ensure that every student in their group understands the answer. Their work is not done until they are sure that every one of their colleagues can leave the room knowing how to do the problem. You don't have to sell every single student on this idea for it to work.

6. Bring it back when you can

Many of the group works in this guide foreshadow future material. When you are lecturing, try to make reference to past group works when it is appropriate. You will find that your students more easily recall a particular problem they discussed with their friends than a particular statement that you made during a lecture.

The above is just the tip of the iceberg. There are plenty of resources available, both online and in print. Don't be intimidated by the literature—start it on the first day of the next semester, and once you are into it, you may naturally want to read what other people have to say!

How to Implement the Discovery Projects

One exciting yet intimidating aspect of teaching a course is projects. An extended assignment gives students the chance to take a focused problem or project and explore it in depth—making conjectures, discussing them, eventually drawing conclusions and writing them up in a clear, precise format. *College Algebra, Fifth Edition* has many Discovery Projects throughout. They are excellent and well thought out, and should be explored if possible. Here are some tips on ensuring that your students have a successful experience.

Time   Students should have two to three weeks to work on any extended out-of-class assignment. This is not because they will need all this time to complete it! But a fifteen-to-twenty-day deadline allows the students to be flexible in structuring their time wisely, and allows the instructors to apply fairly strict standards in grading the work.

Groups   Students usually work in teams and are expected to have team meetings. The main problem students have in setting up these meetings is scheduling. Four randomly selected students will probably find it very hard to get together for more than a few hours, which may not be sufficient. One way to help your students is to clearly specify a minimum number of meetings, and have one or all group members turn in summaries of what was accomplished at each meeting. A good first grouping may be by location.

Studies have shown that the optimal group size is three people, followed by four, then two. I advocate groups of four whenever possible. That way, if someone doesn't show up to a team meeting, there are still three people there to discuss the problems.

Before the first project, students should discuss the different roles that are assumed in a team. Who will be responsible for keeping people informed of where and when they meet? Who will be responsible for making sure that the final copy of the report is all together when it is supposed to be? These types of jobs can be assigned within the team, or by the teacher at the outset.

Tell the students that you will be grading on both content and presentation. They should gear their work toward an audience that is bright, but not necessarily up-to-speed on this problem. For example, they can think of themselves as professional mathematicians writing for a manager, or as research assistants writing for a professor who is not necessarily a mathematician.

If the students are expected to put some effort into the project, it is important to let them know that some effort was put into the grading. Both form and content should be commented on, and recognition of good aspects of their work should be included along with criticism.

One way to help ensure cooperation is to let the students know that there will be an exam question based on the project. If every member of the group does well on that particular question, then they can all get a bonus, either on the exam or on the project grade.

Providing Assistance   Make sure that the students know when you are available to help them, and what kind of help you are willing to provide. Students may be required to hand in a rough draft ten days before the due date, to give them a little more structure and to make sure they have a solid week to write up the assignment.

Individual Accountability   It is important that the students are individually accountable for the output of their group. Giving each student a different grade is a dangerous solution, because it does not necessarily encourage the students to discuss the material, and may actually discourage their working together. A better alternative might be to create a feedback form. If the students are given a copy of the feedback form ahead of time, and they know that their future group placement will be based on what they do in their present group, then they are given an incentive to work hard. One surprising result is that when a group consists of students who were previously slackers, that group often does quite well. The exam question idea discussed earlier also gives individuals an incentive to keep up with their colleagues.

How to Use the Review Sections and Chapter Tests

Review sections for chapters of a textbook are often assigned to students the weekend before a test, but never graded. Students realize they won't be evaluated on this work and often skip the exercises in place of studying previous quizzes and glancing at old homework. A more useful activity for students is to use the review sections in *College Algebra, Fifth Edition* to discover their precise areas of difficulty. Implemented carefully, these are a useful resource for the students, particularly for helping them to retain the skills and concepts they've learned. To encourage more student usage, try the following alternatives:

1. As the course goes on, note the types of exercises which caused difficulties. During a review session, assign students to work on similar exercises in the review sections and go over them at the end of class. Also assign exercises reminiscent of the ones you plan to have on the exam.

2. Use the review section problems to create a game. For instance, break students into groups and have a contest where the group that correctly answers the most randomly picked review questions "wins". One fun technique is to create a math "bingo" game. Give each group a 5×5 grid with answers to review problems. If you laminate the cards, and give the students dry-erase markers, then you can use them year after year. Randomly pick review problems, and write the questions on the board. Make sure that for a group to win, they must not only have the correct answers to the problems, but be able to give sound explanations as to how they got the answers.

3. A very "low-maintenance" way to give students an incentive to look at the chapter tests is to use one of the problems, verbatim, for an exam question, and make no secret of your intention to do so. It is important that students have an opportunity to get answers to any questions they have on the chapter tests before the exam is given; otherwise, this technique loses a great deal of its value.

CHAPTER P   Prerequisites

■ Suggested Time and Emphasis

$\frac{1}{2} - 1$ class. Review material.

■ Points to Stress

1. Going from a verbal description of a quantity to an algebraic formulation of that quantity.

2. Using an algebraic formula to solve word problems.

■ Sample Questions

- **Text Question:** The textbook finds and uses several algebraic formulas. Give an example of one of the formulas you read about.

- **Drill Question:** Find a formula for the distance you travel in a car in terms of the car's speed and the number of hours traveled.

  Answer: distance = (speed) × (number of hours traveled), where distance is measured in any unit of length and speed in measured in those same units of length per hour.

■ In-Class Materials

- Implicit in this section is the concept of converting from specific examples to general algebraic formulas. For example, assume that a movie theater sells adult tickets for eight dollars, student tickets for six dollars, and child tickets for three dollars. Find a formula for the amount of revenue from one show. Start with some specific examples (such as 5 adults, 24 students, and 3 children, for a total of $193) and move to the formula $P = 8a + 6s + 3c$. Then give them time to come up with a formula that will work for any choice of ticket prices. Try to guide them to the general formula $P = xa + ys + zc$. Perhaps use the formula to find the sales if five adult tickets were sold for $10 each, twenty-four student tickets were sold for $8 each, and three child tickets were sold for $6 each. (Answer: $260)

- Foreshadow a few properties in the next section by describing them in words and having the students attempt to represent them algebraically. For example, state that "If you are multiplying two numbers together, the order in which you do it doesn't matter," and see if the students can come up with the formula $ab = ba$.

- Derive or remind the students of the formula $d = rt$. Now pose the question: You have to travel 240 miles. How fast do you have to travel to make the trip in 4 hours? In 3 hours? In 2 hours? Discover that if there is a series of these questions, the easiest way to solve them is to create the formula $r = 240/t$. Now ask the following whimsical question: What if we wanted to make it in a half hour? Fifteen minutes? Ten minutes? Ask the student what happens to the rate as we make the time demands more and more unrealistic.

- Assume a student has received the following test scores: 82, 68, and 79. A common question is "What do I need to get on the fourth test to get a B?" Assuming the grade is based on the average of the four tests, have the students figure out the answer (if 80 is a B, then the answer is 91). Derive the formula $A = \dfrac{229 + s}{4}$ and use it to show the devastating effect a 0 has on one's average. If homework is part of the students' grade, this is a lesson they should learn early in the semester!

▪ Example

A formula for the sum of the first n odd integers can be obtained from looking at a table of values:

$$1 = 1$$
$$1 + 3 = 4$$
$$1 + 3 + 5 = 9$$
$$1 + 3 + 5 + 7 = 16$$

The sum of the first n odd integers $= n^2$

The pattern is not the same thing as a proof, of course. (This formula is proved later in the text.)

▪ Group Work 1: The Hourly Rule of Thumb

The students should not only leave this activity having had practice translating real-world problems into algebraic formulas, but they should also be able to quickly convert hourly to annual salaries. Many of them will not realize that one can multiply by 2000 in one's head. Make it explicit — double the number, add the zeros. When the activity is over, the students should be able to go from 7 dollars per hour to $14,000 per year (and back) quickly and easily.

Answers:

1. The first job, since it is worth $30,000 per year **2.** $24,000 per year **3.** $A = 2000P$ **4.** $P = \frac{1}{2000}A$

▪ Group Work 2: Does Speeding Save You Time?

In this activity students will come up with a formula that I have not seen in any textbook and which occasionally comes in handy. During the introduction, make sure they understand the distinction between the total amount of time a trip takes if you speed, and the amount of time you save by speeding. Hand out the parts one at a time, only giving a group the next part when you are convinced that they understand the previous one. Make sure to have a class discussion when all the students are finished with Part 1. Discuss how, for short trips, speeding doesn't really save a significant amount of time. Question 1 of the second part is not necessarily difficult, but it will be unfamiliar. By attempting it, the students should learn the process of creating an algebraic formula as a way of generalizing repetitive examples.

Answers:

Part 1

1. An hour and a half **2.** Approximately 0.21 hours (about 13 minutes) **3.** Five minutes
4. Approximately 0.71 minutes (about 43 seconds) **5.** Approximately 0.57 hours (about 34 minutes)
6. Since you are travelling for a longer time in the slow case, more time is saved. To contrast: In the case of going out for doughnuts, the travel time is so short that the time saved by speeding is negligible.

Part 2

1. $T = 1.5 - 90/(60 + S)$

2. The formula gives the right answer for $S = 10$ ($T = 0.21$). When $S = 0$ we should get zero, because if we do not speed, then no time is saved.

3. $T = \dfrac{D}{L} - \dfrac{D}{L + S}$. You may want to have your students simplify the formula: $T = \dfrac{DS}{L(L + S)}$. We can check our work by using the formula to solve the problems on the first part. Notice that $T = 0$ when $S = 0$, regardless of the values of D and L.

Part 3

1. $17.14\,\mathrm{mi/h}$ **2.** $3.53\,\mathrm{mi/h}$ **3.** $S = (TL^2)/(D - TL)$

▪ Group Work 3: Adding Them Up

This activity allows the students to attempt to find a useful, non-obvious algebraic formula. The proof that this formula is valid is given later in the text.

The pattern isn't immediately recognizable, but the students can eventually get it. It may help to ask the students to draw diagrams such as the one below, and to think about areas.

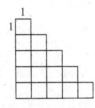

The partial sums of this series are often called triangular numbers because they can be represented as above.

Ano ther way to think about the problem would be to consider the mean of the summands $\left(\dfrac{n+1}{2}\right)$, and

realize that the sum will be the mean times the number of summands $\left(n \cdot \dfrac{n+1}{2}\right)$.

There are many ways to approach this problem. Try not to give too much guidance at first, besides the obvious hint that "Giving Up" is rarely a productive strategy!

Answers:

$$1 = 1$$
$$1 + 2 = 3$$
$$1 + 2 + 3 = 6$$
$$1 + 2 + 3 + 4 = 10$$
$$1 + 2 + 3 + 4 + 5 = 15$$
$$1 + 2 + 3 + 4 + 5 + \cdots + n = \dfrac{n(n+1)}{2}$$

▪ Homework Problems

Core Exercises: 3, 11, 21

Sample Assignment: 2, 3, 7, 8, 11, 12, 16, 21, 25

GROUP WORK 1, SECTION P.1
The Hourly Rule of Thumb

1. You are looking for work and have two competing job offers. One of them offers you $15 per hour. The other offers you $23,000 per year. Assume for the moment that you will work 8 hours a day, 5 days a week, and have two weeks (unpaid) vacation per year. Which job is offering you more money?

2. The conversion between an hourly rate of pay and an annual rate of pay comes up quite often. When people discuss salaries, they often go back and forth. It is handy to find a formula that allows us to convert one to the other. Let's try another example. Assume you were offered 12 dollars per hour. How much would that be per year, assuming the same things we did in Problem 1?

3. Now come up with a formula that will find an annual salary, given an hourly rate of pay.

4. Sometimes the reverse is useful: You have an annual salary and you want to figure out the rate of pay per hour. Find a formula that will provide your hourly rate of pay.

5. Redo Problem 1, this time using your formula. Was it easier or harder?

GROUP WORK 2, SECTION P.1
Does Speeding Save You Time?

Part 1: The Warm-Up

1. You are traveling on a road where the speed limit is 60 miles per hour. Your destination is 90 miles away. How long does it take for you to get there, assuming that you travel at the speed limit?

2. Your friend riding shotgun, who often tries to get you to do bad things, urges you to exceed the speed limit by 10 miles per hour. Your other friend, who is relegated to the back seat, says that you don't really save any time by speeding. How much time would you save by going 70 miles per hour?

3. You arrive at your destination, and all is well. You are going to drive to the store to get doughnuts. It is a five-mile drive. You are going at 60 miles per hour. How long does it take you to arrive?

4. How much time would you save by going 10 miles per hour faster?

5. Now it is time to make the 90 mile trip back. There is construction! Oh no! The new speed limit is 35 miles per hour. Again, your Bad friend wants you to go 45 mi/h, and your Good friend wants you to go 35 mi/h. How much time do you save by speeding?

6. Why is it that speeding by 10 miles per hour gives you different time savings for the trip there and the trip back? Shouldn't the savings be the same?

Part 2: Generalizing the Parameters

When I was a student, my friend Ed noticed that when we did homework together, I would usually solve the first two problems much more slowly than he did, but then I would finish the entire assignment faster. The reason was that I would always try to work out how to do things in general, which takes longer than solving one particular problem as fast as you can, but then I could use my general methods on the rest of them. It is analogous to taking the time to learn the special features of a word-processing program. It takes you a long time to write that first letter, much longer than it would just typing it out, but then the rest of your letters go quickly.

Assume that the speed limit is 60 miles per hour, and the trip is going to be 90 miles, and you are going to speed. Let S be the amount (in miles per hour) by which you are going to exceed the speed limit.

1. Find a formula for the amount of time you save by going S miles per hour over the limit.

2. When generalizing a problem, it always pays to check your work. If we allow S to be ten, then we are back in the situation we had in the first problem. Does your formula give you the right answer for $S = 10$? What should the answer be if S is zero? Do you get that answer? What, physically, does it mean for S to be zero?

3. So now you have a formula that gives you time-savings for any amount of speeding. It is still not as useful as it could be. There is nothing special about a 90 mile trip. Let's let the trip length be D. Also, not all speed limits are 60 miles per hour. Let's let the speed limit be L. Now, find a formula that gives you the time-savings for a trip where the speed limit is L, the trip length is D, and you are speeding by S miles per hour over the limit. How can you check your work?

Part 3: Generalizing the Concept

You should be proud of your formula. You may even want to take it, and a calculator, with you on your next trip. The next thing that we should do is think, "Is this formula as useful as it can possibly be?" In one sense, it is—you want to know the effect of speeding, and it tells you. But in another sense, it is not—it does not tell you how fast to go.

Often, we want to get to our destination by a specific time. Here's a sample situation. We have a 90 mile trip to make, and the speed limit is 60 miles per hour. So that means it will take an hour and a half to get there. Unfortunately, we need to be at our destination in an hour and ten minutes. (I know I shouldn't advocate speeding. I'll tell you what—in the passenger seat you have a kidney that needs to get to the hospital so a little girl can live, and this very little girl will someday grow up to cure a major disease.)

1. By how much should you exceed the speed limit to save 20 minutes?

2. Assume that you had to be there in an hour and twenty five minutes. By how much should you exceed the speed limit to save 5 minutes?

3. So it looks like it would be handy to have a formula where you specify a trip distance D, a speed limit L, and a time savings T, and you find out by how much you need to speed to save T minutes. Try to find such a formula.

GROUP WORK 3, SECTION P.1
Adding Them Up

In this activity, we ask you to find a formula that is not obvious, but we have faith that you can do it.

1. We are going to be looking at sums of the following form: $1 + 2 + 3 + 4 + 5 + 6$. Our ultimate goal is to find a general formula for the sum of the first n numbers. First, we do a few examples. Fill out the following table:

$$1 = 1$$
$$1 + 2 = 3$$
$$1 + 2 + 3 = $$
$$1 + 2 + 3 + 4 = $$
$$1 + 2 + 3 + 4 + 5 = $$

2. We want to find an algebraic formula for $1 + 2 + 3 + 4 + 5 + \cdots + n$. If we plug $n = 1$ into our formula, we want to get the answer 1. If we plug $n = 2$ into our formula, we want to get the answer 3, and so forth. Find such a formula. This will take a bit of thought.

■ **Suggested Time and Emphasis**

1 class. Review material.

■ **Points to Stress**

1. The various subsets of the real number line.

2. The algebraic properties of real numbers.

■ **Sample Questions**

- **Text Question:** Consider the figure below from the text.

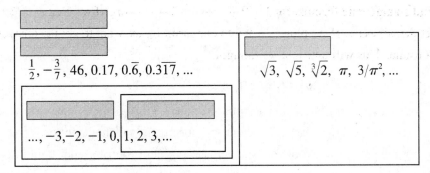

Fill in each gray box with a label from the following list: integers, irrational numbers, natural numbers, rational numbers, and real numbers.

Answer:

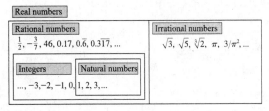

- **Drill Question:** Compute $\frac{1}{5} - \frac{2}{35}$ and reduce your answer.

  Answer: $\frac{1}{7}$

■ **In-Class Materials**

- Point out that the set hierarchy in Figure 1 in the text isn't as simple as it may appear. For example, two irrational numbers can be added together to make a rational number ($p = 2 + \sqrt{3}$, $q = 2 - \sqrt{3}$) but two rational numbers, added together, are always rational (see Exercise 58). Similarly, mathematicians have long known that the numbers π and e ($\pi \approx 3.14159265\ldots$, $e \approx 2.718281828\ldots$) are irrational numbers, but it is unknown whether $\pi + e$ is rational or irrational. As people go farther in mathematics, they break the real numbers down into other types of sets such as the transcendentals, the algebraics, the normals, the computables, and so forth.

- The students probably already know how to multiply binomial expressions together; some of them already using the acronym FOIL to avoid thinking about the process altogether. Use the properties in this section to demonstrate why FOIL works:

$$
\begin{aligned}
(a+b)(c+d) &= a(c+d) + b(c+d) && \text{Distributive Property} \\
&= ac + ad + b(c+d) && \text{Distributive Property on the first term} \\
&= ac + ad + bc + bd && \text{Distributive Property on the second term}
\end{aligned}
$$

If the example in the previous bullet item is used, then p and q can be multiplied together using FOIL to foreshadow the idea of conjugates.

- Warn the students that certain things cannot be rewritten. For example, an expression like $\dfrac{u}{u+1}$ cannot be simplified, while $\dfrac{u+1}{u}$ can also be expressed as $1 + \dfrac{1}{u}$. Similarly, there is no way to simplify $a + bc$. Another common pitfall can be pointed out by asking the question: "Is $-a$ a positive or negative number?" and having the students write their answer down before you go on to explain.

Examples

- $\dfrac{3}{35} + \dfrac{6}{55} = \dfrac{15}{77}$ • $\dfrac{3}{35} - \dfrac{1}{5} = -\dfrac{4}{35}$ • $\dfrac{11}{35} \cdot \dfrac{7}{55} = \dfrac{1}{25}$ • $\dfrac{11}{35} \div \dfrac{7}{55} = \dfrac{121}{49}$

Group Work 1: Foil the Happy Dolphin

The second page to this activity is optional, and should be given to a class that seems to have enjoyed working on the first page. If a group finishes early, ask them this surprisingly difficult follow-up question: "Write a paragraph explaining the answer to Problem 1 in such a way that a fourth-grader could understand it." The students may not succeed here, but the process of trying will help them to understand the concepts.

Answers:

1. It is easiest to explain by allowing the number to be x:

We start with	x
Adding 4 gives	$x+4$
Multiplying by 2 gives	$2(x+4) = 2x+8$
Subtracting 6 gives	$2x+2$
Dividing by 2 gives	$\frac{1}{2}(2x+2) = x+1$
Subtracting the original number gives	$x+1-x=1$

2. Answers will vary.

3. Let a be the first three digits of a phone number and b be the last four. So the phone number has value $10^5 a + b$. Now we follow the steps:

   1. We don't actually need a calculator here.
   2. This is a.
   3. $80a$
   4. $80a+1$
   5. $20{,}000a + 250$
   6. $20{,}000a + b + 250$

7. $20,000a + 2b + 250$

8. $20,000a + 2b$

9. $10,000a + b$, the original phone number.

■ Group Work 2: A Strange Result

Note that $0.99999\overline{9} = 1$. Not "is approximately equal to"—"equals." If a student does not believe it, ask them to find a number between $0.99999\overline{9}$ and 1.

Answers:

1. $\dfrac{1}{9}$ **2.** $\dfrac{4}{9}$ **3.** $\dfrac{5}{9}$ **4.** 1

■ Homework Problems

Core Exercises: 15, 29

Sample Assignment: 2, 5, 6, 14, 15, 23, 25, 26, 29, 32, 33, 34, 46

Foil the Happy Dolphin

When I was in fourth grade, the following was written in a sidebar in my textbook, in a very friendly font next to a picture of a happy dolphin:

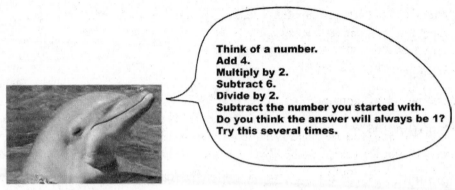

Think of a number.
Add 4.
Multiply by 2.
Subtract 6.
Divide by 2.
Subtract the number you started with.
Do you think the answer will always be 1?
Try this several times.

Think!

I tried it several times, and (can you believe it?) the answer was always 1. I was fascinated, because I had no idea why this was true. Later, when I learned about fractions, I tried it with $\frac{1}{2}$ and $\frac{2}{3}$ and it worked again. Much later, I learned about negative numbers and thought that surely this wondrous machine would break if I put in -2. But no, I still wound up with 1.

1. Does the Happy-Dolphin Procedure (HDP) always yield one? Show why it must be true, or find a number for which the HDP fails.

2. Come up with your own, more complicated, procedure that always gives the answer 1.

GROUP WORK 1, SECTION 1.2
Foil the Happy Dolphin (Part 2)

Here is a chain email that has been going around:

```
From:  "Mia G. Nyuss" <mia@mensa.org>
To:  "Doug Shaw" <doug@dougshaw.com>
Date:  Fri, 14 Dec 2007 11:55:14 -0600
Subject:  Wow, this is spooky

UNBELIEVABLE MATH PROBLEM
Here is a math trick so unbelievable that it is guaranteed to stump you.
(At least, it stumped me, and I have a degree in math from Yale.)
Personally I would like to know who came up with this and where they had the
time to figure this out.  I still don't understand it!

1.  Grab a calculator.  (You won't be able to do this one in your head.)
2.  Key in the first three digits of your phone number (NOT the area code.)
3.  Multiply by 80.
4.  Add 1.
5.  Multiply by 250.
6.  Add the last 4 digits of your phone number.
7.  Add the last 4 digits of your phone number again.
8.  Subtract 250.
9.  Divide number by 2.

Do you recognize this number?  Forward this email to twenty of your friends
and you get a magic wish.
```

3. What is the result of following the directions in the email? Prove that the result will be the same regardless of the phone number.

Express the following repeating decimals as rational numbers.

1. $0.1111\overline{1}$

1. $0.4444\overline{4}$

1. $0.5555\overline{5}$

1. $0.9999\overline{9}$

▓ Suggested Time and Emphasis

1 class. Review material.

▓ Points to Stress

1. Closed and open intervals of real numbers, and their unions and intersections.

2. Absolute value and distance.

▓ Sample Questions

- **Text Question:** Why is there no largest number in an open interval?

  Answer: There is always a number closer to the upper limit of the interval than any given number.

- **Drill Question:** (a) Find $(2, 5] \cup [3, 8)$.   (b) Find $(2, 5] \cap [3, 8)$.

  Answer: (a) $(2, 8)$ (b) $[3, 5]$

▓ In-Class Materials

- Example 5(e) should be discussed: $|3 - \pi| = \pi - 3$. It touches on the ideas of distance, the absolute value of a negative number, and that we don't need to write out π to infinite precision to deduce that it is larger than three.

- Note that we never see intervals of the form $[3, \infty]$ or $(52, 3)$ and explain why they are not well-formed.

▓ Examples

- A nontrivial union of intervals: Let $S = \{x \mid x > 0, x \neq 1/n$, where n is a positive integer$\}$. This set is an infinite union of open intervals: $(1, \infty) \cup \left(\frac{1}{2}, 1\right) \cup \left(\frac{1}{3}, \frac{1}{2}\right) \cup \cdots$. Notice that each individual interval in the union is well-behaved and easy to understand. Also notice that the intersection of S with any positive open interval such as $(0.1, 5)$ becomes a finite union.

▓ Group Work 1: What are the Possibilities?

Many questions in this activity are not very challenging, but will show you the extent to which the class understands unions and intersections. The answers to the last few questions are actually very subtle, and while fun to think about, are not expected to be answered completely by the students. It is nice to establish early on that the students can be given questions to discuss in class which are worthwhile to think about even if they won't be on the exam. If a group finishes early and has some of the answers incorrect, point out that they need to fix something, without telling them which problem to fix.

Answers:

1. $(1, 3) \cup (2, 4)$ is one interval. $(1, 3) \cup (4, 5)$ is two intervals. It is not possible to choose values to make zero intervals or a single point.

2. $[1, 3] \cap [2, 4]$ is one interval. It is not possible to choose values to make two intervals. $[1, 3] \cap [4, 6]$ does not consist of any intervals. $[1, 3] \cap [3, 5]$ is the single number 3.

3. Yes

4. No. Choose $(0, \infty)$ and $(-\infty, 2)$.

5. No

6. No

7. No

8. Surprisingly, yes! Consider the union of all intervals of the form $\left[\dfrac{1}{n}, 2 - \dfrac{1}{n}\right]$ where n is a positive integer. The union of all such closed intervals is $(0, 2)$. Every number between zero and two is in infinitely many of the intervals, yet zero and two themselves are not in any of them.

▪ Group Work 2: Real-World Examples

Reinforce the distinction between closed and open intervals by trying to get the class to come up with real-world examples where each kind of interval is appropriate. Open the activity by referring to or copying the table above Example 5 from the text onto the board. Perhaps give them an example such as the following: "If the speed limit on a highway is 55 miles per hour and the minimum speed is 45 miles per hour, then the set of allowable speeds $[45, 55]$ is a closed interval." Gauge your class—don't let them start until they are clear as to what they will be trying to do. As the activity goes on, you can stop them halfway and let groups share one or two of their answers with the whole class to prevent groups from getting into mental ruts. Make sure to leave enough time for the students to discuss their answers. If you can foster an atmosphere of pride and kudos this early in the semester, it will make the group work easier later on.

Answers:

These will vary. Some typical answers can include the following:

- Given that water freezes at $32\,°\text{F}$ and boils at $212\,°\text{F}$ ($0\,°\text{C}$ and $100\,°\text{C}$ respectively), the set of temperatures at which water is a liquid is then $(32, 212)$, an open interval.
- If an apple-flavored product advertises that it contains real apple juice then the percentage of apple juice it contains is in $(0, 100]$, a half-open interval.
- The set of all possible temperatures (in $°\text{C}$) that can be achieved in the universe is $[-273.16\ldots, \infty)$, a half-open infinite interval.

▪ Homework Problems

Core Exercises: 27, 33, 47, 53, 61

Sample Assignment: 2, 8, 10, 16, 26, 27, 29, 30, 31, 32, 33, 41, 47, 53, 54, 58, 61, 63, 68

GROUP WORK 1, SECTION P.3
What are the Possibilities?

1. Assume we have two intervals (a, b) and (c, d). Is it possible to choose a, b, c, and d so that $(a, b) \cup (c, d)$ can be expressed as a single interval? If so, how? Can it consist of two intervals? Zero intervals? Can it consist of a single point?

2. Assume we have two intervals $[a, b]$ and $[c, d]$. Is it possible to choose a, b, c, and d so that $[a, b] \cap [c, d]$ can be expressed as a single interval? If so, how? Can it consist of two intervals? Zero intervals? Can it consist of a single point?

3. Is the union of two infinite intervals always infinite?

4. Is the intersection of two infinite intervals always infinite?

5. Is it possible to take the union of two open intervals and get a closed interval? If so, how?

6. Is it possible to take the union of two closed intervals and get an open interval? If so, how?

7. Is it possible to take the union of infinitely many open intervals and get a closed interval? If so, how?

8. Is it possible to take the union of infinitely many closed intervals and get an open interval? If so, how?

GROUP WORK 2, SECTION P.3
Real-World Examples

Your textbook describes nine types of intervals. These are not just mathematical abstractions; there are real-world phenomena that represent each type of interval. Your task is to find quality examples of each type in the real world. For instance, if you have to be at least $5'\,10''$ to ride a roller coaster, then the set of allowable heights in inches (according to the policy) is $[70, \infty)$, which is of the third type. (In practice, of course, a twenty foot tall person would be unable to ride the roller coaster, but the rule does not specifically prohibit it.)

1. (a, b)

2. $[a, b]$

3. $[a, b)$

4. $(a, b]$

5. (a, ∞)

6. $[a, \infty)$

7. $(-\infty, b)$

8. $(-\infty, b]$

9. $(-\infty, \infty)$

Suggested Time and Emphasis

$\frac{1}{2}$ – 1 class. Review material.

Points to Stress

1. Definition of a^n in the cases where n is a positive or negative integer, or zero.

2. Algebraic properties of exponents.

3. Scientific notation and its relationship to significant digits.

Sample Questions

• **Text Questions:**

  1. Why is it true that $a^m a^n = a^{m+n}$?

  2. Write 125,000,000 in scientific notation.

  3. Why is scientific notation useful?

  Answers:

  1. $a^m a^n = \underbrace{(a \cdot a \cdots \cdot a)}_{m \text{ factors}} \underbrace{(a \cdot a \cdots \cdot a)}_{n \text{ factors}} = \underbrace{a \cdot a \cdot a \cdots \cdot a}_{m+n \text{ factors}} = a^{m+n}$

  2. $125,000,000 = 1.25 \times 10^8$

  3. It provides a compact way of writing very large numbers and very small numbers.

• **Drill Question:** Simplify $\left(\dfrac{a}{3}\right)^{-3} a^5$.

  Answer: $27a^2$

In-Class Materials

• It is straightforward for the students to blindly memorize the rules of exponents. The problem is that they often forget the rules as quickly as they were memorized. One way to help retention is to assign each student a different rule to present to the class, emphasizing that the student has to explain *why* the rule is true. Make sure that the students have time to ask you (or each other) questions before the presentations.

• One non-rigorous way to justify the way negative exponents work is to start a table such as this:

$$
\begin{array}{ll}
2^5 & 32 \\
2^4 & 16 \\
2^3 & 8 \\
2^2 & 4 \\
2^1 & 2
\end{array}
$$

Note that every step we are dividing by two, and continuing the pattern we get $2^0 = 1$ and $2^{-1} = \frac{1}{2}$.

• When George Everest measured the mountain that bears his name (he never actually climbed it) he used the techniques that were state-of-the-art at the time. According to his measurements, Mount Everest was exactly 29,000 ft tall (to the nearest foot). He was afraid that people would think that it was an estimate: that he was merely saying that the mountain was between 28,500 ft and 29,500 ft tall. He was proud of his work. Discuss how he could have reported his results in such a way that people would know that he was not estimating the height of the mountain. (Historically, he lied and said that it was 29,002 ft tall, so that people would know there were five significant figures. Since the 1950s, the height has been listed at 29,028 ft, although as of 1999 some scientists want to add seven feet to that number.)

• When people talk about groups of objects, they often use the word "dozen" for convenience. It is easier to think about 3 dozen eggs than it is to think about 36 eggs. Chemists use a similar word for atoms: a "mole". There are a mole of atoms in 22.4 L of gas. (You can bring an empty 1 L bottle to help them picture it) and a mole of atoms in 18 mL of water. (Bring in a graduated cylinder to demonstrate.) A mole of atoms is 6.02×10^{23} atoms. Ask the students which is bigger:

1. A mole or the number of inches along the Mississippi River

2. A mole or a trillion

3. A mole or the number of stars visible from Earth

4. A mole or the number of grains of sand on Earth

5. A mole or the number of sun-like stars in the universe

The answer for all five is "a mole".

▧ Examples

• A product whose answer will be given by a calculator in scientific notation:

$$(4,678,200,000)\,(6,006,200,000) = 28,098,204,840,000,000,000$$

• A product whose answer contains too many significant figures for many calculators to compute accurately:

$$(415,210,709)\,(519,080,123) = 215,527,625,898,637,207$$

▧ Group Work 1 Exponential Growth

This activity will foreshadow Section 5.1 and give the students practice working with the rules for manipulating exponents. If the students get stuck, give them the hint sheet.

Answers:

1. a
2. $\sqrt[5]{12} \approx 1.64375$
3. $a = 3$, $B = 40$
4. Answers will vary, given the fuzziness of real-world data. B is approximately 38 and a is approximately 2.5.

▧ Group Work 2: Guess the Exponent

This exercise will give the students a feel for orders of magnitude. Put them into groups of three or four, and have them discuss the questions. Some are easy, some are very tricky. When the groups seem to have achieved consensus, scramble them up, trying to make sure everybody is with two or three new people. Have the new groups try to achieve agreement. If they disagree, allow the groups to vote. For each problem, poll the groups, and then give the answer.

Answers:

1. 2 **2.** 8 **3.** 3 **4.** 6 **5.** 0 **6.** 7 **7.** 4 **8.** 1 **9.** 3 **10.** 1 **11.** 5

12. 7 **13.** 8 **14.** 21 **15.** 5 **16.** 10 **17.** 5 **18.** 4 **19.** 2 **20.** 4 **21.** 3 **22.** 3

23. The answer, my friend, is blowing in the wind. Forty-two is an acceptable answer, as is "seven" if written in confident handwriting.

▓ Homework Problems

Core Exercises: 13, 15, 19, 37, 41, 45, 47, 61, 63, 67, 73, 75, 81, 83, 91

Sample Assignment: 2, 3, 11, 12, 13, 15, 19, 37, 41, 45, 47, 48, 53, 58, 61, 63, 67, 73, 75, 78, 81, 83, 84, 89, 91, 100, 102, 106, 108

GROUP WORK 1, SECTION P.4
Exponential Growth

The Warm-Up

1. Simplify the expression $\dfrac{Ba^{n+1}}{Ba^n}$.

2. If we know that $a^5 = 12$, find a.

Many types of populations grow this way: They start out growing slowly, then more quickly, then very, very quickly. For example, assume we put some water bears (a very cute microscopic organism) in a petri dish. Here is a table showing their population over time:

Day	Population
1	120
2	360
3	1080
4	3240
5	9720
6	29,160
7	87,480
8	262,440
9	787,320
10	2,361,960

The Water Bears

3. This type of growth is called **exponential growth**. After n days, there are Ba^n water bears. B and a are constants that we have to figure out. (Oh, by the way: in this context the word "we" actually means "you".) Find B and a.

4. The previous table wasn't really accurate. A true table of exponential growth might look more like this:

Day	Population
1	95
2	238
3	594
4	1484
5	3711
6	9277
7	23,190
8	57,980
9	144,960
10	362,390

Now calculate the real values of B and a.

The Hint Sheet

1. Calculate this ratio: The water-bear population on Day 3 over the population on Day 2.

2. Now calculate the ratio of the population on Day 4 over the population on Day 3.

3. One more: calculate the ratio of the population on Day 5 over the population on Day 4.

4. How about in general? What is the ratio of the population on Day $n + 1$ over the population on Day n?

5. Recall that the population at day n is given by Ba^n. (This is the definition of exponential growth.) Write an algebraic formula describing water-bear populations. The left-hand side of the formula will be Ba^n.

6. Use the above to find a, and then find B.

GROUP WORK 2, SECTION P.4
Guess the Exponent

Most math problems ask you to figure out if the answer is 4, 5 or 6. Not these! We are going to give you the questions *and* the answers. For your comfort and convenience, the answers will be written in scientific notation. The only thing you have to do is supply the exponent. How hard can that be? How hard, indeed...

1. Approximately how many countries are there in the world?

   Answer: $1.9 \times 10^{\Box}$

2. How many major credit cards are currently issued in the United States?

   Answer: $2.25 \times 10^{\Box}$

3. How many crochet stitches are there in an adult-sized mitten?

   Answer: $1.73 \times 10^{\Box}$

4. How many people lived in the United States in 1800?

   Answer: $5.08 \times 10^{\Box}$

5. How many president's faces are on Mount Rushmore?

   Answer: $4 \times 10^{\Box}$

6. Approximately how many species of insect are there in the world?

   Answer: $3.0 \times 10^{\Box}$

7. According to the Internet Movie Database, how many different television series have been released in the world, as of 2003?

   Answer: $2.4 \times 10^{\Box}$

8. How many breeds of domestic cat are there?

   Answer: $4.6 \times 10^{\Box}$

9. What is the longest a Redwood tree can live?

   Answer: $2 \times 10^{\Box}$ years

10. How many playing cards are there in a hand of bridge?

    Answer: $1.3 \times 10^{\Box}$

11. The average human head has how many hairs?

    Answer: Between $0.8 \times 10^{\Box}$ and $1.2 \times 10^{\Box}$

12. How many books are there in the United States Library of Congress?

    Answer: $1.8 \times 10^{\Box}$

13. How many documents are there in the United States Library of Congress (including books, manuscripts, recordings, photographs, etc.)?

    Answer: $1.2 \times 10^{\boxed{}}$

14. How many sun-like stars (stars that have planets) are there in the universe?

    Answer: $1 \times 10^{\boxed{}}$

15. How far is it from the earth to the moon (on average)?

    Answer: $2.5 \times 10^{\boxed{}}$ miles

16. Approximately how many neurons are there in a human brain?

    Answer: $1 \times 10^{\boxed{}}$

17. How many words are there in the English language?

    Answer: $8.16 \times 10^{\boxed{}}$

18. How many words are there in a typical novel?

    Answer: Between $4.5 \times 10^{\boxed{}}$ and $15 \times 10^{\boxed{}}$

19. How many paintings did the artist Van Gogh create?

    Answer: $8 \times 10^{\boxed{}}$

20. How many feet down is the deepest spot in the ocean (the Mariana Trench in the Pacific Ocean)?

    Answer: $3.60 \times 10^{\boxed{}}$

21. How many miles long is the Mississippi River?

    Answer: $2.350 \times 10^{\boxed{}}$

22. How many miles long is the Nile River?

    Answer: $4.15 \times 10^{\boxed{}}$

23. How many seas must the white dove sail before she sleeps in the sand?

    Answer:

▪ Suggested Time and Emphasis

$\frac{1}{2}$ –1 class. Review material.

▪ Points to Stress

1. Definition of a^n in the cases where n is a rational number.

2. Rationalizing denominators.

▪ Sample Questions

- **Text Question:** What is the definition of $a^{3/4}$?

  Answer: $a^{3/4} = \sqrt[4]{a^3}$

- **Drill Question:** Simplify $\dfrac{\sqrt[3]{a^2}}{\sqrt[3]{a}} a^5$.

  Answer: $a^{16/3}$

▪ In-Class Materials

- Write "$\sqrt{ab} = \sqrt{a}\sqrt{b}$" on the board, and ask the students if this statement is always true. Point out (or have them discover) that this is a false statement when a and b are negative.

- There is a cube root magic trick that illustrates an interesting property of the cube function. A student takes a two-digit integer, cubes it, and gives you the answer (for example, 274,625). You knit your brow, think, and give the cube root (65) using the power of your mind. If the students are not impressed, stop there. If they are, do it a second time, getting the answer wrong by 1. Try it a third time, and again get the correct answer. Have them try to figure the trick out, and promise to reveal the secret if they do well on a future quiz or test.

  The trick is as follows. Memorize the first ten cubes:

x	0	1	2	3	4	5	6	7	8	9
x^3	0	1	8	27	64	125	216	343	612	729

  Notice that the last digit of each cube is unique, and that they aren't very well scrambled (2's cube ends in 8 and vice versa; 3's ends in 7 and vice versa). So the last digit of the cube root is easily obtained (274,625 ends in 5, so the number you were given is of the form ?5). Now the first digit can be obtained by looking at the first three digits of the cube, and seeing in which range they are. (274 is between 6^3 and 7^3, so the number you were given is 65). Make sure to tell the students that if they do this trick for other people, they should not get the answer too fast, and they should get it wrong in the last digit occasionally. This will make it seem like they really can do cube roots in their heads.

- After doing some standard examples of rationalizing the denominator, try doing a few examples involving multiplying by a conjugate such as

$$\frac{5}{2+\sqrt{3}} = \frac{5}{2+\sqrt{3}}\left(\frac{2-\sqrt{3}}{2-\sqrt{3}}\right) = \frac{10-5\sqrt{3}}{4-9} = -2-\sqrt{3}$$

▣ Example

A fractional exponent simplification that works out nicely: $\dfrac{\sqrt[3]{8^5}}{\sqrt[3]{8^4}} = \sqrt[3]{\dfrac{8^5}{8^4}} = \sqrt[3]{8} = 2$.

▣ Group Work 1: Find the Error

The student is invited to pick a hole in someone else's reasoning. Many students do not understand, at first, what they are trying to do—they will tend to point at the conclusion and say words to the effect of "$-1 \neq 1$, so that is the error," or they will start at a given step, proceed differently, and not wind up with a paradox. They will have to be guided to the idea that they must actually analyze *someone else's* reasoning, and find where that other person made the mistake.

Answer: The definition $a^{m/n} = \sqrt[n]{a^m}$ is valid only if m/n is in lowest terms.

▣ Group Work 2: Constructing $\sqrt{2}$

This activity could be expanded by a discussion of straight-edge and compass constructions, but the main idea is to remind the students of the Pythagorean Theorem. Introduce the activity by showing how it is easy (using a ruler) to make a line segment that is 1 inch, 2 inches, or 3 inches long. Hand out rulers and protractors, and have them try to make a segment that is $\sqrt{2}$ inches long. If they are stuck, suggest that they make a right triangle, and remind them of the Pythagorean Theorem. If a group finishes early, ask them to try and get a segment $\sqrt{5}$ units long, and then $\sqrt{3}$ units long. This can be made into an out-of-class project by asking the students to research and discuss the Wheel of Theodorus, which is a lovely extension of the concepts addressed in this activity.

Answer

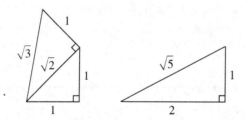

▣ Homework Problems

Core Exercises: 17, 19, 31, 33, 39, 53, 61, 65, 71, 81, 83, 87

Sample Assignment: 2, 10, 11, 16, 17, 19, 20, 25, 26, 31, 33, 39, 40, 42, 53, 61, 65, 71, 81, 83, 84, 86, 87, 90, 94

GROUP WORK 1, SECTION P.5
Find the Error

It is a beautiful Autumn day. Everyone around you is happy and excited because school has begun, and it is time to begin the joy of learning and hard work as opposed to the long summer of idle hooliganism. You are particularly happy because you are taking College Algebra. You sit at a picnic table, set up your thermos of cold milk and a peanut-butter and banana sandwich, and start reading where you had left off. Suddenly, you are aware of an odd odor, and turn around to see a wild-eyed ten-year old boy licking a giant lollipop. "What are you reading?" he asks.

"I am reading *College Algebra, Fifth Edition*," you say. "It is a bit advanced for you, but it is jam-packed with useful and important information. Worry not, lad, the day will come when you, too, are able to read this wonderful book."

"I've already read it," the boy says smugly, "and think it is full of LIES."

"What do you mean?" you ask incredulously. "James Stewart, Lothar Redlin and Saleem Watson have taken some of the greatest knowledge of our civilization, melted it down, mixed it with love, and put it into my textbook."

"Great knowledge, huh?" he asks. "Tell me, what is $(-1)^1$?"

"Why, that is equal to -1," you answer. "Any number to the first power is itself. I knew that even before taking College Algebra!"

"Okay then, what is $(-1)^{6/6}$?"

"Well, by the definition of rational roots, that would be $\sqrt[6]{(-1)^6} = \sqrt[6]{1} = 1$."

"I thought you said $(-1)^1 = -1$, and now you are saying that $(-1)^{6/6} = 1$... In other words, you are saying that $-1 = 1$!"

You can't be saying that, can you? The rude stranger must have made a mistake!

What was his mistake? Find the error.

GROUP WORK 2, SECTION P.5
Constructing $\sqrt{2}$

It is possible to use your ruler to make a line segment exactly 2 inches long. Your challenge is to make one that is exactly $\sqrt{2}$ inches long.

■ Suggested Time and Emphasis

$\frac{1}{2}$ – 1 class. Review material.

■ Points to Stress

1. Definition of and algebraic operations with polynomials.
2. Special product formulas.

■ Sample Questions

- **Text Question:**

    (a) Give an example of an expression that is a polynomial.

    (b) Give an example of an expression that is not a polynomial.

- **Drill Question:** Compute $\left(x^2 - x + 2\right)(x - 5)$.

    Answer: $x^3 - 6x^2 + 7x - 10$

■ In-Class Materials

- Remind students of the standard multiplication algorithm (some people don't learn it) by multiplying 352 by 65. Then multiply $3x^2 + 5x + 2$ by $6x + 5$ using the algorithm in the text. If your students are used to "lattice multiplication" this can also be done. One doesn't really need the "lattice" but the process can be put into the same form they are used to.

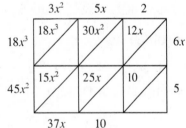

- In chemistry, the pressure, volume, quantity and temperature of a gas are related by the equation

$$PV = nRT$$

where P is pressure, V is volume, n is quantity (in moles), and T is temperature. (R is a constant called the ideal gas constant.) Present the formula this way:

$$P = \frac{nRT}{V}$$

and play with it a bit. If you hold the volume constant and increase the temperature, why would the pressure increase? What does that correspond to in physical terms? What would it mean to decrease the volume and keep the pressure constant. How could that be achieved physically? Would the temperature then increase? There is quite a lot to play with in this algebraic formula, which the students may very well see in a semester or two.

- This is an interesting product to look at with the students:

$$(x-1)\left(1+x+x^2+x^3+x^4+\cdots+x^n\right)=x^{n+1}-1$$

Have them work it out for $n = 2, 3$, and 4 and see the pattern. Once they see how it goes, you can derive

$$\left(1+x+x^2+x^3+x^4+\cdots+x^n\right)=\frac{x^{n+1}-1}{x-1}$$

and use it to estimate such things as $1+\frac{1}{2}+\frac{1}{4}+\frac{1}{8}+\cdots$ or the sum of any geometric series.

- This is a good opportunity to review the previous section's algebraic rules of commutativity, associativity, etc. Have different sections of the class check different rules for polynomial addition and multiplication. Is it commutative? Associative? What would the distributive law translate to in polynomial addition and multiplication?

▨ Example

A cubic product: $\left(3x^3-2x^2+4x-5\right)\left(x^3-2x^2-4x+1\right)=3x^6-8x^5-4x^4-2x^3-8x^2+24x-5$

▨ Group Work 1: Find the Error

This particular paradox was found carved in a cave-wall by Og the Neanderthal Algebra teacher. Even though it is an old chestnut, it is still wonderful for students to think about, if it is new to them. There is some value in tradition!

Answer: $b-a=0$ and one cannot divide by zero.

▨ Group Work 2: Designing a Cylinder

This activity gives students an opportunity to experiment with an open-ended problem requiring approximations and the use of formulas. Answers will vary.

▨ Homework Problems

Core Exercises: 21, 41, 51, 65, 67, 71, 89

Sample Assignment: 2, 3, 8, 11, 12, 13, 14, 15, 16, 21, 22, 24, 30, 37, 41, 44, 51, 58, 65, 67, 71, 72, 89, 91, 92, 95

GROUP WORK 1, SECTION P.6
Find the Error

It is a beautiful autumn day. You are collecting leaf samples for your biology class. Your friend Ed is with you, and every time you collect a leaf he says, "School sure is fun, isn't it?" and you say, "It truly is." After the tenth time, it starts getting old, but you continue to do it. Suddenly, you smell the sweet smell of sticky lollipop and a voice says, "Plenty of fun if you don't mind LIES!" You turn around and there is the wild-eyed boy you've seen before, with a grin on his face that is even stickier than his lolly.

"What are you talking about?" you ask. "Nobody has lied to me today. In chemistry we learned about chemicals, in music we learned about madrigals, in history we learned about radicals, and in mathematics we learned about..." You pause, trying to think of something that rhymes. And as you pause, he interrupts:

"You learned about LIES. Watch me, old-timer, and learn!"

You wince at being called "old-timer" and you wince again when you realize that the boy has snatched a particularly nice maple leaf from Ed's hand. Using a felt-tip pen, he writes:

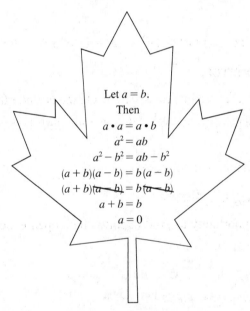

Let $a = b$.
Then
$$a \cdot a = a \cdot b$$
$$a^2 = ab$$
$$a^2 - b^2 = ab - b^2$$
$$(a + b)(a - b) = b(a - b)$$
$$(a + b)\cancel{(a - b)} = b\cancel{(a - b)}$$
$$a + b = b$$
$$a = 0$$

"See that? All those letters and variables bouncing around — it's a waste of time! Because I've just shown that $a = 0$ no matter what you want it to be. Zero. Always zero!"

Is the boy correct? Are all variables equal to zero? That doesn't seem very "variable" of them.

Save all of algebra! Find the error.

GROUP WORK 2, SECTION P.6
Designing a Cylinder

The volume of a right circular cylinder with height h and radius r is given by $V = \pi r^2 h$.

1. Draw such a cylinder.

2. The equation for the area of a circle is $A = \pi r^2$. Why do you think that "πr^2" also appears in the formula for the volume of a cylinder?

3. Assume you are designing a cylindrical can that has a volume of 120 square inches. Find dimensions of such a can, assuming that it cannot be more than 6 inches tall.

4. Find different possible dimensions for a can with a volume of 120 square inches, again assuming it cannot be more than 6 inches tall.

5. Find dimensions of a can with a volume of 120 square inches that is very long and skinny.

6. Find dimensions of a can with a volume of 120 square inches that is very short and fat.

7. Assume that this is going to be a can of Vegetarian Baked Beans to be manufactured in great quantity and sold to grocery stores. Find the dimensions that would be best to use, in your opinion. Why did you pick those dimensions?

Suggested Time and Emphasis

$\frac{1}{2}$ – 1 class. Review material.

Points to Stress

1. Factoring expressions by finding common factors.
2. Factoring quadratics by trial and error.
3. Factoring by recognition of special cases.

Sample Questions

- **Text Question:** What does "factoring" mean?

  Answer: Factoring an expression means writing that expression as a product of simpler ones.

- **Drill Question:** Factor the polynomial $12x^3 + 18x^2y$.

  Answer: $6x^2(2x + 3y)$

In-Class Materials

- Factoring expressions ties into two concepts students have seen before: factoring natural numbers, and expanding expressions. Make those connections explicit. Try to get them to see the direct analogy between writing $75 = 3 \cdot 5 \cdot 5$ and writing $x^2y - 4y = y(x+2)(x-2)$. Try to get them to see the inverse relationship between expanding $y(x+2)(x-2) = x^2y - 4y$ and factoring $x^2y - 4y = y(x+2)(x-2)$.

- After doing some more routine examples, show the students that grouping is not always obvious, as in examples like

  $$2xa + 4y + ay + 8x = (2xa + ay) + (4y + 8x) = a(2x + y) + 4(y + 2x) = (2x + y)(a + 4)$$

  Some of the standard formulas can also be awkward. For example, $x^2 - 2$ can be factored, even though we don't often refer to the number 2 as a "square".

- Show the students that factoring can be taken to extremes. For example, most people would look at $x^4 + 324$ and think it cannot be factored. (Point out that it could be if it was $x^4 - 324$). It can be factored, although the factorization is not obvious:

  $$x^4 + 324 = x^4 + 36x^2 - 36x^2 + 324 = \left(x^2 + 18\right)^2 - 36x^2$$
  $$= \left(x^2 + 18\right)^2 - (6x)^2 = \left(x^2 + 6x + 18\right)\left(x^2 - 6x + 18\right)$$

- It has been proven mathematically that any polynomial can be factored into the products of linear factors and irreducible quadratic factors. It has also been proven that if the degree of the polynomial is greater than four there is no formula (analogous to the quadratic formula) that will allow us to find those factors in general.

- This is a good opportunity to remind the students of polynomial division. Have them try to factor an expression such as $x^3 + 2x^2 - 21x + 18$. Now assume you have the hint that $x - 1$ is a factor. Show the students how you can use the hint by dividing the polynomial by $x - 1$ to get a remaining quadratic which is easy to break down.
  Answer: $(x - 3)(x + 6)(x - 1)$

Examples

- A fourth degree polynomial with integer factors:
  $$(x - 1)(x - 1)(x + 2)(x - 3) = x^4 - 3x^3 - 3x^2 + 11x - 6$$

- A polynomial that can be factored nicely using the method of Materials for Lecture Point 3:
  $$x^4 + 64 = \left(x^2 - 4x + 8\right)\left(x^2 + 4x + 8\right)$$

Group Work: Back and Forth

While expansion and factoring are inverse processes, they are not perfectly symmetrical. It is generally easier to expand than to factor, as illustrated by this activity. Introduce this activity by pointing out that when writing tests, one can't just put up a random polynomial to factor, because the answer might be too hard to find, or too complex to write clearly.

Divide the room into two halves A and B and give each half the corresponding form of the activity. The students expand six expressions and write their answers in the space provided. Emphasize that they should write only their expanded answers, not the work leading up to them, in the blanks. As students finish, they will trade papers, finished As swapping with finished Bs. After the swap, they factor their partner's answer. The pair will then (hopefully) have obtained the original questions back; if not, they should get together and figure out their errors. If a pair finishes early, have them repeat the exercise, making up their own expressions. (If the students are taking a long time, you can have them omit Question 6.)

When closing the activity, note that while it is theoretically possible to do all of them, some (such as Question 6) are extremely difficult to factor.

Homework Problems

Core Exercises: 9, 11, 13, 15, 19, 21, 53, 55, 59, 61, 65, 67, 71, 75, 77, 89, 91

Sample Assignment: 2, 3, 5, 8, 9, 11, 13, 14, 15, 19, 21, 23, 24, 31, 32, 37, 40, 43, 46, 53, 54, 55, 59, 61, 63, 65, 67, 71, 72, 75, 77, 81, 87, 89, 91, 92, 93, 97, 99, 101

Expand the following expressions. Write your answers (the answers only — do not show your work) at the bottom of this sheet, where indicated.

When you are finished, fold the top of the page backward along the dotted line and trade with someone who has finished Form B. Your job will then be to factor the expressions you receive.

1. $\left(x + \sqrt{3}\right)\left(x - \sqrt{3}\right)$

2. $(x + 2)(x + 3)$

3. $(2x + 3)\left(4x^2 - 6x + 9\right)$

4. $(3r + s)(m + 3n)$

5. $(2b - 3)^2(x + 1)$

6. $(x + 1)(x - 1)(x + 2)(x - 2)(x + 3)$

- -

Answers:

1.

2.

3.

4.

5.

6.

Back and Forth (Form B)

Expand the following expressions. Write your answers (the answers only — do not show your work) at the bottom of this sheet, where indicated.

When you are finished, fold the top of the page backward along the dotted line and trade with someone who has finished Form A. Your job will then be to factor the expressions you receive.

1. $(x+3)(x+3)$

2. $(2x-1)(x+2)$

3. $(x-2)(x^2+2x+4)$

4. $(m+4)^2(n-1)$

5. $(2a+b)(r-5s)$

6. $(x+2)(x-2)(x+3)(x-3)(x+1)$

- -

Answers:

1.

2.

3.

4.

5.

6.

■ Suggested Time and Emphasis

$\frac{1}{2} - 1$ class. Review material.

■ Points to Stress

1. Finding the domain of an algebraic expression.

2. Simplifying, adding, and subtracting rational expressions, including compound fractions.

3. Rationalizing numerators and denominators.

■ Sample Questions

- **Text Question:** What is a rational expression?

  Answer: A rational expression is a fractional expression where both the numerator and denominator are polynomials.

- **Drill Question:** Simplify $\dfrac{(x+2)/(x-3)}{x/(x-2)}$.

  Answer: $\dfrac{(x-2)(x+2)}{x(x-3)}$ or $\dfrac{x^2-4}{x^2-3x}$

■ In-Class Materials

- One of the most persistent mistakes students make is confusing the following:

$$\frac{a+b}{c} = \frac{a}{c} + \frac{b}{c}$$

$$\frac{a}{b+c} = \frac{a}{b} + \frac{a}{c} \quad \longleftarrow \quad \mathfrak{Wrong!}$$

Make sure the students understand the difference between these two cases. Perhaps give them the following to work with:

$$\frac{u+1}{u} = 1 + \frac{1}{u}$$

$$\frac{u}{u+1} = \frac{u}{u+1}$$

$$\frac{x^3 + x + \sqrt[3]{x}}{x} = x^2 + 1 + x^{-2/3}$$

$$\frac{x}{x^3 + x + \sqrt[3]{x}} = \frac{x}{x^3 + x + \sqrt[3]{x}}$$

- Ask the students why we like to rationalize the denominator. Note that it is a matter of context; often it is a matter of taste. There is nothing inherently "simpler" about $\frac{\sqrt{2}}{2}$ as opposed to $\frac{1}{\sqrt{2}}$ if they are just sitting there as numbers. However, the students would probably prefer to add $\frac{\sqrt{2}}{2} + \frac{\sqrt{3}}{3} + \frac{1}{6}$ than to add $\frac{1}{\sqrt{2}} + \frac{1}{\sqrt{3}} + \frac{1}{6}$. See if they can come up with other reasons or instances when it is convenient to rationalize a denominator.

• This is a good time to start talking about magnitudes. For example, look at $\dfrac{x+6}{x^2+4}$ and ask the question, "What is happening to this fraction when x gets large? What happens when x gets close to zero? What happens when x is large and negative, such as $-1,000,000$?" The idea is not yet to be rigorous, but to give the students a feel for the idea that a large denominator yields a small fraction, and vice versa. You can pursue this idea with fractions like $\dfrac{x^2+4}{x}$ and $\dfrac{6}{x+(3/x)}$.

■ Examples

• A compound fraction to simplify: $\dfrac{x+(3/b)}{b+(2x/6)} = 3\dfrac{xb+3}{b\,(3b+x)}$

• A denominator to rationalize: $\dfrac{x}{\sqrt{x}+\sqrt{3}} = \dfrac{x\left(\sqrt{x}-\sqrt{3}\right)}{x-3}$

■ Group Work: A Preview of Calculus

In the spirit of Exercises 65-68, this activity gives students practice in some of the types of calculations seen in calculus, and foreshadows the concept of a "difference quotient". The students may not all finish. At any point after they are finished with Problem 5(a) you can close the activity by allowing the students to present their answers.

After the answers are presented, if there is student interest, you can point out that in calculus, we want to see what happens when h gets close to 0. Before we have simplified the expressions, if you let $h = 0$ all of the expressions become the undefined $\dfrac{0}{0}$. After they are simplified, you obtain expressions in x when you allow $h = 0$. Note that technically we cannot allow $h = 0$ after we have factored the expressions, because we would have divided by zero; hence one reason for the existence of calculus.

Answers:

1. $\dfrac{\dfrac{1}{x+h}-\dfrac{1}{x}}{h} = -\dfrac{1}{(x+h)\,x}$ **2.** $\dfrac{(x+h)^2-x^2}{h} = 2x+h$ **3.** $\dfrac{\sqrt{x+h}-\sqrt{x}}{h} = \dfrac{1}{\sqrt{x+h}+\sqrt{x}}$

4. (a) $\dfrac{(x+h)^3-x^3}{h}$ (b) $\dfrac{2\,(x+h)-2x}{h}$ (c) $\dfrac{(x+h)^2+(x+h)-\left(x^2+x\right)}{h}$

(d) $\dfrac{5-5}{h}$ (e) $\dfrac{3^{x+h}-3^x}{h}$

5. (a) $3x^2+3xh+h^2$ (b) 2   (c) $2x+h+1$ (d) 0

(e) $3^x\dfrac{3^h-1}{h}$. We cannot simplify this further, nor could we substitute $h = 0$ even if we wanted to. You can't win 'em all!

■ Homework Problems

Core Exercises: 9, 13, 23, 31, 37, 49, 67, 69, 75, 83, 87, 95

Sample Assignment: 2, 3, 4, 9, 11, 13, 16, 21, 23, 26, 31, 36, 37, 45, 49, 54, 61, 67, 69, 75, 77, 78, 79, 83, 85, 87, 89, 90, 95, 98, 110, 111

Example 8 in the text involves simplifying an expression similar to this one:

$$\frac{\dfrac{1}{x+h} - \dfrac{1}{x}}{h}$$

1. Expressions of this kind occur often in calculus. Without looking at your book, simplify this expression.

2. Now simplify $\dfrac{(x+h)^2 - x^2}{h}$.

3. Now try $\dfrac{\sqrt{x+h} - \sqrt{x}}{h}$. (**Hint:** Rationalize the numerator, as done in Example 11 in the text.)

These types of expressions are called **difference quotients**. We could write the following abbreviations:

$$DQ\left(\frac{1}{x}\right) = \frac{\dfrac{1}{x+h} - \dfrac{1}{x}}{h}$$

$$DQ\left(x^2\right) = \frac{(x+h)^2 - x^2}{h}$$

$$DQ\left(\sqrt{x}\right) = \frac{\sqrt{x+h} - \sqrt{x}}{h}$$

In other words, given an expression with x as the variable, we can write its difference quotient. It isn't just a game that algebra teachers play; the difference quotient turns out to be a very important concept in higher math: given information about a quantity, we can figure out how that quantity is changing over time.

4. Let's see if you've picked up on the pattern. Write out the following difference quotients:

(a) $DQ\left(x^3\right)$

(b) $DQ\left(2x\right)$

(c) $DQ\left(x^2 + x\right)$

(d) $DQ\left(5\right)$

(e) $DQ\left(3^x\right)$

5. Simplify the difference quotients you found above.

CHAPTER 1 Equations and Inequalities

▪ 1.1 | Basic Equations

▪ Suggested Time and Emphasis

$\frac{1}{2} - 1$ class. Essential material.

▪ Points to Stress

1. Solving equations using the techniques of adding constants to both sides of the equation, multiplying both sides of the equation by a constant, and raising both sides of the equation to the same nonzero power.

2. Avoiding the pitfalls of accidentally multiplying or dividing by zero, or introducing extraneous solutions.

▪ Sample Questions

- **Text Question:** Give two different reasons that it is important to check your answer after you have solved an equation such as $2 + \dfrac{5}{x-4} = \dfrac{x+1}{x-4}$.

  Answer: Firstly, we must make sure that our answer is not extraneous, and secondly, we should check that we have not made an error in calculation.

- **Drill Question:** Solve: $(x-2)^2 = 9$.

  Answer: $x = -1$ or $x = 5$

▪ In-Class Materials

- After showing the students how two or three standard linear equations can be solved (such as $4x + 10 = 2$, $2x - 5 = 4$) start introducing other variables such as $4x + 10 = a$ and $4x + a = 2$ and segue to the idea of "solving for x". Once that idea is understood, they should be able to solve $ax + b = c$ for x, by following the pattern of what has been done so far. Then show them how to solve it for b, and ask them to solve it for c. If they understand what the phrase means, the response should be that the equation has already been solved for c, or that we should write $c = ax + b$.

- There are two main pathologies that students may encounter when solving linear equations: $0 = 0$ and $1 = 0$. While it is not a good idea to dwell on the pathologies, as opposed to spending time on the cases where the students will spend a majority of their time, it is good to address them, because they *do* come up, in math class and in real life. Have them attempt to solve the following equations, and check their work:

$$3x + 4 \; = \; x + 6$$
$$3x + 4 \; = \; x + 6 + 2x - 2$$
$$3x + 4 \; = \; x + 6 + 2x + 2$$

By the time this example is presented, most of the students should be able to obtain $x = 1$ for the first equation, and to check this answer. The second one gives $0 = 0$. Point out that $0 = 0$ is always a true statement. (If you like, introduce the term "tautology".) It is a true statement if $x = 1$, it is a true statement if $x = 2$, it is a true statement if the author Lemony Snickett writes another book, it is a true statement if he does not write another book. So the students can test $x = 1$, $x = 2$, $x = -\sqrt{2}$ in the second equation, and all of them will yield truth. The third statement gives $1 = 0$ (actually, it gives $0 = 4$, but we can multiply both sides of the equation by $\frac{1}{4}$). This is a false statement, no matter what value we assign to x. Point out "Currently, it is false to say that this piece of chalk is blue. Now, is there a value I can assign to x to change that?" Again, test various values of x in the third equation to see that, no matter what, we get that the LHS is always 4 less than the RHS.

- If the equation $PV = nRT$ was introduced earlier (where P is pressure, V is volume, n is quantity of gas in moles, T is temperature, and R is a constant called the ideal gas constant) it is a good time to bring it up again. Ask how we could experimentally determine the value of R. (Answer: Measure P, V, n, and T, and solve the equation for R.) Ask the students to solve the equation for T and then for P.

- Modern electrical engineering students learn Kirchoff's Voltage Law: $V = IR$. (Voltage equals current times resistance.) In the 1950s, some employees of the U.S. Navy taught their electrical engineers "Kirchoff's Three Voltage Laws":

$$V = IR$$
$$\frac{V}{I} = R$$
$$\frac{V}{R} = I$$

They were given this mnemonic diagram to help them remember the three laws:

If you want to know, say, Resistance, you cross out the R and are left with $\frac{V}{I}$. Ask the students if modern students are being cheated by only learning about one of these laws, and not learning the diagram. Hopefully they will get the idea that you can obtain the three laws by solving for whichever variable you need.

■ Example

An equation with an extraneous solution:

$$\frac{x^2}{x+1} = \frac{x+2}{x+1}$$

This simplifies to $x^2 - x - 2 = 0$, either by multiplying by $x + 1$ directly or by first subtracting the RHS from the LHS and simplifying. The students don't yet know how to solve quadratic equations, but they can verify that $x = -1$ and $x = 2$ are solutions. $x = -1$ is extraneous.

▪ Group Work 1: Leaving the Nest

This lightly foreshadows the next section, in that students are asked to use an equation to solve a real-world problem. This problem can be modified to make the original savings a parameter instead of the constant 100. If students solve Problems 7 and 8 in different ways, make sure that the class sees the various methods used.

Answers:

1. $\dfrac{1200}{70} = 17.142857$—about 18 months

2. Moving-out time $= \dfrac{1200}{x}$ $\left(\text{technically } \left\lceil \dfrac{1200}{x} \right\rceil \right)$

3. $3 = \dfrac{1200}{x}$ $\Rightarrow$ $x = \$400$ per month

4. $\dfrac{550}{70} \approx 7.86$; 8 months

5. $\dfrac{1300/3 - 100}{70} \approx 4.76$; 5 months

6. $\dfrac{1300/(n+1) - 100}{70} = \left(\dfrac{130}{7(n+1)} - \dfrac{10}{7} \right)$ months

7. $\dfrac{1300/(n+1) - 100}{70} = 3, n = \dfrac{99}{31}$; 4 roommates

8. $\dfrac{1300/(n+1) - 100}{70} = \dfrac{1}{4}, n = \dfrac{473}{47}$; 11 roommates

▪ Group Work 2: The Mathematics of Pizza

The first question isn't an algebra question, but a warm up to make sure that the students remember the formula for the area of a circle (it is also a question that comes up in dorm rooms quite frequently.) If you want to use this as an opportunity to review significant figures, you may want to be strict that all answers should be given to (say) four significant figures.

Answers:

1. The large pizza is larger than two small pizzas—49π in^2 versus 32π in^2.

2. $\pi r^2 = 100$ $\Rightarrow$ $r = \sqrt{\dfrac{100}{\pi}} \approx 5.642$ in. The diameter is about 11.28 in.

3. $d = 2\sqrt{\dfrac{n^2}{\pi}} \approx 1.128n$

4. $n^2 = 49\pi$ $\Rightarrow$ $n \approx 12.41$

▪ Homework Problems

Core Exercises: 17, 21, 43, 47, 53, 59, 61, 63, 73, 83, 85

Sample Assignment: 3, 8, 9, 12, 16, 17, 21, 28, 33, 43, 47, 53, 59, 61, 62, 63, 73, 78, 83, 85, 99

GROUP WORK 1, SECTION 1.1
Leaving the Nest

1. I am a mathematics professor who lives in Minneapolis, where an inexpensive apartment is $650 per month. In order to rent an apartment here, you need the first month's rent up front, and a security deposit equal to the monthly rent. Assume that I have $100 saved up in the bank, and I can save $70 per month from my professorial salary. How long will it be before I can move out of my parent's basement?

2. Depressing thought, eh? Well, one way to move out sooner would be to save more money. How long will it be before I can move out, assuming I can save x dollars per month?

3. How much would I have to save per month if I wanted to move out in three months?

4. Realistically, I can't really save all that much more money. Math supplies do not come cheap. Let's go back to the situation where I am saving $70 per month. Another way I could move out sooner would be to get a roommate. How long would it be before I could move out, assuming a roommate would pay half of the first month's rent and the security deposit?

5. How long would it take if I had 2 roommates?

6. How about n roommates?

7. How many roommates would I have to have if I wanted to move out in three months?

8. For reasons best left to your imagination, it would make things a lot easier if I moved out next week. How many roommates will I need for this to happen?

GROUP WORK 2, SECTION 1.1
The Mathematics of Pizza

1. A small pizza from Raineri's Pizza is 8 inches in diameter. A large pizza is 14 inches in diameter, and costs twice as much. Are you better off buying two small pizzas or one large one, assuming you want as much pizza as possible?

2. Pizzas aren't always round. In Chicago, for example, pizza often comes in rectangles. Assume you make a pizza in a ten-inch by ten-inch pan. If you wanted a round pan that would give you the same amount of pizza, what would the diameter of that round pan be?

3. What would be the radius of a round pan that gave you as much pizza as an $n \times n$ square pizza?

4. How big a square pan would you need to give you as much pizza as a large pizza from Raineri's Pizza?

Suggested Time and Emphasis

1 class. Essential material.

Points to Stress

1. Solving applied problems described verbally.
2. Presenting the solution process in a clear, organized way.

Sample Questions

- **Text Question:** Discuss one of the problems presented in this section. You don't have to know all the specific numbers, but describe the problem and the method of solution.

- **Drill Question:** A car rental company charges $20 a day and 30 cents per mile for renting a car. Janice rents a car for three days and her bill comes to $72. How many miles did she drive?

  Answer: The total cost is $C = 20d + 0.30m$, where d is the number of days and m is the mileage. In this case we have $72 = 20\,(3) + 0.30m \;\Rightarrow\; m = 40$, so Janice drove 40 miles.

In-Class Materials

- Some college algebra students will have seen this material at one point in their lives, and may have many different ideas and habits. It is important to make your requirements explicit: is it acceptable to present an answer with no work at all? With work shown but barely decipherable? Do you require the students to explicitly go through the steps described in the text? Do you require them to write out a table (as in the examples in the text)? Much conflict can be avoided if your requirements are specified in a handout at the outset.

- Here is a simple-sounding problem: A person is currently making $25,000 a year (after taxes) working at a large company, and has an opportunity to quit the job and make $35,000 independently. Is this a good deal financially? Elicit other considerations such as: Insurance tends to cost $400 per month for an individual— the company is no longer paying for that. Taxes will be roughly 30%. The large company probably pays some percentage (say 2%) towards a retirement account. Based on the discussion that your particular class has, come up with a linear equation that converts an annual gross income for an independent contractor to a net income, and then figure out how much the independent contractor would have to charge in order to net $25,000. Other hard-to-quantify considerations may come up such as paid vacations, sick leave, "being one's own boss", the tax benefits of having a home office, quality of life, and so forth. Acknowledge these considerations, and perhaps (for purposes of comparison) try to quantify them. Perhaps assume that the tax benefits for the home office add 5% to the gross income. Ask the class if the pleasure of not having a boss is worth, say, $2000 a year. (On the other hand, would they would get any work done at all without a boss standing over them?) This is a real-life modeling situation that, every year, more and more people find themselves thinking about.

- This section is particularly suited to having students come up with their own problems to solve, or have others solve. Once they understand the concept, with a little (or a lot of) thought, they should be able to come up with practical, relevant problems. If the students need a little prompting (try to get away without such prompting) you can wonder how many recordable CDs one would have to buy to store a hard drive full of music, how many people one could invite to a party that has a firm budget of $200 (have them list fixed costs and per-person costs), how many miles one could drive a car (paying all expenses) for $2000/year, etc.

• Point out that not all behaviors are best modeled linearly. For example, assume that the temperature of a thermos of coffee is 160°F, and after a half hour it is 120°. Show how we can write a linear model: $T = 160 - 80t$. Show that, according to the model, the coffee will reach 0° in two hours and will freeze solid a little less than a half hour after that! A much better model of coffee cooling is be the exponential model $70 + 90 (0.605)^t$, assuming that the temperature of the room is 70°.

▨ Examples

• A straightforward mixture problem: A child makes two quarts of chocolate milk consisting of 30% syrup and 70% milk. It is far too sweet. How much milk would you have to add to get a mixture that is 5% syrup?
Answer: 10 quarts

• A straightforward job-sharing problem: If it takes Mike two hours to mow the lawn, and Al three hours to mow the lawn, how long does it take the two of them, working together?
Answer: 1.2 hours

• A classic (i.e. very old) trick question: If it takes two people three hours to dig a hole, how long does it take one person to dig half a hole?
Answer: You can't dig half a hole. Don't worry; my students did not laugh either.

▨ Group Work 1: How Many People?

This modeling problem has a lot of data, and is designed to teach students to distinguish between fixed and variable costs. As in the real world, some data are irrelevant (e.g. the maximum capacity of the hall) and some seem irrelevant, but are not (e.g. the length of the reception). The problems are deliberately not given in a standard order. Students would normally be asked to do Problem 3 before Problem 2; they are presented in this way to see if the students realize that the easiest way to solve Problem 2 is to come up with an algebraic formula.

Answers:

1. $2,225

2. 114. If a student answers 114.58, they must include an explanation of what they mean by that, given that 0.58 of a person doesn't make sense on the face of it. Note that if a student rounds up to 115, then they may go over budget. Given that there are approximations involved, it would be better to err on the side of caution, perhaps hosting 110 people rather than pushing it to the limit of 114.

3. $C = 12x + 1625$

■ Group Work 2: Some Like it Hot

This is a straightforward mixture problem.

Answers:

1. $\dfrac{25}{10,000} = \dfrac{1}{400}$ gallon

2. $\dfrac{1}{100} = \dfrac{\frac{1}{800} + x}{\frac{1}{2} + x} \quad \Leftrightarrow \quad x = \dfrac{1}{264}$ gallon

■ Homework Problems

Core Exercises: 19, 21, 41, 43, 45, 53, 57

Sample Assignment: 4, 11, 15, 19, 20, 21, 22, 29, 30, 34, 35, 40, 41, 43, 45, 47, 53, 54, 57, 60, 66

GROUP WORK 1, SECTION 1.2
How Many People?

Jessica and Trogdor are getting married! They are planning the reception, and have come up with the following data:

- The reception hall is going to cost $1200 to rent.
- The reception hall will house a maximum of 500 people.
- The reception will take three hours.
- Each person's dinner is going to cost $8.
- On average, every person that drinks alcohol will cost an extra $9.
- About one-third of the attendees will drink alcohol.
- Each piece of wedding cake will cost $1.11.
- 90% of the guests will eat a piece of wedding cake.
- The DJ is going to charge $75 per hour.
- The decorations (flowers, streamers, bobble-head representations of the groom, etc.) are going to cost $200.

Answer the following questions:

1. How much would the reception cost if 50 people attended?

2. How many people could come if Jessica and Trogdor have a total of $3000 to spend?

3. Write an algebraic formula describing the cost of x people attending their reception.

GROUP WORK 2, SECTION 1.2
Some Like it Hot

I like my chili spicier than my sister does. I like mine to be 1% habañero sauce, and she likes it to be 0.25% habañero sauce. Here is the plan: I'm going to make a gallon of chili the way my sister likes it. I'll measure out a half-gallon, and put it in a container for her. Then I will add some more habañero sauce so that the remaining chili will be the way I like it.

1. How much habañero sauce should I put in initially?

2. How much extra habañero sauce should I put in my portion after I've divided it up?

■ Suggested Time and Emphasis

1 class. Essential material.

■ Points to Stress

1. Solving quadratic equations using the techniques of factoring, completing the square, and the quadratic formula.
2. The use of the discriminant to determine the nature of the solutions to a quadratic equation.
3. The zero-product property.

■ Sample Questions

- **Text Question:** What is the difference between a linear and a quadratic equation?

  Answer: A **linear equation** is equivalent to one of the form $ax + b = 0$, where a and b are real numbers. A **quadratic equation** is equivalent to one of the form $ax^2 + bx + c = 0$, where a, b, and c are real numbers with $a \neq 0$.

- **Drill Question:** Solve $x^2 + 3x = -2$ for x.

  Answer: $x = -2$ or $x = -1$

■ In-Class Materials

- The zero-product property is the base upon which the various methods of solving quadratic equations rests. Many errors students make in solving these equations stems from misunderstanding the zero product property. Students should see the difference between these two equations:

$$(x - 2)(x - 3)(x - 4) = 0$$
$$(x - 2)(x - 3)(x - 4) = -24$$

Note how the solution to the first is immediate, while the solution to the second requires some work. ($x = 0$ is the only real solution to the second.)

- Go through an example where the appearance of a quadratic equation may be unexpected. For example, assume that if we charge $200 for a pair of hand-made shoes, we can sell 100 of them. For every five dollars we raise the price, we can sell one fewer pair. (Conversely, for every five dollars we lower the price, we can sell one more.) At what prices will our revenue be $23,520? (Answer: $280, $420) Point out that this is somewhat artificial—in practice we would be more interested in finding a maximum revenue, or (ideally) maximum profit. Later (in Section 3.5) the students will be able to solve such problems.

- Point out that the quadratic formula works for algebraic expressions, too. For example, it can be used to solve $(2A + B)x^2 - 3Bx + (A - B) = 0$ for x.

  Answer: $x = \dfrac{1}{2(2A + B)} 3B \pm \sqrt{(13B^2 - 8A^2 + 4BA)}$

- Notice that the discriminant can tell us information about the most general of quadratic equations. For example, it tells us that if a and c have opposite signs, then $ax^2 + bx + c$ has two real solutions.

■ Examples

- Quadratic equations with zero, one, and two solutions:

  $x^2 - 6x + 11 = 3$ has two solutions, $x = 2$ and $x = 4$.

  $x^2 - 6x + 12 = 3$ has one solution, $x = 3$.

  $x^2 - 5x + 13 = 3$ has no real solution.

- A quadratic equation with a parameter:

  $3x^2 + 5x - 3\gamma = 0$ has solutions $x = \dfrac{-5 \pm \sqrt{25 + 36\gamma}}{6}$.

■ Group Work 1: The Tour

The students may have questions about the setup of this problem. Don't answer them right away; part of the goal of this chapter is to teach the students how to read a paragraph and figure out what it is asking. Conclude by pointing out that in Chapter 4 we find a method of maximizing the profit.

Answers:

1. The equation $-x^2 + 51x - 700 = 0$ has no solution, so it is not possible to make $700.

2. The solutions of $-x^2 + 51x - 494 = 0$ are 13 and 38, so 13 is the smallest number of people that will result in a profit of $700.

3. The solutions of $-x^2 + 47x - 544 = 0$ are approximately 20.6277 and 26.3723, so the answers are (a) 21 and (b) 26. Note that in part (a) we must round up because if we round down, we make slightly less than $700. Similarly, we must round down in part (b).

■ Group Work 2: An Infinite Fraction

Open by writing the fraction from the group work on the board, and allowing a full minute of silence for the students to start to play with it and think about it. Have them think about whether it makes sense, whether it works out to a single number, etc. Then group the students and hand out the activity.

Answers:

1. $\frac{1}{2} = 0.500000$
2. $\frac{1}{3} = 0.333333$
3. $\frac{3}{7} = 0.428571$
4. $\frac{7}{17} = 0.411765$
5. $\frac{17}{41} = 0.414634$
6. Any well-stated answer should count as credit. The idea is the recursion, the self-similarity.
7. Solving $x^2 + 2x - 1 = 0$, we find that $x = -1 \pm \sqrt{2}$. The negative solution is extraneous, so $x \approx 0.414214$.

■ Group Work 3: An Infinite Root

The positive answer to this question is called the golden ratio. One can spend many hours posing questions whose answer is the golden ratio. For example, the limit of the ratios of adjacent Fibonacci numbers is the golden ratio. Many artists have used rectangles in their work whose proportions approximate the golden ratio.

Answers:

1. (a) $\sqrt{1 + \sqrt{1}} \approx 1.41421$

(b) $\sqrt{1 + \sqrt{1 + \sqrt{1}}} \approx 1.55377$

(c) $\sqrt{1 + \sqrt{1 + \sqrt{1 + \sqrt{1}}}} \approx 1.59805$

(d) $\sqrt{1 + \sqrt{1 + \sqrt{1 + \sqrt{1 + \sqrt{1}}}}} \approx 1.61185$

2. (a) $x^2 = 1 + x$

(b) $x^2 - 1 = x$

(c) We solve $x^2 - x - 1 = 0$ to find $x = \frac{1 \pm \sqrt{5}}{2}$.

▨ Homework Problems

Core Exercises: 5, 17, 25, 31, 39, 45, 65, 67, 69, 81, 91, 97

Sample Assignment: 2, 5, 8, 9, 17, 24, 25, 29, 31, 32, 36, 39, 45, 65, 67, 68, 69, 70, 81, 82, 87, 88, 91, 95, 97, 103

GROUP WORK 1, SECTION 1.3
The Tour

There is increasing interest in touring the place of your birth—the places you played, the places you ate, the stores where your food was purchased, etc. And who better to give such tours than you? You decide to charge $50 per person. But that is a bit excessive, so you decide to give group discounts of $1 per person. In other words, if two people go on the tour together, you will charge $49 per person (for a total of $98) and if three people go on the tour you will charge $48 per person (for a total of $144).

1. How many people have to go on the tour in order for you to make $700?

2. You are not satisfied with these measly amounts of money. So you add a fee of $206 per tour group, regardless of size. Now what is the smallest number of people who have to go on the tour in order for you to make $700?

3. If you are going to charge that much for a tour, you should at least give everyone lunch. Assume that each person on the tour is going to eat a $4 lunch, the cost of which comes out of your pocket. Also assume that the caterer is going to charge you a flat fee of $50, regardless of how many people eat.

(a) What is the smallest number of people who have to go on the tour in order for you to make $700, under these circumstances?

(b) If too many people show up, of course, then you will actually be paying *them* to take the tour! You want to make sure to cap the number of people who are allowed to go on the tour. What is the largest number of people who can go on the tour without causing your profit to dip below $700?

GROUP WORK 2, SECTION 1.3
An Infinite Fraction

Consider this odd fraction:

$$\cfrac{1}{2+\cfrac{1}{2+\cfrac{1}{2+\cfrac{1}{2+\cdots}}}}$$

Take a minute to think about it before going on. What does it mean? Do you think it is a number? Infinity? Is it even defined?

We can start to get a handle on this fraction by looking at approximations as follows. Write your answers as decimals with four significant figures.

1. $\dfrac{1}{2}$

2. $\dfrac{1}{2+1}$

3. $\cfrac{1}{2+\cfrac{1}{2+1}}$

4. $\cfrac{1}{2+\cfrac{1}{2+\cfrac{1}{2+1}}}$

5. $\cfrac{1}{2+\cfrac{1}{2+\cfrac{1}{2+\cfrac{1}{2+1}}}}$

Notice that there is definitely a trend here: the answers you are getting are zeroing in on a particular number. Now let's try to find that number. We call that number x, so we can write

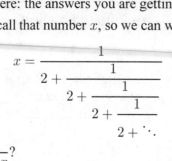

$$x = \cfrac{1}{2 + \cfrac{1}{2 + \cfrac{1}{2 + \cfrac{1}{2 + \cdots}}}}$$

6. Why is it correct to write $x = \dfrac{1}{2 + x}$?

7. Find x. Is it close to what you approximated in Problem 5?

GROUP WORK 3, SECTION 1.3
An Infinite Root

1. Compute the following:

(a) $\sqrt{1 + \sqrt{1}}$

(b) $\sqrt{1 + \sqrt{1 + \sqrt{1}}}$

(c) $\sqrt{1 + \sqrt{1 + \sqrt{1 + \sqrt{1}}}}$

(d) $\sqrt{1 + \sqrt{1 + \sqrt{1 + \sqrt{1 + \sqrt{1}}}}}$

2. You may notice that your answers in Problem 1 seemed to be getting closer and closer to some number. We are going to try to find out that number exactly, using algebra. In other words, we are going to attempt to discover

$$\sqrt{1 + \sqrt{1 + \sqrt{1 + \sqrt{1 + \sqrt{1 + \sqrt{1 + \cdots}}}}}}$$

(a) We let $x = \sqrt{1 + \sqrt{1 + \sqrt{1 + \sqrt{1 + \sqrt{1 + \sqrt{1 + \cdots}}}}}}$. What is x^2 equal to?

(b) What is $x^2 - 1$ equal to?

(c) Find x.

1.4 | Complex Numbers

■ **Suggested Time and Emphasis**

$\frac{1}{2}$ – 1 class. Essential material.

■ **Points to Stress**

1. Arithmetic operations with complex numbers.

2. Complex numbers as roots of equations.

■ **Sample Questions**

• **Text Question:** Write out all solutions (real and complex) to the equation $z^2 = -9$.

  Answer: $z = \pm 3i$

• **Drill Question:** Simplify $\dfrac{3i + 2}{3 + 4i}$.

  Answer: $\frac{18}{25} + \frac{1}{25}i$

■ **In-Class Materials**

• Students often believe that the relationship between real and complex numbers is similar to the relationship between rational and irrational numbers—they don't see that the number 5 can be thought of as complex ($5 + 0i$) as well as real. Perhaps show them this extension of Figure 1 in Section P.2:

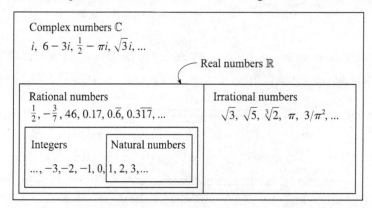

• One doesn't have to think of complex numbers as a philosophical abstraction. Many applied fields use complex numbers, because the result of complex arithmetic leads to real-world understanding. One can think of complex numbers as points in the plane with the real and imaginary axes replacing the x- and y-axes. (In that sense, the complex numbers become a geometric extension of a number line.) Now we can model walking two feet North and one foot East as $1 + 2i$, and one foot North and three feet East as $3 + i$. Adding the numbers now has a physical significance: how far have you walked in total? Multiplication has a meaning too: when we multiply two complex numbers (thinking of them as points on the plane) we are multiplying their distances from the origin and adding their vector angles. So when we say $i^2 = -1$ we are really just saying that a 90° angle plus a 90° angle is a 180° angle. The statement $i = \sqrt{-1}$ is then a notational aid. Engineers represent waves of a fixed frequency as a magnitude and a phase angle. This interpretation of a complex number is well suited to that model.

- The text states an important truth: that every quadratic equation has two solutions (allowing for multiplicities) if complex numbers are considered. Equivalently, we can say that every quadratic expression $ax^2 + bx + c$ can be factored into two linear factors $(x - z_1)(x - z_2)$, where z_1 and z_2 are complex numbers (and possibly real). An important, easy-to-understand generalization is the Fundamental Theorem of Algebra: every nth degree polynomial can be factored into n linear factors, if we allow complex numbers. (If we do not, it can be shown that every nth degree polynomial can be factored into linear factors and irreducible quadratic factors) The Fundamental Theorem will be covered explicitly in Section 4.4.

- There is a certain similarity to dividing complex numbers and rationalizing denominators. Make this similarity explicit by having the students do these two problems:

  - Rationalize the denominator of $\dfrac{8}{3 + \sqrt{2}}$. (Answer: $\frac{24}{7} - \frac{8}{7}\sqrt{2}$)

  - Simplify $\dfrac{8}{3 + 2i}$. (Answer: $\frac{24}{13} - \frac{16}{13}i$)

■ Example

Sample operations with complex numbers: Let $a = 3 + 2i$ and $b = 7 - 2i$. Then

$$a + b = 10$$
$$a - b = -4 + 4i$$
$$ab = 25 + 8i$$
$$\frac{a}{b} = \frac{17}{53} + \frac{20}{53}i$$

■ Group Work 1: Complex Roots

Students should be encouraged, in solving the first problem, to try things out and to explore. Make sure they know in advance that there isn't some method out there that they should have learned and can look up in the textbook. A sufficiently clever student may solve the first problem without the use of the hint sheet. If this happens, have the student attempt to find the square root of $-3 - 4i$ without the hint sheet. After the students have given Problem 1 the "old college try", hand out the hint sheet.

Problem 2 on the hint sheet may require the students to solve $b^4 - 3b^2 + 2 = 0$. Allow them to figure out how to solve it—it is a good foreshadowing of the next section. You may want to give them the hint that it can be factored as $(b^2 - x)(b^2 - y)$.

Answer:

$\pm\frac{\sqrt{2}}{2}(1 + i)$. Note that students are not expected to get this problem without going through the hint sheet.

Hint Sheet Answers:

1. $(a^2 - b^2) + (2ab)i = 0 + 1i$ $\Leftrightarrow$ $a^2 - b^2 = 0$ and $2ab = 1$ $\Leftrightarrow$ $a = \pm\frac{1}{\sqrt{2}}, b = \pm\frac{1}{\sqrt{2}}$. The square roots of i are $\frac{\sqrt{2}}{2} + \frac{\sqrt{2}}{2}i$ and $-\frac{\sqrt{2}}{2} - \frac{\sqrt{2}}{2}i$.

2. $\sqrt{-3 - 4i} = 1 - 2i$ and $-1 + 2i$, using the same method.

■ Group Work 2: Find the Error

This is another "old standard" that will show the students that it is important to be careful when manipulating complex numbers. The students should write their answer out completely, so you can make sure that they really understand the error—it will be very easy for them to write vague statements that dance around the mistake without actually explaining it. If students finish early, ask them if it is true that $\frac{1}{i} = -i$.

Answer:

The rule $\sqrt{\dfrac{a}{b}} = \dfrac{\sqrt{a}}{\sqrt{b}}$ works only if a and b are real and positive. It is true that $\frac{1}{i} = -i$. Also, when writing $\sqrt{z}$ for complex values of z, it is unclear which of the two possible values is the principal square root.

■ Homework Problems

Core Exercises: 5, 9, 15, 19, 25, 33, 47, 49, 51, 57, 59, 65

Sample Assignment: 2, 5, 9, 15, 19, 21, 22, 25, 26, 27, 33, 34, 37, 47, 49, 50, 51, 57, 59, 65, 69, 70, 77, 82

GROUP WORK 1, SECTION 1.4
Complex Roots

So far we have learned how to find square roots of real numbers. For example, $\sqrt{9} = 3$ or -3. Also, $\sqrt{-9} = 3i$ or $-3i$, if we allow $i = \sqrt{-1}$. We can check our work: $3^2 = 9$ and $(-3)^2 = 9$ so we know that we were right when we said that $\sqrt{9} = \pm 3$. Similarly $(3i)^2 = -9$ and $(-3i)^2 = -9$ so we know that we were right when we said $\sqrt{-9} = \pm 3i$.

It turns out that, once we are in the world of complex numbers, real numbers aren't the only ones that have square roots.

Find $\sqrt{i}$. Notice that "$\sqrt{i}$" is not a sufficient answer—it is simply restating what we are trying to find! "$i^{1/2}$" has the same problem. We are looking for a complex number $x = a + bi$ with the property that $x^2 = i$.

Finding $\sqrt{i}$ isn't easy, huh? But you can do it with the knowledge you have of complex numbers. We want to find $a + bi$ with the property that it is the square root of i. In other words:

$$(a + bi)^2 = i$$

We can write this as

$$(a + bi)^2 = 0 + 1i$$

You know how to simplify the left-hand side. You will get an expression with two parts: a real part and an imaginary part. Set the real part equal to zero, the imaginary part equal to one, and find a and b which satisfy the equation.

1. The square roots of 9 are $3 + 0i$ and $-3 + 0i$.

The square roots of -9 are $0 + 3i$ and $0 - 3i$.

The square roots of i are ____ + ____i and ____ + ____i.

2. You can now find the square root of *any* complex number!

The square roots of $-3 - 4i$ are ____ + ____i and ____ + ____i.

3. Check your answers to Problem 2 by squaring them.

It is a beautiful autumn day. You and your friends are playing horseshoes, and to make it even more fun, you are playing the rule that after every toss you have to mention something that you learned in school. "Shakespeare wrote in iambic pentameter," says one friend as her horseshoe lands three feet from the post. "Theodore Roosevelt backed antitrust legislation, our national park system, and was the first US citizen to win the Nobel Peace Prize," says another friend, quickly, as his horseshoe lands nine inches from the post. "Mathematicians use the symbol i to denote the square root of negative one, and everything works out," you say, as your horseshoe lands a foot from the post. Another horseshoe sails over your head and rings the post as a small voice yells, "LIES!"

The three of you turn around to see a wild-eyed boy, with several horseshoes in one hand, and his lollipop in the other. "What do you mean, lies?" you ask. "Complex numbers aren't the most intuitive things in the world, hence the use of the adjective 'complex,' but they are certainly consistent with the rest of mathematics, if we allow the concept of i."

"LIES I say, and LIES I mean!" yells the boy. He takes a horseshoe and writes the following in the dirt:

$$\frac{-1}{1} = \frac{1}{-1}$$

"True or false?" demands the boy. You say "True," and your friends nod in assent. They love you. You are their leader.

The boy then says, "And we can take the square root of both sides?"

$$\sqrt{\frac{-1}{1}} = \sqrt{\frac{1}{-1}}$$

"Of course," you say. Your friends do not have to agree with you out loud, because they are looking on you with admiration and respect.

The boy continues to write in the dirt:

$$\frac{\sqrt{-1}}{\sqrt{1}} = \frac{\sqrt{1}}{\sqrt{-1}}$$

$$\frac{i}{1} = \frac{1}{i}$$

"Fine by me!" you say, wondering why the boy continues to write such obvious banalities. "Fine by us!" chorus your friends.

The boy asks you for help with his cross-multiplying. You oblige:

$$i \cdot i = 1 \cdot 1$$

$$-1 = 1$$

There is an uncomfortable pause. You look to your friends, but they are not making eye contact. A single tear is about to run down one of their cheeks. Is all of mathematics a big lie? Are negative numbers really the same as positive numbers? If that is true, could you please write a letter to my credit card company, telling them that they actually owe *me* a few thousand dollars?

Or is it possible that somewhere, somehow, someone made a mistake? Find the error.

1.5 | Other Types of Equations

■ Suggested Time and Emphasis

$\frac{1}{2}$ – 1 class. Essential material. More time is necessary if the students have not yet mastered quadratic equations.

■ Points to Stress

1. Solving generalized quadratic equations.

2. Solving equations by factoring.

3. Solving equations involving fractional expressions.

■ Sample Questions

- **Text Question:** Solve: $\dfrac{1}{x+4} = \dfrac{1}{2x}$.

  Answer: $x = 4$

- **Drill Question:** Solve: $(x+3)^2 + 2(x+3) = -1$.

  Answer: $x = -4$

■ In-Class Materials

- For two resistors in series, the total resistance is easy to find: $R = R_1 + R_2$. Have the students solve the following straightforward problem: "Two resistors are in series. The total desired resistance is $100 \ \Omega$. The first resistor needs to have a resistance $45 \ \Omega$ greater than the second. What should their resistances be?"
  Answer: The equation is $R_1 + (R_1 - 45) = 100$, so $R_1 = 72.5$ and $R_2 = 27.5$.

  Things get more complicated if the resistors are in parallel. In that case we have $\dfrac{1}{R} = \dfrac{1}{R_1} + \dfrac{1}{R_2}$. Have the students try to set up and solve the same problem, only with the resistors in parallel.
  Answer: $R_1 = 225$ and $R_2 = 180$. There is also an extraneous solution.

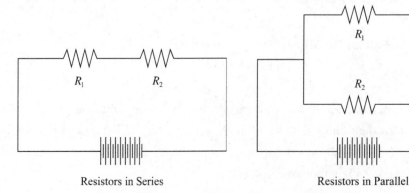

Resistors in Series   Resistors in Parallel

SECTION 1.5 Other Types of Equations

- One can demonstrate an equation involving two square roots. For example:

  The square root of a number, plus one more than that number, is exactly 5. Find the number.

  Answer: $\sqrt{x} + (x+1) = 5 \iff \sqrt{x} = 4 - x \iff x = 16 - 8x + x^2 \iff x^2 - 9x + 16 = 0$. The solutions to the quadratic are approximately 2.438 and 6.562. The latter proves to be extraneous, leaving 2.438 as the answer.

- One can approximate the complicated function $\cos x^2$ by $1 - \frac{1}{2}x^4 + \frac{1}{24}x^8$ near $x = 0$. It would be difficult to solve $\cos x^2 = \frac{1}{6}$ algebraically, but we can approximate the answer by solving $1 - \frac{1}{2}x^4 + \frac{1}{24}x^8 = \frac{1}{6} \iff x^8 - 12x^4 + 20 = 0 \iff (x^4 - 2)(x^4 - 10) = 0 \iff x = \pm\sqrt[4]{2}$ or $\pm\sqrt[4]{10}$. The answer is $\pm\sqrt[4]{2}$. The other answer is too far from zero for the approximation to be accurate.

▪ Examples

- An equation that can be solved by factoring: $x^4 + x^3 - 6x^2 = 0 \implies x = -3, x = 0$, or $x = 2$.
- An equation in quadratic form: $\left(x^2 + 4x + 5\right)^2 - 3\left(x^2 + 4x + 5\right) + 2 = 0 \implies x = -3, x = -2$, or $x = -1$.

▪ Group Work: The Joint Gift

The difficult part of this problem will be setting it up. Once the students have done so, they will have to solve $928 + 16n - \dfrac{1920}{n} = 960$, which can be put into quadratic form by multiplying both sides by n. This problem is similar to Exercises 69 and 70 in the text.

Answer: $(n - 2)\left(\dfrac{960}{n} + 16\right) = 960 \implies 12$ people worked in the office originally.

▪ Homework Problems

Core Exercises: 5, 15, 19, 29, 37, 39, 45, 75, 83

Sample Assignment: 2, 5, 11, 12, 15, 19, 21, 22, 29, 31, 32, 37, 39, 45, 56, 75, 76, 78, 83, 86, 87

GROUP WORK, SECTION 1.5
The Joint Gift

A group of computer programmers in an office decide to get together to get a gift for their beloved boss. The gift will cost $960. Everyone is okay with this gift, because they like their boss, and they are dividing the cost equally. Unfortunately, two days before they are due to buy the gift, one of them makes the boss' tea too hot, and gets fired. The day before they are due to buy the gift, one of them makes the boss' tea too cold, and gets fired. Now everybody's share has gone up by $16 each, which is a full day's pay!

How many people worked in the office originally?

Suggested Time and Emphasis

1 class. Essential material.

Points to Stress

1. Definition of inequalities.

2. Manipulation of linear and nonlinear inequalities.

Sample Questions

- **Text Question:** Solve the inequality $(x - 1)(x - 3) < 0$.
  Answer: $1 < x < 3$
- **Drill Question:** Solve the pair of inequalities $5 \leq 4x - 7 < 17$.
  Answer: $3 \leq x < 6$

In-Class Materials

- There are dozens of silly mnemonics to help students distinguish between "$<$" and "$>$". Even though most of your students may know the difference, it doesn't hurt to present a mnemonic. One can think of each as a mouth aimed at the bigger number, or as an arrow pointing to the smaller number. Also, some students aren't aware that $2 < x < 4$ actually constitutes two inequalities. Five minutes spent on the simple things may save a lot of time later.

- Just as a quadratic equation can have zero, one, or two solutions, quadratic inequalities can have zero, one, or infinitely many solutions. A good way to clarify this point is to solve the following with the students:

$$x^2 + 2x \leq 0$$
$$x^2 + 2x + 1 \leq 0$$
$$x^2 + 2x + 1 < 0$$
$$x^2 + 2x + 2 \leq 0$$

- A nice comparison is the difference between these two inequalities:

$$\frac{x}{x^2 + 4} < 0$$
$$\frac{x}{x^2 - 4} < 0$$

- Ask the students if there is an inequality that is true for every value of x *except* a single number, say 22. See if they can come up with something like $(x - 22)^2 > 0$.

Example

Solve $-5 < x^2 + 3x + 2 < 10$.
Answer: $-\frac{3}{2} - \frac{1}{2}\sqrt{41} < x < -\frac{3}{2} + \frac{1}{2}\sqrt{41}$

◼ Group Work: Sketching Solution Sets

This activity is designed to help students sketch solution sets, and get a feel for working with inequalities. Before handing this out, warn the students to be particularly careful on the second problem.

Answers:

1. (a) $(0, 1) \cup (3, \infty)$

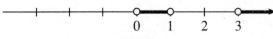

(b) $[0, 1] \cup [3, \infty)$

(c) $(-\infty, 0] \cup [1, 3]$

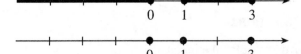

(d) $\{0, 1, 3\}$

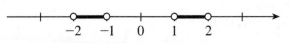

2. (a) $(-2, -1) \cup (1, 2)$

(b) $(-2, -1] \cup [1, 2)$

(c) $(-\infty, -2) \cup [-1, 1] \cup (2, \infty)$

(d) $\{\pm 1\}$

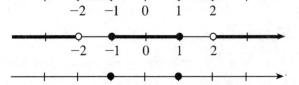

◼ Homework Problems

Core Exercises: 19, 29, 39, 77, 79

Sample Assignment: 1, 6, 17, 18, 19, 29, 33, 34, 38, 39, 40, 44, 53, 54, 73, 75, 77, 78, 79, 82, 83, 89, 93, 96

Solve the following inequalities and equations, and graph their solution sets.

1. (a) $x^3 - 4x^2 + 3x > 0$

(b) $x^3 - 4x^2 + 3x \geq 0$

(c) $x^3 - 4x^2 + 3x \leq 0$

(d) $x^3 - 4x^2 + 3x = 0$

2. (a) $\dfrac{x^2 - 1}{x^2 - 4} < 0$

(b) $\dfrac{x^2 - 1}{x^2 - 4} \leq 0$

(c) $\dfrac{x^2 - 1}{x^2 - 4} \geq 0$

(d) $\dfrac{x^2 - 1}{x^2 - 4} = 0$

Suggested Time and Emphasis

$\frac{1}{2}$ – 1 class. Essential material.

Point to Stress

Solving inequaiities of the form $|A| < B$ and $|A| > B$.

Sample Questions

- **Text Question:** The text says that $|a| = \begin{cases} a & \text{if } a \geq 0 \\ -a & \text{if } a < 0 \end{cases}$ By this definition, is it possible for $|a|$ to be negative? Why or why not?

  Answer: No. If $a \geq 0$, then $|a| = a \geq 0$. If $a < 0$, then $|a| = -a > 0$. In either case, $a \geq 0$.

- **Drill Question:** Solve $|3x + 5| = 14$.

  Answer: $x = -\frac{19}{3}$ or $x = 3$

In-Class Materials

- Point out that there is a bit of asymmetry in this topic. The expression $|x| < 5$ corresponds to one interval, while $|x| > 5$ corresponds to two. If the group work "The Tour" was covered in Section 1.3, then it can be redone now using the language that was learned in this section.

- One of the themes of this chapter is taking verbal descriptions and translating them into algebraic equations. Assume that we know that a length of tubing (to three significant figures) is 11.6 cm. Because of significant figures, there is a range of possible exact lengths of tubing. For example, if the actual length is 11.6000323 cm, we would report the length as 11.6 cm. Have the students try to express the range of values as an absolute value inequality: $|x - 11.6| \leq 0.05$.

- Have half the class solve $|2x - 8| < 16$ and the other half solve $|8 - 2x| < 16$. See if they can explain why both problems have the same answer.

- There is a particular type of inequality that shows up often in higher mathematics: $0 < |x - a| < \delta$. Ask the students to graph $0 < |x - 3| < \frac{1}{10}$ and similar inequalities, emphasizing the idea that x is close to 3, but not equal to 3. For fun, you can now write the definition of "limit" on the blackboard, and see what you and the students can do with it at this stage. Note that $\dfrac{x^2 - 9}{x - 3}$ is not defined at $x = 3$, but is close to 6 when x is close to three. Then write the formal definition:

  > **We say** $\displaystyle\lim_{x \to 3} \dfrac{x^2 - 9}{x - 3} = 6$ **because for every** $\varepsilon > 0$, **there is a** δ **such that** $\left| \dfrac{x^2 - 9}{x - 3} - 6 \right| < \varepsilon$ **whenever** $0 < |x - 3| < \delta$.

Examples

Quadratic inequalities involving absolute values that require thoughtful analysis:

- $\left|x^2 - 8x + 6\right| < 6 \implies x \in (0, 2) \cup (6, 8)$
- $\left|x^2 - 8x + 6\right| \geq 6 \implies x \in (-\infty, 0] \cup [2, 6] \cup [8, \infty)$

Group Work: Teaching Tolerance

Before they start this activity, you may want to remind them that the volume of a sphere is given by $\frac{4}{3}\pi r^3$. After this activity is over, you might want to mention the following: According to engineers at NASA, the roundness tolerance of ball bearings used in the space shuttle is 0.000005 inches. For example, if a ball bearing is supposed to have diameter 0.7867 in., it must meet the requirement that no matter where you measure the diameter, it is greater than 0.786695 inches and less than 0.786705 inches.

Answers:

1. $\left|\frac{1}{3}x - 15\right| \leq 0.1 \implies 44.7 \leq x \leq 45.3$
2. $\left|\frac{4}{3}\pi r^3 - 10\right| \leq \frac{1}{5} \implies 1.3275345 \leq r \leq 1.3453559$. Or, $\frac{1}{10}\sqrt[3]{7350}\pi^{-1/3} \leq r \leq \frac{1}{10}\sqrt[3]{7650}\pi^{-1/3}$.

Homework Problems

Core Exercises: 13, 17, 27, 33, 57

Sample Assignment: 4, 7, 8, 13, 14, 17, 18, 25, 26, 27, 33, 34, 55, 56, 57, 58

GROUP WORK, SECTION 1.7
Teaching Tolerance

When manufacturing items, we often have varying degrees of allowable tolerance. For example, assume a piece of metal needs to be 2 cm wide. If the metal is being used to make an attractive bracelet, any value between 1.9 cm and 2.1 cm would probably be okay. If it is being used to make a ruler, any value between 1.95 cm and 2.05 cm would probably be acceptable. If it is being used in an automobile engine, it would probably be best to have it measure between 1.999 cm and 2.001 cm.

We can express these possible ranges as $|x - 2| \leq 0.1$, $|x - 2| \leq 0.05$, and $|x - 2| \leq 0.001$.

1. Assume that we have a process where for every 3 cm^3 of batter we start with, we wind up with 1 cm^3 of Belderon. Assume that we want to wind up with 15 cm^3 of Belderon, with a tolerance of 0.1 cm^3. What is the allowable range of quantity of batter?

2. Now assume we are manufacturing steel ball bearings. We want to manufacture ball bearings with a volume between 9.8 mm^3 and 10.2 mm^3. What is the allowable range of the radius of each bearing?

CHAPTER 2

Coordinates and Graphs

| The Coordinate Plane

▪ Suggested Time and Emphasis

$\frac{1}{2}-1$ class. Essential material.

▪ Points to Stress

1. Plotting points.

2. The distance and midpoint formulas.

▪ Sample Questions

- **Text Question:** The text derives the distance formula by using the Pythagorean Theorem to show that the distance between A and B is $d(A, B) = \sqrt{|x_2 - x_1|^2 + |y_2 - y_1|^2}$.

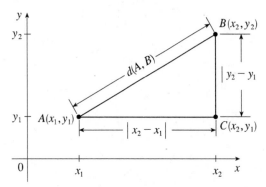

Why can we remove the absolute value signs to find $d(A, B) = \sqrt{(x_2 - x_1)^2 + (y_2 - y_1)^2}$?

Answer: The square of any nonzero real number is positive, so the the absolute value bars are not needed.

- **Drill Question:** Let $P = (1, -3)$ and $Q = (7, 5)$.

  (a) What is the distance between these two points?

  (b) What is the midpoint of these two points?

  Answer: (a) 10 (b) $(4, 1)$

▪ In-Class Materials

- Pass out graph paper. After plotting a few points with integer values with the students, have them try to plot rational points such as $\left(\frac{1}{2}, 0\right)$ and $\left(-\frac{2}{3}, \frac{1}{3}\right)$. Then see what they can do with points such as $\left(\sqrt{2}, -\pi\right)$.

- Obtain a transparency of a local map, and overlay it with an appropriately-sized grid. Try to estimate the walking distance between the classroom and various points of interest. Then use the distance formula to find the distance "as the crow flies". This is discussed in Exercise 51 in the text.

- Assume that a meter stick is situated as in the diagram at right. Ask the students to find the 50 cm mark, and then the 25 cm mark.

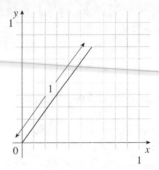

- I have always found this interesting, and your students may, too. Many modern cities are laid out in a grid similar to René Descartes' coordinate system. Paris, however, looks like this:

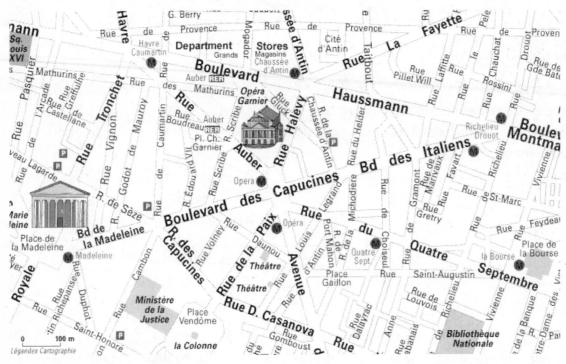

One can imagine René Descartes looking at such a map and saying, "There *must* to be a more organized way to arrange points in a plane!"

Example

Investigate the trapezoidal region given by the inequalities $x > 2$, $y > \frac{3}{2}x - 3$, $y > -x + 7$, and $y < -x + 12$.

Group Work 1: Connect the Dots

Gauge your class carefully. This exercise may be extremely useful to your students, or it may be a waste of their time, depending on their experience level. One variant would be to have them create a connect-the-dots problem for others to solve—perhaps even another class. The difficulty level can be increased by describing points instead of listing them, for example, "The midpoint of $(5, 5)$ and $(-1, -1)$". Points may also be given in polar coordinates.

Answer: It looks like a hand.

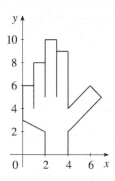

▪ Group Work 2: Taxicab Geometry

Taxicab geometry was first invented in the late 1800s, and is an accessible example of non-Euclidean geometry. In taxicab geometry, we assume a grid where we are allowed to travel only along the roads, and we define "distance" as driving distance. For example, in taxicab geometry, the distance between the point $(0, 0)$ and the point $(5, 6)$ is 11, because we would have to drive five blocks north and six blocks east to get from $(0, 0)$ to $(5, 6)$. There are analogues to circles, parabolas, and all the conic sections in taxicab geometry. This activity explores the distance formula in this context, and then checks to see whether the student really understands the definition of a circle.

If Chapter 11 is to be covered, note at that time that one can draw taxicab ellipses, hyperbolas, and parabolas.

Answers:

1. No, you are a four-mile drive away.

2.

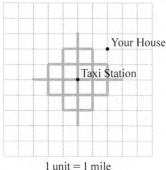

1 unit = 1 mile

3.

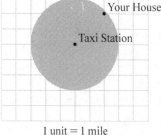

1 unit = 1 mile

4. $d = |x_1 - x_2| + |y_1 - y_2|$

▪ Homework Problems

Core Exercises: 7, 9, 25, 39, 43

Sample Assignment: 3, 5, 6, 7, 9, 11, 12, 13, 20, 23, 25, 32, 36, 39, 43, 44, 53, 57, 58

GROUP WORK 1, SECTION 2.1
Connect the Dots

Plot the following points in order and connect the dots. What do you see?

$(2,0), (2,2), (0,3), (0,6), (1,6), (1,4), (1,8), (2,8), (2,5), (2,10),$

$(3,10), (3,5), (3,9), (4,9), (4,4), (6,6), (7,5), (4,2), (4,0)$

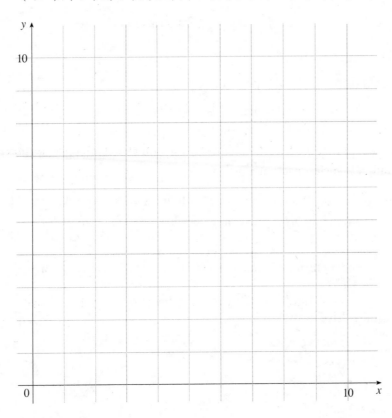

GROUP WORK 2, SECTION 2.1
Taxicab Geometry

Assume you live in a town where the streets form a grid.

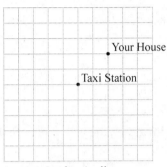

1 unit = 1 mile

1. The taxi dispatcher is willing to let the taxis travel only 3 miles to pick up a customer. Will she allow a taxi to leave her station to pick you up at your house?

2. Shade the region consisting of all points where the cab is allowed to make a pickup.

3. Now assume that, instead of a city, the taxi station and your house are located on a huge expanse of pavement, extending for miles in every direction, with no obstacles in sight. Shade the region where a cab would be allowed to make a pickup.

4. Create a "distance formula" the dispatcher could use to find how far the cab would travel.

Suggested Time and Emphasis

$2 - 2\frac{1}{2}$ classes. Essential material.

Points to Stress

1. The relationship between a two-variable equation and its graph. (This is the most crucial concept.)

2. Sketching graphs by plotting points, using intercepts and symmetry.

3. Equations of circles and their graphs, including the technique of completing the square.

Sample Questions

- **Text Question:** Circle the type of types of symmetry exhibited by each of the following figures.

(a)

(b)

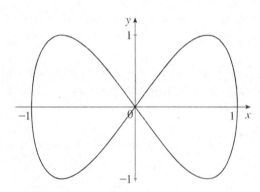

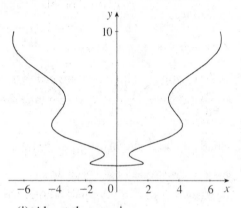

(i) About the x-axis

(ii) About the y-axis

(iii) About the origin

(i) About the x-axis

(ii) About the y-axis

(iii) About the origin

Answer: (a) (i), (ii), and (iii)   (b) (ii)

- **Drill Question:** Graph the circle with equation $x^2 + 2x + y^2 - 4y = 20$.

Answer:

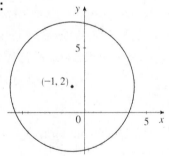

In-Class Materials

- Graph $y = ||x| - 1| - 2$ by plotting points. This is a nice curve because it is easy to get points, but the students will not immediately see what the curve should look like. Have different students obtain different points, and plot them on a common graph on the board.

Answer:

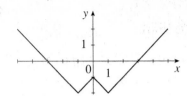

- Exploring symmetry is an excellent way of examining the close relationship between a function and its graph. For example, obtain the graph of $y = \frac{1}{2}x$ by plotting points. Then show its origin symmetry both algebraically and geometrically. (The old "rotate the graph 180 degrees and it looks the same" point of view works very well.) Similarly, explore the symmetries of $y = |x|$, $y = x^2$, and $y = x^3$. Note how things go wrong when algebraically exploring the curve $y = x^{1/2}$. Follow up by looking at a simple implicit curve such as $y^2 = x$.

- Point out that it is not always trivial to find intercepts. For example, first do $y = x^3 - x$ but then point out that finding the x-intercept of $y = x^3 + 2x^2 + 10x - 40$ would be very tough.

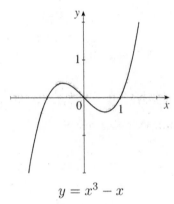

$$y = x^3 - x$$

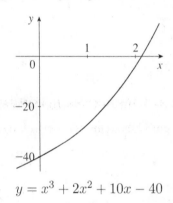

$$y = x^3 + 2x^2 + 10x - 40$$

- Emphasize that the equation $(x - 2)^2 + (y + 3)^2 = 100$ and the equation $x^2 - 4x + y^2 + 6y = -3$ have the same graph — the same points satisfy both equations. Perhaps test $(2, 7)$ and $(1, 1)$ in both equations and notice that $(2, 7)$ satisfies both, and $(1, 1)$ fails to satisfy either. The only difference between the two equations is the form: it is easier to work with the first than the second.

Example

A curve with a lot of intercepts: $y = x^5 - 15x^4 + 85x^3 - 225x^2 + 274x - 120$ looks frightening until students are told it factors to $y = (x - 1)(x - 2)(x - 3)(x - 4)(x - 5)$.

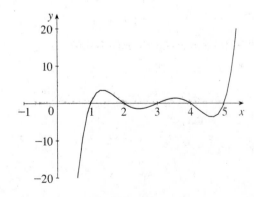

▪ Group Work 1: Discovering the Shift

This group work foreshadows Section 3.4: Transformations of Functions. The curves are obtainable by plotting points, although other techniques may be used. The first part deals with functions, although it doesn't use the term "function". The second part deals with $y^2 = x$, whose graph is also easily obtainable by plotting points.

Answers (Part One):

1. $y = x^2$: x- and y-intercepts $(0,0)$

$y = (x - 1)^2$: x-intercept $(1, 0)$, y-intercept $(0, 1)$

$y = (x - 2)^2$: x-intercept $(2, 0)$, y-intercept $(0, 4)$

$y = (x - 3)^2$: x-intercept $(3, 0)$, y-intercept $(0, 9)$

$y = (x - 4)^2$: x-intercept $(4, 0)$, y-intercept $(0, 16)$

2.

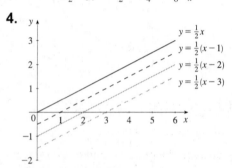

3. $y = \frac{1}{2}x$: x- and y-intercepts $(0,0)$

$y = \frac{1}{2}(x - 1)$: x-intercept $(1, 0)$, y-intercept $\left(0, -\frac{1}{2}\right)$

$y = \frac{1}{2}(x - 2)$: x-intercept $(2, 0)$, y-intercept $(0, -1)$

$y = \frac{1}{2}(x - 3)$: x-intercept $(3, 0)$, y-intercept $\left(0, -\frac{3}{2}\right)$

4.

5.

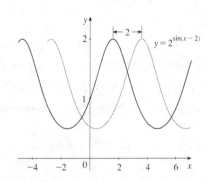

6. Replacing x with $x - k$ shifts a graph k units to the right.

Answers (Part Two):

1. $y^2 = x$: x- and y-intercepts $(0,0)$.

$(y - 1)^2 = x$: x-intercept $(0, 1)$, y-intercept $(1, 0)$

$(y - 2)^2 = x$: x-intercept $(0, 2)$, y-intercept $(4, 0)$

$(y - 3)^2 = x$: x-intercept $(0, 3)$, y-intercept $(9, 0)$

$(y - 4)^2 = x$: x-intercept $(0, 4)$, y-intercept $(16, 0)$

2.

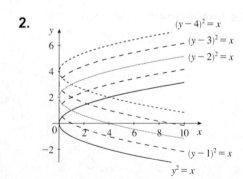

3. $y = \frac{1}{2}x$: x- and y-intercepts $(0,0)$

$y - 1 = \frac{1}{2}x$: x-intercept $(0,1)$, y-intercept $(-2,0)$

$y - 2 = \frac{1}{2}x$: x-intercept $(0,2)$, y-intercept $(-4,0)$

$y - 3 = \frac{1}{2}x$: x-intercept $(0,3)$, y-intercept $(-6,0)$

4.

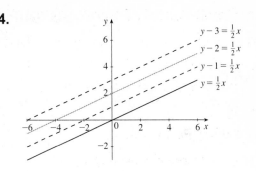

5.

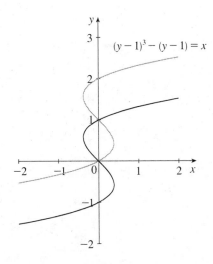

6. Replacing y with $y - k$ shifts a graph k units up.

7. The graph would be shifted 4 units down.

▪ Group Work 2: Symmetry

Don't succumb to the temptation to give hints too early here; this activity should be accessible to any student who has read the material and does not want to give up. If a group finishes early, ask them to write out reasons that certain graphs do not exist.

Answers:

Answers will, and should vary. Problems 5, 6 and 7 are impossible. A straightforward way of showing this is the following pointwise argument: If (x, y) is on the curve, then $(-x, y)$ must also be on it (by symmetry about the x-axis), and then $(x, -y)$ must be on it (by symmetry about the origin), forcing symmetry about the y-axis.

▪ Homework Problems

Core Exercises: 15, 19, 31, 43, 49, 51, 55, 59, 65, 77, 79, 81, 83

Sample Assignment: 4, 8, 15, 17, 19, 23, 24, 28, 31, 32, 38, 40, 43, 49, 51, 53, 55, 56, 57, 59, 63, 65, 67, 70, 73, 77, 79, 80, 81, 83, 86, 93

GROUP WORK 1, SECTION 2.2
Discovering the Shift

Part One

1. Find the x- and y-intercepts of the curves $y = x^2$, $y = (x-1)^2$, $y = (x-2)^2$, $y = (x-3)^2$, and $y = (x-4)^2$.

2. Sketch the graph of each equation in Problem 1.

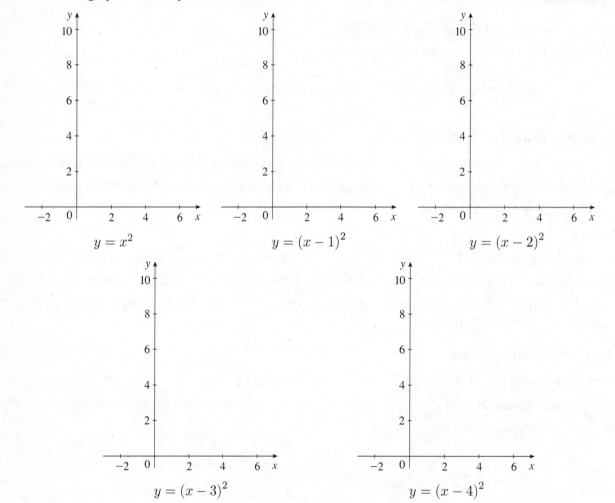

$y = x^2$

$y = (x-1)^2$

$y = (x-2)^2$

$y = (x-3)^2$

$y = (x-4)^2$

3. Find the x- and y-intercepts of the curves $y = \frac{1}{2}x$, $y = \frac{1}{2}(x-1)$, $y = \frac{1}{2}(x-2)$, and $y = \frac{1}{2}(x-3)$.

4. Sketch the graph of each equation in Problem 3.

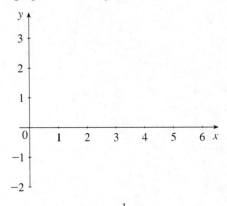

$$y = \frac{1}{2}x$$

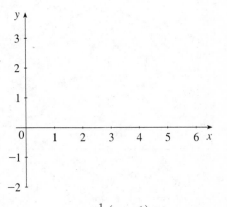

$$y = \frac{1}{2}(x-1)$$

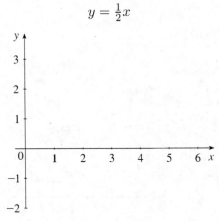

$$y = \frac{1}{2}(x-2)$$

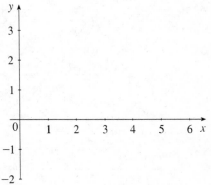

$$y = \frac{1}{2}(x-3)$$

5. This is a graph of the complicated equation $y = 2^{\sin x}$.

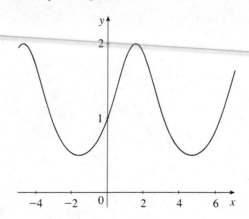

On the same axes, sketch a graph of $y = 2^{\sin(x-2)}$. You don't need to know what "sin" means to do this problem.

6. This activity demonstrates an important principle about replacing x by $x - k$. What is that principle?

Part Two

1. Find the x- and y-intercepts of the curves $y^2 = x$, $(y-1)^2 = x$, $(y-2)^2 = x$, $(y-3)^2 = x$, and $(y-4)^2 = x$.

2. Sketch the graph of each equation in Problem 1.

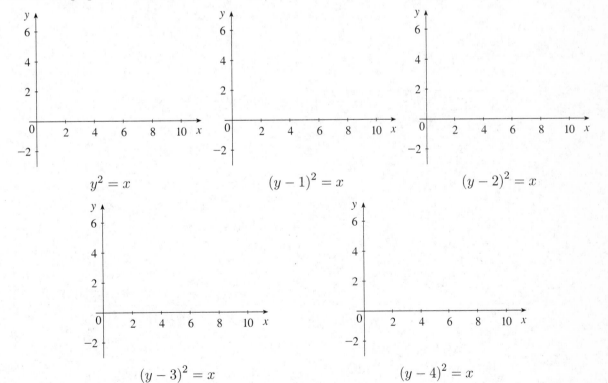

$y^2 = x$

$(y-1)^2 = x$

$(y-2)^2 = x$

$(y-3)^2 = x$

$(y-4)^2 = x$

3. Find the x- and y-intercepts of the curves $y = \frac{1}{2}x$, $y - 1 = \frac{1}{2}x$, $y - 2 = \frac{1}{2}x$, and $y - 3 = \frac{1}{2}x$.

4. Sketch the graph of each equation in Problem 3.

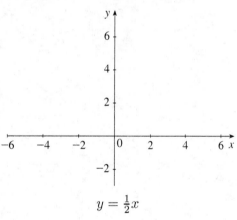

$$y = \frac{1}{2}x$$

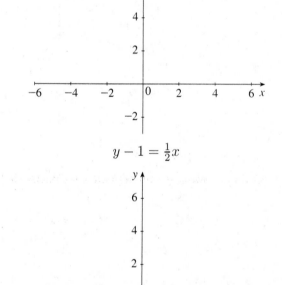

$$y - 1 = \frac{1}{2}x$$

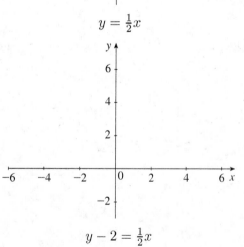

$$y - 2 = \frac{1}{2}x$$

$$y - 3 = \frac{1}{2}x$$

5. This is a graph of the complicated equation $y^3 - y = x$.

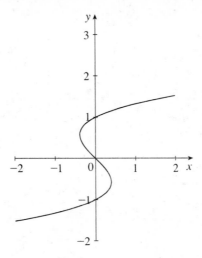

On the same axes, sketch a graph of $(y - 1)^3 - (y - 1) = x$.

6. This activity was designed to demonstrate an important principle about replacing y by $y - k$. What is that principle?

7. What do you think would happen if we replaced y by $y + 4$?

GROUP WORK 2, SECTION 2.2
Symmetry

For this activity you are asked to draw several graphs. If a question asks you to draw something that does not exist, write "Does not exist".

1. Draw a graph that is symmetrical with respect to the x-axis, the y-axis, and the origin.

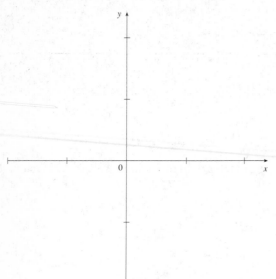

2. Draw a graph that is symmetrical with respect to the x-axis.

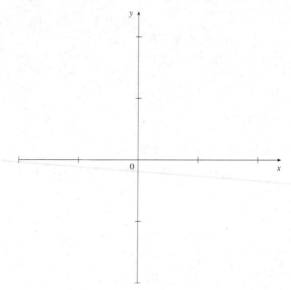

3. Draw a graph that is symmetrical with respect to the y-axis only.

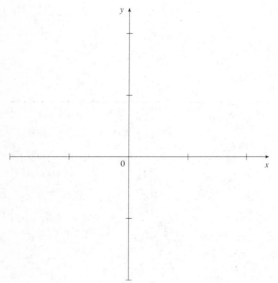

4. Draw a graph that is symmetrical with respect to the origin.

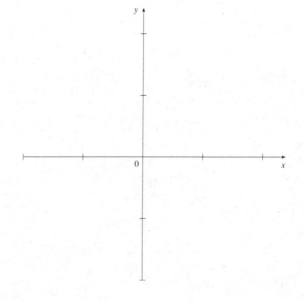

5. Draw a graph that is symmetrical with respect to the x-axis and the y-axis, but not the origin.

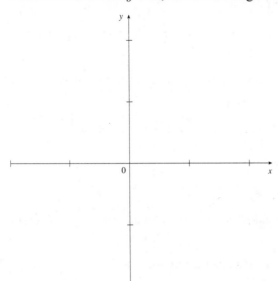

6. Draw a graph that is symmetrical with respect to the x-axis and the origin, but not the y-axis.

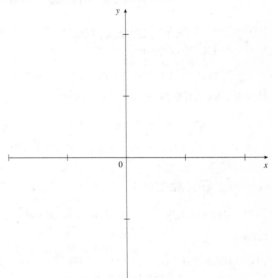

7. Draw a graph that is symmetrical with respect to the y-axis and the origin, but not the x-axis.

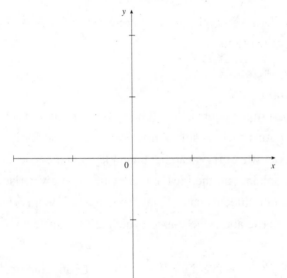

8. Draw a graph that is *not* symmetrical with respect to the x-axis, nor the y-axis, nor the origin.

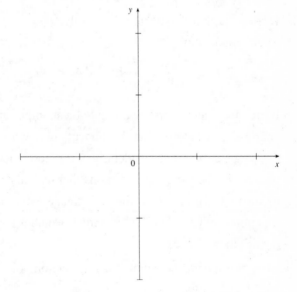

2.3 | Graphing Calculators; Solving Equations and Inequalities Graphically

■ Suggested Time and Emphasis

1 class. Recommended material.

■ Points to Stress

1. Approximating the solution to an equation by finding the roots of an expression graphically.

2. Approximating the solution to an inequality by graphing both sides of the inequality.

■ Sample Questions

- **Text Question:** Give an advantage of solving an equation graphically, and an advantage of solving an equation algebraically.

- **Drill Question:** Solve the equation $x^3 - \sqrt{x} = 2x - 1$ to the nearest thousandth.
  Answer: $x \approx 0.2556$ or $x \approx 1.464$

■ In-Class Materials

- Have the students find an viewing rectangles for $y = 3x + 1$, $y = -x^2 + 2$, and $y = x^6 - 100x^4 + 50$.

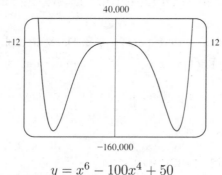

$$y = x^6 - 100x^4 + 50$$

- If graphing calculators are going to be an important part of the course, do not hurry the concept of finding appropriate windows. Let the students play with functions such as $\sin x$, $\ln x$, $\cos^{-1} x$, and so forth. At this stage, don't ask the students to worry too much about what they mean; let them play. Let them develop the idea of the variety of functions their calculators contain, and the idea that each function gives rise to its own special curve. In the unfortunate event that your students can't "play," perhaps ask them which functions are bounded or unbounded, which are symmetric about the y-axis, which are symmetric about the origin, and so on.

- Have the students determine the intersection points of $y = x^2 - 2$ and $y = -x^2 + 5x + 1$ both graphically and algebraically.
  Answers: $x = -\frac{1}{2}$, $x = 3$

- Have the students compare the values of $100x^2$ and $x^4 + 1$ for $x = 0$, $x = \frac{1}{2}$, $x = 1$, and $x = 2$. Then ask the question: For what values of x is $100x^2 > x^4 + 1$? See if they can use their calculators to approximate the answer.

Answers: $100x^2 > x^4 + 1$ for $x \in [-10, -0.1] \cup [0.1, 10]$, approximately.

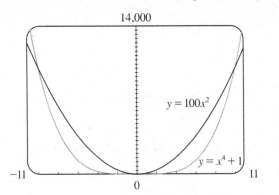

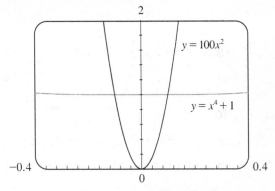

Notice that it is possible to find the right windows by trial and error, but sometimes plugging a number or two into the functions can give a clue as to the best y-range.

■ Examples

Graphs that some calculators get wrong:

- $y = \sqrt{x - 2}\sqrt{x - 4}$ Some calculators do not give a graph with the correct domain.

- $y = \sin x + \frac{1}{100}\cos 100x$ The "standard" viewing rectangle misses the bumps that a rectangle of $[-0.1, 0.1] \times [-0.1, 0.1]$ will catch.

- $y = x^{1/3}$ Some calculators dislike taking negative numbers to rational powers, even when it is possible.

- $y = \dfrac{\sin\left(x - \sqrt{2}\right)}{x - \sqrt{2}}$ Calculators are not good at graphing functions with holes.

■ Group Work 1: Some Interesting Curves

The idea here is to give the students some idea of the variety of functions that their calculator can create, and of some of the calculator's limitations as well. It is also an exercise in putting parentheses in the correct places. If a group finishes early, ask them to come up with their own interesting curve.

Answers:

1.

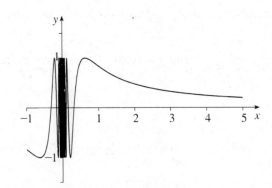

2.

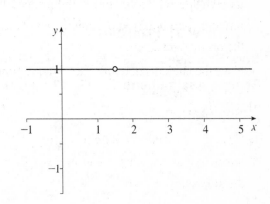

3.

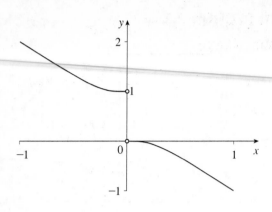

$y = \dfrac{1}{1 - 2^{1/x}}$ is not defined at $x = 0$ because the exponent is undefined there.

4.

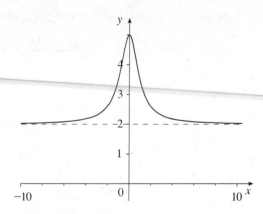

It appears that as x gets very large,

$y = \dfrac{3}{1 + x^2} + 2$ approaches 2.

5.

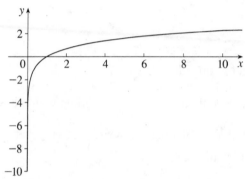

The graph does *not* approach any particular y-value. If it did, then we would have $\ln x < y_0$ for some y_0. But at $x = e^{y_0+1}$, the y-coordinate of the graph is $y = \ln x = \ln e^{y_0+1} = y_0 + 1 > y_0$. This shows that the graph continues to rise indefinitely.

■ Group Work 2: The Small Shall Grow Large

If a group finishes early, ask them to similarly compare x^3 and x^4.

Answers:

1. $x^6 \geq x^8$ for $-1 \leq x \leq 1$

2. $x^3 \geq x^5$ for $-\infty < x \leq -1, 0 \leq x \leq 1$

3. $x^3 \geq x^{105}$ for $-\infty < x \leq -1, 0 \leq x \leq 1$. If the exponents are both even, the answer is the same as for Problem 1; if the exponents are both odd, the answer is the same as for Problem 2.

■ Homework Problems

Core Exercises: 5, 23, 27, 31, 35, 43, 59, 61, 73

Sample Assignment: 3, 5, 7, 9, 10, 17, 18, 22, 23, 25, 26, 27, 29, 30, 31, 34, 35, 36, 41, 43, 47, 48, 59, 61, 69, 70, 72, 73, 77

GROUP WORK 1, SECTION 2.3
Some Interesting Curves

1. Sketch the graph of $y = \sin \dfrac{1}{x}$. Pay particular attention to what happens when x is close to zero.

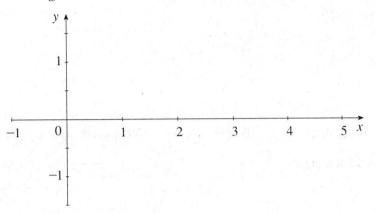

2. Sketch the graph of $y = \dfrac{x - 1.5}{x - 1.5}$. Be careful!

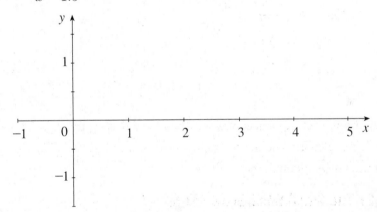

3. Sketch the graph of $y = \dfrac{1}{1 - 2^{1/x}}$. Chose a viewing window that best shows what the graph looks like.

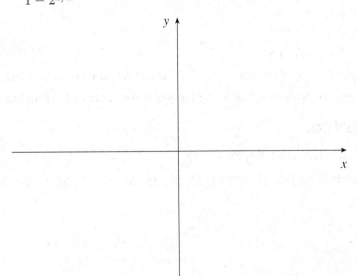

4. Sketch the graph of $y = \dfrac{3}{1 + x^2} + 2$. As x becomes very large, does this graph approach a specific y-value?

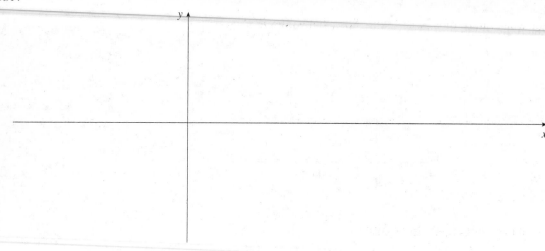

5. Sketch the graph of $y = \ln x$. As x becomes very large, does this graph approach a specific y-value?

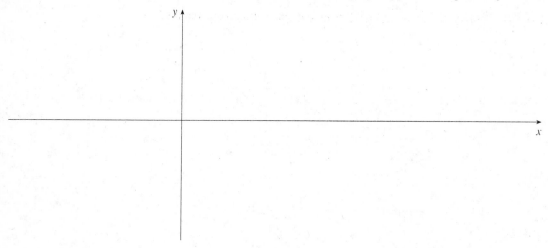

The Small Shall Grow Large

1. For what values of x is $x^6 \geq x^8$? For what values is $x^6 \leq x^8$?

2. For what values of x is $x^3 \geq x^5$?

3. For what values of x is $x^3 \geq x^{105}$? Can you generalize your results?

Suggested Time and Emphasis

1 class. Essential material.

Points to Stress

1. Computing equations of lines in their various forms, given information such as a point and a slope, or two points.
2. The concepts of parallel, perpendicular, slope, vertical, horizontal, and rate of change as reflected in equations of lines.
3. Graphing lines from their equations.

Sample Questions

- **Text Question:** Which of the three lines graphed below has the largest slope?

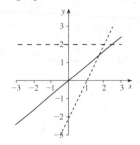

  Answer: The dotted line
- **Drill Question:** Find an equation of the line through the points $(2, 4)$ and $(3, -1)$.
  Answer: $y = -5x + 14$

In-Class Materials

- One good way to get students used to slope is to have them do quick estimates. Stand in front of the class, raise your arm at various angles, and have them write down (or call out) estimates. Students should be able to tell a positive from a negative slope, and if a slope is closer to $\frac{1}{3}$ than it is to 3. Also note that if the x- and y-scales on a graph are different, the appearance of the slope can be misleading.
- A classic example is to have the students come up with conversion formulas from Fahrenheit to centigrade and vice-versa, using the fact that in centigrade measurement, water freezes at $0°$ and boils at $100°$ ($-32°$ F and $212°$ F respectively.) Other conversion formulas can be found, using facts such as the following: 3 ft ≈ 0.914 m, 1 L ≈ 0.264 gal (US), a 250-calorie snack is equivalent to 0.992 BTU, etc.
- Go over an interpolation with the students. For example, compare your school's budget this year with that of ten years ago. Find the equation of the appropriate line. Then try to predict the budget five years ago, and see if a linear model was appropriate. (Linear models will be discussed more thoroughly in the next section.)
- Ask the students to figure out if three given points are vertices of a right triangle. They can go ahead and plot them, to get a guess going. Ask them to come up with a strategy, and reveal (or ideally elicit) the idea of writing equations of lines between each pair of points, and checking for perpendicular lines. $(3, 4)$, $(3, 12)$, and $(6, 5)$ do not form a right triangle; $(-2, -1)$, $(-2, 8)$, and $(8, -1)$ do.

- Don't neglect to give the students horizontal and vertical lines to explore—they often find equations of vertical lines challenging.

▓ Examples

Equations of some standard lines:

- Through $(3, 5)$ and $(-1, 13)$: $y = -2x + 11$
- Through $(6, -5)$ with a slope of $\frac{1}{3}$: $y = \frac{1}{3}x - 7$

▓ Group Work 1: I've Grown Accustomed to Your Growth

This activity uses the students' skills in finding equations of lines to foreshadow the idea that some growth is linear, and some is not linear.

Answers:

1. Yes $(m = 1)$, no, yes $(m \approx 2.08)$, yes $(m \approx 2.01)$

2. Equally spaced changes in x-values result in equally spaced changes in y-values.

▓ Group Work 2: Read Between the Lines

This is a drill-oriented activity, probably best worked on by the students individually, using their groups to check their work. It just goes over various bits of information that suffice to give the equation of a line.

Answers:

1. $y = -\frac{15}{2}x + 35$ **2.** $x = 4$ **3.** $y = -2x + 7$ **4.** $y = 3$

5. $x = 2$ **6.** $y = -2x + 7$ **7.** $y = -\frac{1}{3}x + \frac{11}{3}$ **8.** $x = 2$

9. Not enough information given   **10.** $y = \frac{1}{2}x$ **11.** $y = 4x - 11$

▓ Group Work 3: Lines and Slopes

In this age of graphing calculators, students usually see graphs where the x- and y-scales are the same. This activity allows them to explore slopes when the scales are different, and allows them to connect linear relationships to the real world.

Answers:

1. (b), (a), (c)

2. (a), (c), (b)

3. Answers will vary. Make sure your students' answers are consistent with the slopes of the lines. Possible answers:

(a) The accumulation of rain or snow during a storm.

(b) The distance a jet plane has traveled from a given point in time.

(c) The force exerted by a spring as it stretches.

▓ Homework Problems

Core Exercises: 5, 19, 23, 25, 31, 35, 41, 47, 53, 57, 69, 73

Sample Assignment: 2, 5, 10, 11, 13, 17, 18, 19, 22, 23, 24, 25, 28, 31, 35, 41, 42, 47, 49, 50, 51, 52, 53, 57, 69, 70, 72, 73

GROUP WORK 1, SECTION 2.4
I've Grown Accustomed to Your Growth

1. Some of the following four tables of data have something in common: linear growth. By trying to find equations of lines, determine which of them represent linear growth. Which table has the slowest growth?

x	y
1	2
2	3
3	4
4	5

x	y
21.5	4.32
32.6	4.203
43.7	4.090
54.8	3.980

x	y
−3	1.1
−2.5	2.14
−2	3.18
−1.5	4.22

x	y
1	−5.00
3	−0.98
6	5.05
8	9.07

2. In a sentence, describe a property of linear growth that can be determined from a table of values.

Read Between the Lines

Find the equations of the following lines. If there is not enough information given, write "Not enough information given".

1. The line through the points $(4, 5)$ and $(6, -10)$.

2. The line through the points $(4, 5)$ and $(4, -10)$.

3. The line through the point $(2, 3)$ with a slope of -2.

4. The horizontal line through the point $(2, 3)$.

5. The vertical line through the point $(2, 3)$.

6. The line through the point $(2, 3)$ that is parallel to the line $y = -2x + 11$.

7. The line through the point $(2, 3)$ that is perpendicular to the line $3x - y + 12 = 0$.

8. The line through the point $(2, 3)$ that is perpendicular to the line $y = 5$.

9. The line parallel to the line $y = -2x + 11$ and perpendicular to the line $y = \frac{1}{2}x + 12$.

10. The line with slope $\frac{1}{2}$ that passes through the origin.

11. The line parallel to the line $y = 4x - 2$ which passes through the point of intersection of the lines $y = x - 2$ and $y = 2x - 5$.

GROUP WORK 3, SECTION 2.4
Lines and Slopes

1. Sort the following three lines from smallest slope to largest slope.

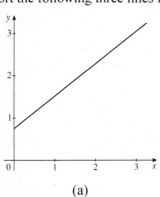

(a)

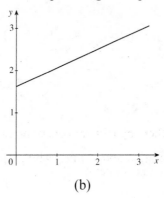

(b)

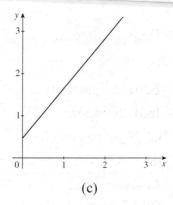

(c)

2. Sort the following three lines from smallest slope to largest slope.

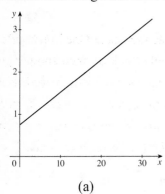

(a)

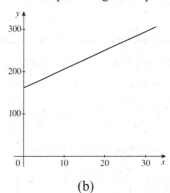

(b)

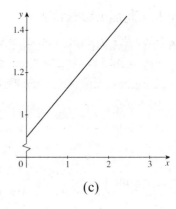

(c)

3. For each of the following graphs, describe a possible real-world situation that it might model. Make sure your answer is realistic.

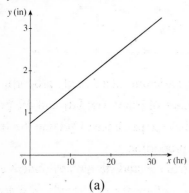

(a)

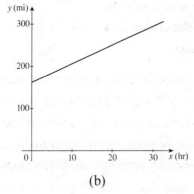

(b)

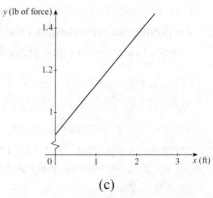

(c)

▪ Suggested Time and Emphasis

1 class. Recommended material.

▪ Point to Stress

Direct and inverse proportionality.

▪ Sample Questions

- **Text Question:**

    (a) If y is proportional to x, must there be a linear equation relating y and x?

    (b) If there is a linear equation relating y and x, must y be proportional to x?

    Answer: (a) Yes   (b) No

- **Drill Question:** The mass of a memo is proportional to the number of pages it contains. If a 100-page memo measures 89 g, how much mass would a 35 page memo have?

    Answer: $(0.89)\,35 = 31.15\,\text{g}$

▪ In-Class Materials

- Have the students come up with as many examples of proportionality as they can. One quick, effective way would be to give them a minute to write down as many as they could think of, then another couple of minutes to discuss their list with a neighbor, generating more, and finally write down their answers on the board. With luck, some will accidentally give examples that are not proportional or that are inversely proportional. If these don't come up, you can ask, "What about the height of a person and that person's average rent?" or, "What about the cost of a computer and its weight, all other things being equal?"

- Point out that proportionality is a model, just like a linear model or any other kind of model. For example, show them an example of a scatter plot such as the one below (from Figure 1 in the Discovery Project "Visualizing Data" after Section 2.1 in the text).
  Clearly there is no straight line that will go through the points, but we can model the relationship by a straight line to try to make predictions.

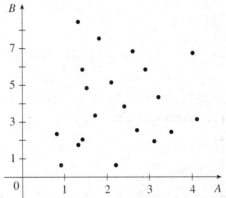

- Discuss the difference between a general linear relationship and direct variation: in a directly proportional relationship, the origin is a data point. For example, the number of cans of beans you buy and the price you pay are in direct proportion—zero cans costs zero dollars. If you have to pay a fee to get into the store (as in some discount stores) the two quantities are no longer in direct proportion.

- There are many proportional and inversely proportional relationships that the students already understand, but may not have thought about using that vocabulary. For example, the area of a circle is directly proportional to the square of its radius. The area of a rectangle is jointly proportional to its length and width. The time it takes to make a trip (of fixed distance) is inversely proportional to the average speed.

Examples

- Newton's Law: The rate of change of temperature of an object is proportional to the difference between the current temperature of the object and the temperature of its surroundings.
- Torricelli's Law: The velocity at which liquid pours out of a cylindrical container (like orange juice out of a can with a hole at the bottom) is proportional to the square root of its height in the container.
- Einstein's Law: The energy of a photon is directly proportional to its frequency.
- Einstein's Theory of Relativity: The energy of a particle is proportional to its mass. (The constant of proportionality being the speed of light, squared.)

Group Work 1: Powers of Magnification

All of these are real measurements taken by the author's brother, except for the second, which was altered slightly to make the inverse relationship work more closely. If a group finishes early, or if you want to go into more detail, point out that the measurement was actually "$100\times = 20$ microns" and discuss whether an inverse variation model is still appropriate.

Notice the premise of the problem: the mathematician doesn't quite understand the application, but understands the mathematics enough to answer the question. In industry, people who model often are not given the "big picture," but are still expected to answer questions based on the information they have, and on the underlying principles of mathematics.

Answers:

1. This is inversely proportional, since the larger the magnification, the smaller the pointer.
2. The constant is approximately 1600. The first three data points give 1600 exactly. The last point would give 1600 if it were actually 1.6. (If we are talking about a tenth of a micron, we can't rule out experimental error.)
3. 8 microns

Group Work 2: Circular Reasoning

Make sure that there are several circles of different sizes around the room. Show the students how to measure perimeter of a circle the careful way (wrapping a string, and measuring the string) or the sloppy way (holding a ruler to the edge and rolling it around) based on your preference. The students already know the formula $C = \pi d$ but may not recognize it in this context. When they are finished, congratulate them and point out that they have just approximated π.

If this activity is too simple, have the students try to find the constant acceleration due to gravity (9.8 m/s^2), the constant of a spring, or the formula for the volume of a cylinder.

Homework Problems

Core Exercises: 17, 19, 29, 35, 41

Sample Assignment: 3, 7, 8, 9, 12, 17, 18, 19, 21, 25, 29, 31, 32, 35, 41, 42, 48, 49

GROUP WORK 1, SECTION 2.5
Powers of Magnification

I received this email from my brother, an amateur scientist, last month:

```
From:  "Melvin Shaw" <melvin@melvinshaw.com>
To:  "Doug Shaw" <doug@dougshaw.com>
Date:  Sat, 17 Nov 2007 14:11:54 -0600
Subject:  Math help needed!

Hey bro.  I took the following measurements of the pointer in my eyepiece at
the powers of magnification shown on the left:

40X = 40 microns
100X = 16 microns
400X = 4 microns
1000X = 1.5 microns

Are these random numbers, or are they related in some way?
```

Frankly, I didn't know what he was talking about; I didn't know what the $\times$ meant, nor what the pointer in the eyepiece was, exactly (Was it shrinking? Why?) But I knew some mathematics, and recognized this as a proportional relationship.

1. Was this a directly proportional relationship, or an inversely proportional relationship? How do you know?

2. Approximately what is the constant of proportionality?

3. If my brother had a $200\times$ lens, predict the "pointer measurement".

GROUP WORK 2, SECTION 2.5
Circular Reasoning

Find three differently sized circles in the room, or make them yourself using a compass.

1. What are the diameters of your three circles?

2. What are the circumferences of your three circles?

3. Many people believe that the circumference of a circle is directly proportional to its diameter. Do you think this is true? Using your data, approximate the constant of proportionality.

CHAPTER 3   Functions

■ Suggested Time and Emphasis

$\frac{1}{2}$ – 1 class. Essential material.

■ Points to Stress

1. The idea of function, viewed as the dependence of one quantity on a different quantity.

2. The notation associated with numeric functions, including piecewise-defined functions.

3. Domains and ranges from an algebraic perspective.

4. Four different representations of functions (verbally, algebraically, visually, and numerically).

■ Sample Questions

• **Text Question:** What is a function?

Answer: Answers will vary. Anything that gets at the idea of assigning an element in one set to an element in another set should be given full credit.

• **Drill Question:** Let $f(x) = x + \sqrt{x}$. Find $f(0)$ and $f(4)$.

Answer: $f(0) = 0$, $f(4) = 6$

■ In-Class Materials

• If students are using calculators, discuss the ties between the idea of a function and a calculator key. The keys such as sin, cos, tan, and $\sqrt{}$ represent functions. It is easy to compute and graph functions on a calculator. Contrast this with equations such as $y^3 - x^3 = 2xy$ which have graphs, but are not easy to work with, even with a calculator. (Even symbolic algebra calculators such as the TI-89 do not do well with all general relations.) Point out that the calculator often gives approximations to function values—applying the square root function key to the number 2 gives 1.4142136 which is close to, but not equal to, $\sqrt{2}$.

• This course emphasizes functions where both the domain and range sets are numerical. One could give a more abstract definition of function, where D and R can be any set. For example, there is a function mapping each student in the class to his or her birthplace. A nice thing about this point of view is that it can be pointed out that the map from each student to his or her telephone number may *not* be a function, since a student may have more than one telephone number, or none at all.

• Function notation can trip students up. Start with a function such as $f(x) = x^2 - x$ and have your students find $f(0)$, $f(1)$, $f(\sqrt{3})$, and $f(-1)$. Then have them find $f(\pi)$, $f(y)$, and (of course) $f(x + h)$. Some students will invariably, some day, assume that $f(a + b) = f(a) + f(b)$ for all functions, but this can be minimized if plenty of examples such as $f(2 + 3)$ are done at the outset.

- Discuss the straightforward things to look for when trying to find the domain of a function: zero denominators and negative even roots. Discuss the domain and range of a function such as

$$f(x) = \begin{cases} x^2 & \text{if } x \text{ is an integer} \\ 0 & \text{if } x \text{ is not an integer} \end{cases}$$ If the class seems interested, perhaps let them think about

$$f(x) = \begin{cases} x^2 & \text{if } x \text{ is rational} \\ 0 & \text{if } x \text{ is irrational} \end{cases}$$

- Let $f(x) = \dfrac{x(x-2)}{x-2}$ and $g(x) = x$. Ask students if the functions are the same function. If they say "yes", ask them to compare the domains, or to compute $g(2)$ and $f(2)$. If they say "no" ask them to find a value such that $f(x) \neq g(x)$. [This activity assumes that students know the equation of a circle with radius r. If they do not, this may be a good opportunity to introduce the concept.]

Examples

- Real-world piecewise functions:

  1. The cost of mailing a letter that weighs x ounces (see Exercise 90 in Section 3.2)

  2. The cost of making x photocopies (given that there is usually a bulk discount)

  3. The cost of printing x pages from a computer (at some point the toner cartridge must be replaced)

- A function with a non-trivial domain: $\sqrt{\dfrac{x^2 - 5x + 6}{x^2 - 2x + 1}}$ has domain $(-\infty, 1) \cup (1, 2] \cup [3, \infty)$.

Group Work 1: Choosing a Calling Plan

This activity will require some advance work on the part of your students, but it will be worth it. It anticipates Example 7 in Section 3.2. Television is full of advertisements for long-distance services and cell phone plans. They often have a figure such as "five cents per minute," but there are a lot of details behind the figure. There may or may not be a monthly fee. There may or may not be a minimum call length. (One commercial offered a 20-minute call for $1, but did not mention that a three-minute call also cost $1.) There may or may not be a fee change after a certain time. (One plan costs five cents per minute for the first twenty minutes and seven cents per minute thereafter.) There may also be a rate increase after a certain base number of minutes are used.

Have each student pick a plan (or you can assign plans to them) and research exactly how the plan works. In addition to the myriad cell phone and long distance plans, there are collect call plans such as 1-800-COLLECT and 1-800-CALL ATT. Students can also research the cost of an operator-assisted long distance call. After they have done so, this group work can be handed out.

Part 1 is for this section and is algebraic in nature. Part 2 is for the next section (although it can be done earlier) and involves drawing a graph of a piecewise function. Note that you may not want to discuss the greatest integer function at this point. In that case, you can let students assume that the call lengths are all an integral number of minutes.

You may have to "keep students honest" here—a careless student may take the phrase "five cents per minute" at face value and not worry about the fine print. Being able to listen carefully to a commercial or a salesperson and translate the pitch into mathematics is not a trivial skill.

It might be a good idea to collect students' findings and distribute them. Students can then be assigned to decide which plan is best for them, taking into account their average call length, and the amount of calling they do each month. (The monthly fees become important to a person who doesn't use the phone often.) An alternative form of this group work is provided that deals with text messages.

Group Work 2: Finding a Formula

Make sure that students know the equation of a circle with radius r, and that they remember the notation for piecewise-defined functions. Divide the class into groups of four. In each group, have half of them work on each problem first, and then have them check each other's work. If students find these problems difficult, have them work together on each problem.

Answers: 1. $f(x) = \begin{cases} -x - 2 & \text{if } x \le -2 \\ x + 2 & \text{if } -2 < x \le 0 \\ 2 & \text{if } x > 0 \end{cases}$ **2.** $g(x) = \begin{cases} x + 4 & \text{if } x \le -2 \\ 2 & \text{if } -2 < x \le 0 \\ \sqrt{4 - x^2} & \text{if } 0 < x \le 2 \\ x - 2 & \text{if } x > 2 \end{cases}$

Group Work 3: Rounding the Bases

On the board, review how to compute the percentage error when estimating π by $\frac{22}{7}$. (Answer: 0.04%) Have them work on the problem in groups. If a group finishes early, have them look at $h(7)$ and $h(10)$ to see how fast the error grows. Students have not seen exponential functions before, but Problem 3 is a good foreshadowing of Section 5.1.

Answers: 1. 17.811434627, 17, 4.56% **2.** 220.08649875, 201, 8.67% **3.** 45.4314240633, 32, 29.56%

Homework Problems

Core Exercises: 13, 17, 19, 27, 35, 43, 47, 51, 65, 71

Sample Assignment: 2, 3, 8, 13, 17, 18, 19, 20, 26, 27, 29, 35, 43, 47, 50, 51, 52, 60, 61, 65, 67, 71, 72, 75, 84

GROUP WORK 1, SECTION 3.1
Choosing a Calling Plan

1. You have been assigned to research a calling plan. What is the name of the plan you've investigated?

2. Is there a monthly fee?

For Questions 3–7, do not include monthly fees.

3. How much would it cost to make a twenty-minute call using your plan?

4. How much would it cost to make a five-minute call?

5. How much would it cost to make a one-minute call?

6. How much would it cost to make a three-hour call?

7. Write a function $c(t)$, where t is the duration of the call in minutes and $c(t)$ is the cost of the call.

8. How much would it cost to make 20 five-minute calls in a month? (Include the monthly fee.)

9. How much would it cost to make 2 fifty-minute calls in a month? (Include the monthly fee.)

10. Is this plan suitable for you? Why or why not?

Choosing a Text Message Plan

1. You have been assigned to research a text message plan. What is the name of the plan you've investigated?

2. Is there a monthly fee?

For Questions 3–5, do not include monthly fees.

3. How much would it cost to send twenty messages in one month using your plan?

4. How much would it cost to send three hundred messages in one month?

5. How much would it cost to send just one message in one month?

6. Is there a maximum message length?

7. Now including the monthly fee, how much would it cost to send 20 messages in one month. 300 messages? A single message?

8. What is the average cost per message under this plan if you send 20 messages in one month. 300 message? A single message?

9. Write a function $c(n)$ modeling the total monthly cost c if n messages are sent that month.

10. Is this plan suitable for you? Why or why not?

Find formulas for the following functions:

1.

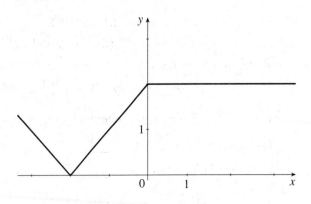

2.

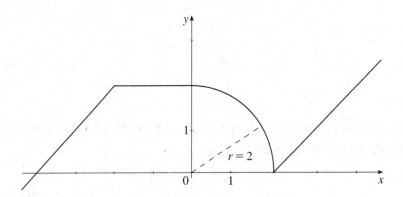

GROUP WORK 3, SECTION 3.1
Rounding the Bases

1. For computational efficiency and speed, we often round off constants in equations. For example, consider the linear function

$$f(x) = 3.137619523x + 2.123337012$$

In theory, it is very easy and quick to find $f(1)$, $f(2)$, $f(3)$, $f(4)$, and $f(5)$. In practice, most people doing this computation would probably substitute

$$f(x) = 3x + 2$$

unless a very accurate answer is called for. For example, compute $f(5)$ both ways to see the difference.

The actual value of $f(5)$: _____

The "rounding" estimate: _____

The percentage error: _____

2. Now consider

$$g(x) = 1.12755319x^3 + 3.125694x^2 + 1$$

Again, one is tempted to substitute $g(x) = x^3 + 3x^2 + 1$.

The actual value of $g(5)$: _____

The "rounding" estimate: _____

The percentage error: _____

3. It turns out to be very dangerous to similarly round off exponential functions, due to the nature of their growth. For example, let's look at the function

$$h(x) = (2.145217198123)^x$$

One may be tempted to substitute $h(x) = 2^x$ for this one. Once again, look at the difference between these two functions.

The actual value of $h(5)$: _____

The "rounding" estimate: _____

The percentage error: _____

■ **Suggested Time and Emphasis**

1 class. Essential material.

■ **Points to Stress**

1. The Vertical Line Test.

2. Graphs of piecewise-defined functions.

3. The greatest integer function.

■ **Sample Questions**

- **Text Question:** Your text discusses the greatest integer function $[\![x]\!]$. Compute $[\![2.6]\!]$, $[\![2]\!]$, $[\![-2.6]\!]$, and $[\![-2]\!]$.

  Answer: $[\![2.6]\!] = 2$, $[\![2]\!] = 2$, $[\![-2.6]\!] = -3$, $[\![-2]\!] = -2$

- **Drill Question:** Let $f(x) = x^2 + |x|$. Which of the following is the graph of f? How do you know?

(a)
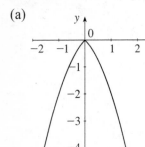

(b)
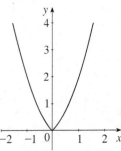

(c)
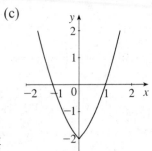

(d)
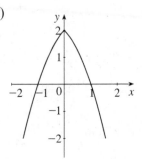

Answer: (b) is the graph of f, because $f(x) \geq 0$ for all x.

■ **In-Class Materials**

- Draw a graph of fuel efficiency versus time on a trip, such as the one below. Lead a discussion of what could have happened on the trip.

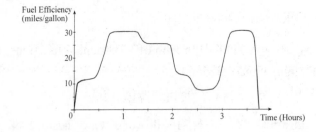

- In 1984, United States President Ronald Reagan proposed a plan to change the United States personal income tax system. According to his plan, the income tax would be 15% on the first $19,300 earned, 25% on the next $18,800, and 35% on all income above and beyond that. Describe this situation to the class, and have them graph (marginal) tax rate and tax owed versus income for incomes ranging from $0 to $80,000. Then have them try to come up with equations describing this situation.

- In the year 2000, Presidential candidate Steve Forbes proposed a "flat tax" model: 0% on the first $36,000 and 17% on the rest. Have your students do the same analysis, and compare the two models. As an extension, perhaps have them look at a current tax table and draw similar graphs.

• Discuss the shape, symmetries, and general "flatness" near 0 of the power functions x^n for various values of n. Similarly discuss $\sqrt[n]{x}$ for n even and n odd. A blackline master is provided at the end of this section, before the group work handouts.

▨ Examples

• A continuous piecewise-defined function

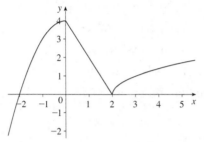

$$f(x) = \begin{cases} 4 - x^2 & \text{if } x < 0 \\ 4 - 2x & \text{if } 0 \le x \le 2 \\ \sqrt{x-2} & \text{if } x > 2 \end{cases}$$

• A discontinuous piecewise-defined function

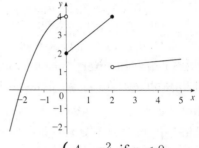

$$f(x) = \begin{cases} 4 - x^2 & \text{if } x < 0 \\ x + 2 & \text{if } 0 \le x \le 2 \\ \sqrt[3]{x} & \text{if } x > 2 \end{cases}$$

• Classic rational functions with interesting graphs

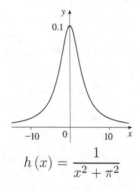

$$h(x) = \frac{1}{x^2 + \pi^2}$$

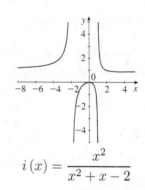

$$i(x) = \frac{x^2}{x^2 + x - 2}$$

▨ Group Work 1: Every Picture Tells a Story

Put students in groups of four, and have them work on the exercise. If there are questions, encourage them to ask each other before asking you. After going through the correct matching with them, have each group tell their story to the class and see if it fits the remaining graph.

Answers:

1. (b)   **2.** (a)   **3.** (c)

4. The roast was cooked in the morning and put in the refrigerator in the afternoon.

▨ Group Work 2: Functions in the Classroom

Before starting this one, review the definition of "function". Some of the problems can be answered only by polling the class after they are finished working. Don't forget to take leap years into account for the eighth problem. For an advanced class, anticipate Section 3.7 by quickly defining "one-to-one" and "bijection", then determining which of the functions have these properties.

Answers:

Chairs: Function, one-to-one, bijection (if all chairs are occupied)

Eye color: Function, not one-to-one

Mom & Dad's birthplace: Not a function; mom and dad could have been born in different places

Molecules:

Function, one-to-one (with nearly 100% probability); inverse assigns a number of molecules to the appropriate student.

Spleens: Function, one-to-one, bijection. Inverse assigns each spleen to its owner.

Pencils: Not a function; some people may have more than one or (horrors!) none.

Social Security Number: Function, one-to-one; inverse assigns each number to its owner.

February birthday: Not a function; not defined for someone born on February 29.

Birthday: Function, perhaps one-to-one.

Cars: Not a function; some have none, some have more than one.

Cash: Function, perhaps one-to-one.

Middle names: Not a function; some have none, some have more than one.

Identity: Function, one-to-one, bijection. Inverse is the same as the function.

Algebra instructor: Function, not one-to-one.

▪ Group Work 3: Rational Functions

Remind students of the definition of a rational function as a quotient of polynomials. Students should be able to do this activity by plotting points and looking at domains and ranges.

Answers:

1. 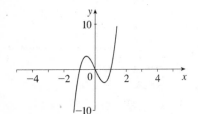 **2.** (d)   **3.** (b)   **4.** (e)   **5.** (c)   **6.** (a)

▪ Homework Problems

Core Exercises: 11, 15, 19, 23, 35, 51, 57, 61, 69, 81

Sample Assignment: 4, 11, 15, 16, 19, 20, 23, 26, 28, 31, 35, 36, 40, 45, 50, 51, 57, 60, 61, 64, 69, 81, 83

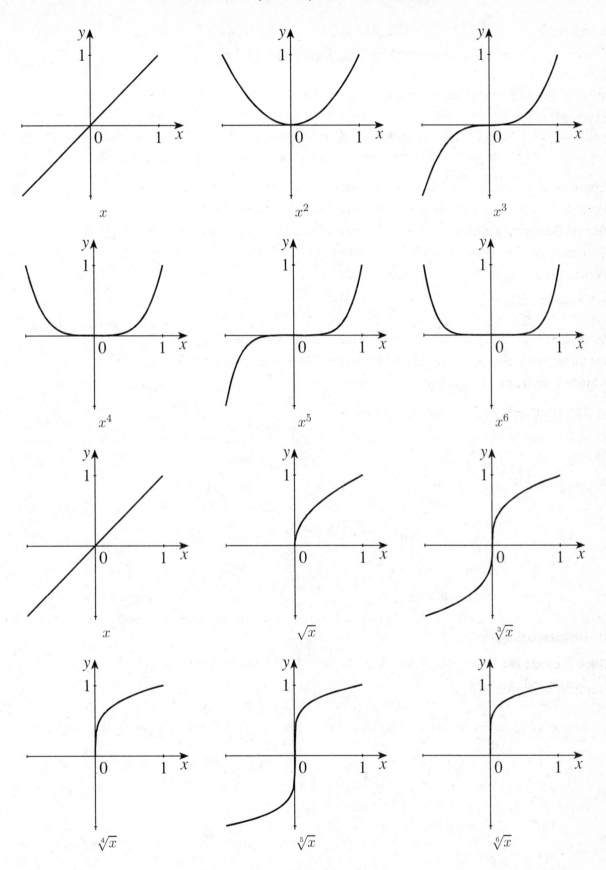

GROUP WORK 1, SECTION 3.2
Every Picture Tells a Story

One of the skills you will be learning in this course is the ability to take a description of a real-world occurrence, and translate it into mathematics. Conversely, given a mathematical description of a phenomenon, you will learn how to describe what is happening in plain language. Here follow four graphs of temperature versus time and three stories. Match the stories with the graphs. When finished, write a similar story that would correspond to the final graph.

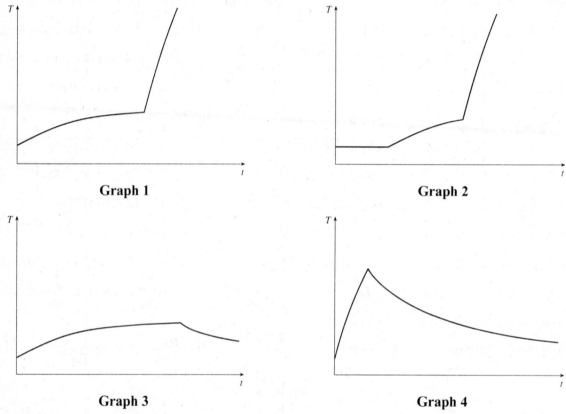

Graph 1   Graph 2

Graph 3   Graph 4

(a) I took my roast out of the freezer at noon, and left it on the counter to thaw. Then I cooked it in the oven when I got home.

(b) I took my roast out of the freezer this morning, and left it on the counter to thaw. Then I cooked it in the oven when I got home.

(c) I took my roast out of the freezer this morning, and left it on the counter to thaw. I forgot about it, and went out for Chinese food on my way home from work. I put it in the refrigerator when I finally got home.

GROUP WORK 2, SECTION 3.2
Functions in the Classroom

Which of the following relations are functions?

Domain	Function Values	Function
All the people in your classroom	Chairs	f (person) = his or her chair
All the people in your classroom	The set {blue, brown, green, hazel}	f (person) = his or her eye color
All the people in your classroom	Cities	f (person) = birthplace of their mom and dad
All the people in your classroom	ℝ, the real numbers	f (person) = number of molecules in their body
All the people in your classroom	Spleens	f (person) = his or her own spleen
All the people in your classroom	Pencils	f (person) = his or her pencil
All the people in the United States	Integers from 0–999999999	f (person) = his or her Social Security number
All the living people born in February	Days in February, 2007	f (person) = his or her birthday in February 2007
All the people in your classroom	Days of the year	f (person) = his or her birthday
All the people in your classroom	Cars	f (person) = his or her car
All the people in your classroom	ℝ, the real numbers	f (person) = how much cash he or she has
All the people in your college	Names	f (person) = his or her middle name
All the people in your classroom	People	f (person) = himself or herself
All the people in your classroom	People	f (person) = his or her algebra instructor

GROUP WORK 3, SECTION 3.2
Rational Functions

The functions below are sad and lonely because they have lost their graphs! Help them out by matching each function with its graph. One function's graph is not pictured here; when you are done matching, go ahead and sketch that function's graph.

1. $\dfrac{x^3 - x}{0.125}$

2. $\dfrac{x^2 - 1}{x^2 - 4}$

3. $\dfrac{x^2 - 4}{x^2 - 1}$

4. $\dfrac{x^2 - 1}{x + 0.5}$

5. $\dfrac{5x\left(x^2 - 1\right)}{x^2 + 1}$

6. $\dfrac{5x\left(x^2 - 1\right)}{-x^2 - 1}$

(a)

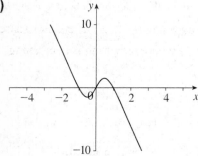

(b)

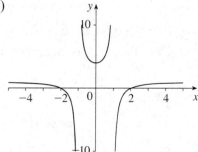

(c)

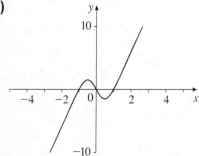

(d)

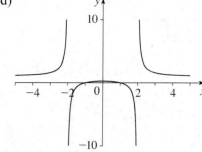

(e)

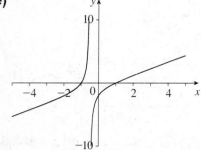

Suggested Time and Emphasis

1 class. Essential material.

Points to Stress

1. Gaining information about a function from its graph, including finding function values, domain and range.

2. Algebraic and geometric definitions of increasing and decreasing.

3. Finding local extrema of a function from its graph.

Sample Questions

- **Text Question:** Draw a graph of a function with domain $[-10, 10]$ and range $[-2, 2]$. There should be at least one interval where the graph is increasing and at least one interval where the graph is decreasing.

  Answer: Answers will vary.

- **Drill Question:** If $f(x) = -x^2 + 9x + 2$, find the extreme value of f. Is it a maximum or a minimum?
  Answer: $f\left(\frac{9}{2}\right) = \frac{89}{4}$ is a maximum.

In-Class Materials

- Explore domain and range with some graphs that have holes, such as the graphs of some of the functions in the previous section.

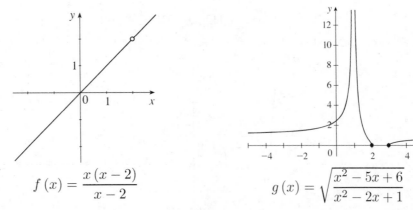

$$f(x) = \frac{x(x-2)}{x-2} \qquad\qquad g(x) = \sqrt{\frac{x^2 - 5x + 6}{x^2 - 2x + 1}}$$

- Draw a graph of electrical power consumption in the classroom versus time on a typical weekday, pointing out important features throughout, and using the vocabulary of this section as much as possible.

- Notice that it is fairly easy to tell where some functions are increasing and decreasing by looking at their graphs. For example, the graph of $f(x) = x^4 - 8x^2$ makes things very clear. Note that in this case, the intervals are not immediately apparent from looking at the formula. However, for many functions such as $g(x) = x^3 - 3x^2 + x + 1$, it is very difficult to find the exact intervals where the function is increasing/decreasing. In this example, the endpoints of the intervals will occur at precisely $x = 1 \pm \frac{1}{3}\sqrt{6}$.

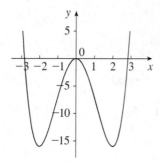

$$f(x) = x^4 - 8x^2$$

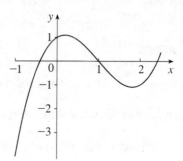

$$g(x) = x^3 - 3x^2 + x + 1$$

- Revisit $f(x) = \begin{cases} x^2 & \text{if } x \text{ is rational} \\ 0 & \text{if } x \text{ is irrational} \end{cases}$ pointing out that it is neither increasing nor decreasing near $x = 0$. Stress that when dealing with new sorts of functions, it becomes important to know the precise mathematical definitions of such terms.

Examples

- A function with two integer turning points and a flat spot:

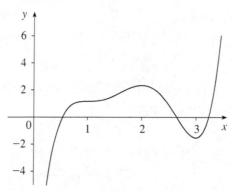

$$\tfrac{1}{6}\left(12x^5 - 105x^4 + 340x^3 - 510x^2 + 360x - 90\right)$$

- A function with several local extrema: $f(x) = x^4 + x^3 - 7x^2 - x + 6 = (x+3)(x+1)(x-1)(x-2)$

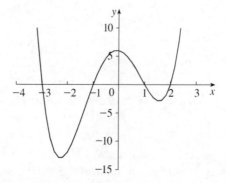

The extrema occur at $x \approx -2.254$, $x \approx -0.0705$, and $x \approx 1.5742$.

▪ Group Work 1: Calculator Exploration

This gives students a chance to graph things on their calculator and make conclusions. It will also serve as a warning that relying on calculator graphs without understanding the functions can lead one astray.

Notice that in calculus, when we say a function is increasing, we are saying it is increasing at every point on its domain. In this context, we are talking about increasing over an interval, which is slightly different. The curve $-1/x$, for example, is increasing at every point in its domain. Can we say it is decreasing over the interval $[-10, 1]$? No, because it is not defined in that interval. So the curve $-1/x$ is increasing over every interval for which it is defined.

Answers:

1. (c)   **2.** (a)   **3.** (a) (assuming positive intervals)   **4.** (c)   **5.** (c)   **6.** (a)   **7.** (b)   **8.** (a)   **9.** (c)
10. (c)

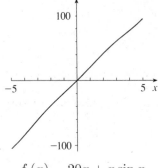

$$f(x) = 20x + x\sin x$$

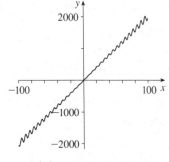

$$f(x) = 20x + x\sin x$$

▪ Group Work 2: The Little Dip

In this exercise students analyze a function with some subtle local extrema. After they have tried, reveal that there are two local maxima and two local minima.

After students have found the extrema, point out that if they take calculus, they will learn a relatively simple way to find the exact coordinates of the extrema.

Answers:

1.

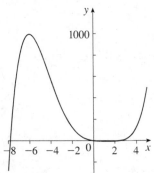

2. There are local maxima at $x = -6$ and $x = \frac{5}{4}$, and local minima at $x = 1$ and $x = \frac{3}{2}$.

▪ Homework Problems

Core Exercises: 5, 15, 29, 35, 45, 53

Sample Assignment: 4, 5, 6, 7, 15, 27, 28, 29, 33, 35, 37, 40, 42, 45, 49, 53, 56

GROUP WORK 1, SECTION 3.3
Calculator Exploration

Graph the following curves on your calculator. For each curve specify which of the following applies.

(a) The graph of f is increasing over every interval (assuming the curve is defined everywhere in that interval).

(b) The graph of f is decreasing over every interval (assuming the curve is defined everywhere in that interval).

(c) The graph of f is increasing over some intervals and decreasing over others.

1. $f(x) = x^2$

2. $f(x) = x^3$

3. $f(x) = \sqrt{x}$

4. $f(x) = \sin x$

5. $f(x) = \cos x$

6. $f(x) = \tan x$

7. $f(x) = e^{-x}$

8. $f(x) = \ln x$

9. $f(x) = 5x^4 - 1.01^x$

10. $f(x) = 20x + x \sin x$

GROUP WORK 2, SECTION 3.3
The Little Dip

Consider $f(x) = \frac{1}{5}x^5 + \frac{9}{16}x^4 - \frac{143}{24}x^3 + \frac{207}{16}x^2 - \frac{45}{4}x$.

1. Draw a graph of f.

2. Estimate the x-values of all local extrema. Make sure your estimates are accurate to three decimal places.

■ **Suggested Time and Emphasis**

$\frac{1}{2}$–1 class. Essential material.

■ **Points to Stress**

1. Average rate of change.

■ **Sample Questions**

• **Text Question:**

Let $f(t) = 3t + 2$.

(a) What is the average rate of change of f from $t = 1$ to $t = 3$?

(b) What is the average rate of change of f from $t = 1$ to $t = \pi$?

Answer: (a) 3   (b) 3

• **Drill Question:** If $f(t) = \left|t^2 - |3t|\right|$, what is the average rate of change between $t = -3$ and $t = -1$?

Answer: 1

■ **In-Class Materials**

• Students should see the geometry of the average rate of change — that the average rate of change from $x = a$ to $x = b$ is the slope of the line from $(a, f(a))$ to $(b, f(b))$. Armed with this knowledge, students now have a way of estimating average rate of change: graph the function (making *sure* that the x- and y-scales are the same), plot the relevant points, and then estimate the slope of the line between them.

• It is possible, at this point, to foreshadow calculus nicely. Take a simple function such as $l(t) = t^2$ and look at the average rate of change from $t = 1$ to $t = 2$. Then look at the average rate of change from $t = 1$ to $t = \frac{3}{2}$. If students work in parallel, they should be able to fill in the following table:

From	To	Average Rate of Change
$t = 1$	2	3
$t = 1$	1.5	2.5
$t = 1$	1.25	2.25
$t = 1$	1.1	2.1
$t = 1$	1.01	2.01
$t = 1$	1.001	2.001

Note that these numbers seem to be approaching 2. This idea is pursued further in Group Work 2.

• Assume that a car drove for two hours and traversed 120 miles. The average rate of change is clearly 60 miles per hour. Ask the students if it was possible for the car to have gone over 60 mph at some point in the interval, and explain how. Ask the students if it was possible for the car to have stayed under 60 mph the whole time. Ask the students if it was possible for the car never to have gone exactly 60 mph. Their intuition will probably say that the car had to have had traveled exactly 60 mph at one point, but it will be hard for them to justify. The truth of this statement is an example of the Mean Value Theorem from calculus.

▪ Example

If $f(x) = x^3 - x$, the average rate of change from $x = 1$ to $x = 4$ is

$$\frac{f(4) - f(1)}{4 - 1} = \frac{(4^3 - 4) - (1^3 - 1)}{3} = \frac{(64 - 4) - (1 - 1)}{3} = \frac{60}{3} = 20$$

▪ Group Work: Small Intervals

If you have the time, and really wish to foreshadow calculus, have the students find the limit starting with $x = 1$ and then again with $x = 3$. Then see if they can find the pattern, and discover that the average value is going to approach $3a^2$ if we start at a.

Students won't remember every detail of this problem in a year, obviously. So when you close, try to convey the main idea that as we narrow the interval, the average values approach a single number, and that everything blows up if we make the interval consist of a single point. You may want to mention that exploring this phenomenon is a major part of the first semester of calculus.

Answers:

1. 19 **2.** 15.25 **3.** 12.61 **4.** 12.0601 **5.** 12.006001 **6.** 11.9401 **7.** 12 **8.** You get $\frac{0}{0}$, which is undefined.

▪ Homework Problems

Core Exercises: 11, 15, 25

Sample Assignment: 3, 4, 6, 11, 12, 15, 18, 19, 20, 25, 30, 31

GROUP WORK, SECTION 3.4
Small Intervals

Let us consider the curve $y = x^3$. Assume I am interested only in what is happening near $x = 2$. It is clear that the function is getting larger there, but my question is, how quickly is it increasing? One way to find out is to compute average rates of change.

1. Find the average rate of change between $x = 2$ and $x = 3$.

2. The number 2.5 is even closer to the number 2. Remember, I only really care about what is happening very close to $x = 2$. So compute the average rate of change between $x = 2$ and $x = 2.5$.

3. We can get closer still. Compute the average rate of change between $x = 2$ and $x = 2.1$.

4. Can we get closer? Sure! Compute the average rate of change between $x = 2$ and $x = 2.01$.

5. Compute the average rate of change between $x = 2$ and $x = 2.001$.

6. We can also approach 2 from the other side. Compute the average rate of change between $x = 2$ and $x = 1.99$.

7. Your answers should be approaching some particular number as we get closer and closer to 2. What is that number?

8. Hey, the closest number to 2 is 2 itself, right? So go ahead and compute the average rate of change between $x = 2$ and $x = 2$. What happens?

■ Suggested Time and Emphasis

1 class. Essential material.

■ Points to Stress

1. Transforming a given function to a different one by shifting, stretching, and reflection.

2. Using the technique of reflection to better understand the concepts of even and odd functions.

■ Sample Questions

• **Text Question:** What is the difference between a vertical stretch and a vertical shift?

  Answer: A vertical stretch extends the graph in the vertical direction, changing its shape. A vertical shift simply moves the graph in the vertical direction, preserving its shape.

• **Drill Question:** Given the graph of $f(x)$ below, sketch the graph of $\frac{1}{2}f(x) + 1$.

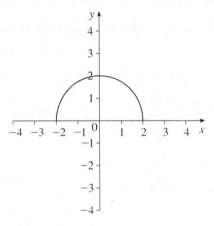

Answer:

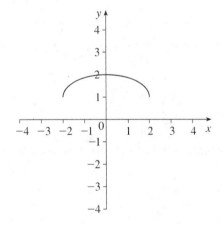

■ In-Class Materials

• Students will often view this section as a process of memorizing eight similar formulas. While it doesn't hurt to memorize how to shift, reflect, or stretch a graph, emphasize to students the importance of understanding what they are doing when they transform a graph. Group Work 1: Discovering the Shift (in Section 2.2) and Group Work 1: Stretching (in this section) should help students understand and internalize. Tell students that if worse comes to worst, they can always plot a few points if they forget in which direction the graphs should move.

- Show the class a function they have not learned about yet, such as $f(x) = \sin x$. (If students know about sin, then show them arctan or e^{-x^2}—any function with which they are unfamiliar.) Point out that even though they don't know a lot about $\sin x$, once they've seen the graph, they can graph $\sin x + 3$, $\sin(x - 1)$, $2\sin x$, $-\sin x$, etc.

- Graph $f(x) = x^2$ with the class. Then anticipate Section 4.1 by having students graph $(x - 2)^2 - 3$ and $(x + 1)^2 + 2$, finally working up to $g(x) = (x - h)^2 + k$. If you point out that any equation of the form $g(x) = ax^2 + bx + c$ can be written in this so-called *standard form*, students will have a very good start on the next section in addition to learning this one.

- This is a good time to start discussing parameters. Ask your students to imagine a scientist who knows that a given function will be shaped like a stretched parabola, but has to do some more measurements to find out exactly what the stretching factor is. In other words, she can write $f(x) = -ax^2$, noting that she will have to figure out the a experimentally. The a is not a variable, it is a parameter. Similarly, if we are going to do a bunch of calculations with the function $f(x) = \sqrt[3]{x + 2}$, and then do the same calculations with $\sqrt[3]{x + 3}$, $\sqrt[3]{x - \pi}$, and $\sqrt[3]{x - \frac{2}{3}}$, it is faster and easier to do the set of calculations just once, with the function $g(x) = \sqrt[3]{x + h}$, and then fill in the different values for h at the end. Again, this letter h is called a parameter. Ask the class how, in the expression $f(t) = t + 3s$, they can tell which is the variable, and which is the parameter—the answer may encourage them to use careful notation.

■ Example

A distinctive-looking, asymmetric curve that can be stretched, shifted and reflected:

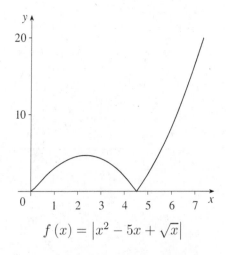

$$f(x) = \left| x^2 - 5x + \sqrt{x} \right|$$

■ Group Work 1: Label Label Label, I Made It Out of Clay

Some of these transformations are not covered directly in the book. If the students are urged not to give up, and to use the process of elimination and testing individual points, they should be able to complete this activity.

Answers: 1. (d) **2.** (a) **3.** (f) **4.** (e) **5.** (i) **6.** (j) **7.** (b) **8.** (c) **9.** (g) **10.** (h)

■ Group Work 2: Which is the Original?

The second problem has a subtle difficulty: the function is defined for all x, so some graphs show much more of the behavior of $f(x)$ than others do.

Answers: 1. $2f(x+2), 2f(x), f(2x), f(x+2), f(x)$ **2.** $2f(x), f(x), f(x+2), f(2x), 2f(x+2)$

■ Homework Problems

Core Exercises: 11, 13, 15, 17, 19, 21, 23, 25, 27, 29, 53, 65, 67, 69

Sample Assignment: 9, 11, 13, 15, 17, 19, 21, 23, 25, 27, 28, 29, 41, 44, 49, 52, 53, 61, 65, 67, 69, 74

This is a graph of the function $f(x)$:

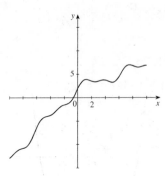

Give each graph below the correct label from the following:

(a) $f(x+3)$ (b) $f(x-3)$ (c) $f(2x)$ (d) $2f(x)$ (e) $|f(x)|$

(f) $f(|x|)$ (g) $2f(x)-1$ (h) $f(2x)+2$ (i) $f(x)-x$ (j) $1/f(x)$

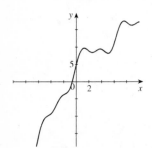
Graph 1

Graph 2

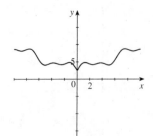
Graph 3

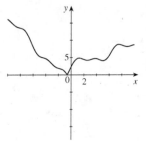
Graph 4

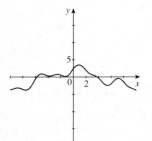
Graph 5

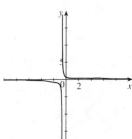
Graph 6

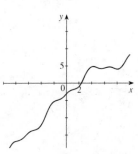
Graph 7

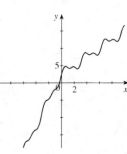
Graph 8

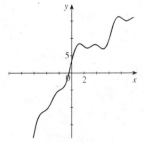
Graph 9

Graph 10

GROUP WORK 2, SECTION 3.5
Which is the Original?

Below are five graphs. One is the graph of a function $f(x)$ and the others include the graphs of $2f(x)$, $f(2x)$, $f(x+2)$, and $2f(x+2)$. Determine which is the graph of $f(x)$ and match the other functions with their graphs.

1.

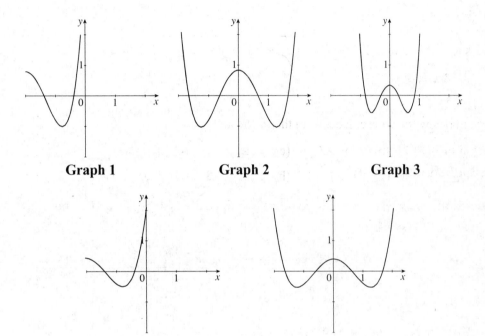

Graph 1   Graph 2   Graph 3

Graph 4   Graph 5

2.

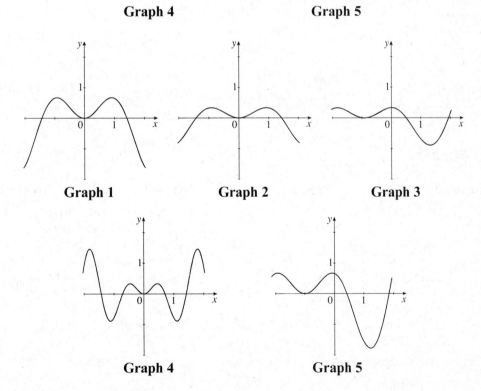

Graph 1   Graph 2   Graph 3

Graph 4   Graph 5

Suggested Time and Emphasis

$\frac{1}{2}$–1 class. Essential material.

Points to Stress

1. Addition, subtraction, multiplication, and division of functions.

2. Composition of functions.

3. Finding the domain of a function based on analysis of the domain of its components.

Sample Questions

- **Text Question:** The text describes addition, multiplication, division, and composition of functions. Which of these operations is represented by the following diagram?

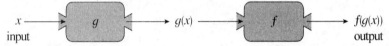

Answer: Composition

- **Drill Question:** Let $f(x) = 4x$ and $g(x) = x^3 + x$.

  (a) Compute $(f \circ g)(x)$.

  (b) Compute $(g \circ f)(x)$.

  Answer: (a) $4\left(x^3 + x\right) = 4x^3 + 4x$ (b) $(4x)^3 + 4x = 64x^3 + 4x$

In-Class Materials

- Do the following problem with the class:

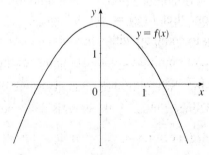

From the graph of $y = f(x) = -x^2 + 2$ shown above, compute $f \circ f$ at $x = -1$, 0, and 1. First do it graphically, then algebraically.

138

- Show the tie between algebraic addition of functions and graphical addition. For example, let $f(x) = 1 - x^2$ and $g(x) = x^2 + \frac{1}{2}x - 1$. First add the functions graphically, as shown below, and then show how this result can be obtained algebraically: $\left(1 - x^2\right) + \left(x^2 + \frac{1}{2}x - 1\right) = \frac{1}{2}x$.

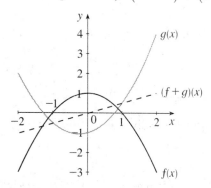

- Point out that it is important to keep track of domains, especially when doing algebraic simplification. For example, if $f(x) = x + \sqrt{x}$ and $g(x) = 3x^2 + \sqrt{x}$, even though $(f - g)(x) = x - 3x^2$, its domain is not $\mathbb{R}$ but $\{x \mid x \geq 0\}$.

- Function maps are a nice way to explain composition of functions. To demonstrate $g \circ f(x)$, draw three number lines labeled x, $f(x)$, and $g(x)$, and then indicate how each number x goes to $f(x)$ which then goes to $g(f(x))$. For example, if $f(x) = \sqrt{x}$ and $g(x) = 2x - 1$, the diagram looks like this:

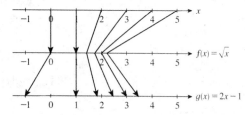

- After doing a few basic examples of composition, it is possible to foreshadow the idea of inverses, which will be covered in the next section. Let $f(x) = 2x^3 + 3$ and $g(x) = x^2 - x$. Compute $f \circ g$ and $g \circ f$ for your students. Then ask them to come up with a function $h(x)$ with the property that $(f \circ h)(x) = x$. They may not be used to the idea of coming up with examples for themselves, and so the main hints they will need might be "don't give up," "when in doubt, just try something and see what happens," and "I'm not expecting you to get it in fifteen seconds." If the class is really stuck, have them try $f(x) = 2x^3$ to get a feel for how the game is played. Once they have determined that $h(x) = \sqrt[3]{\dfrac{x - 3}{2}}$, have them compute $(h \circ f)(x)$ and have them conjecture whether, in general, if $(f \circ g)(x) = x$ then $(g \circ f)(x)$ must also equal x.

■ Example

Combined functions with graphs: Let $f(x) = x^2 - 3x + 2$ and $g(x) = -\sqrt{x}$.

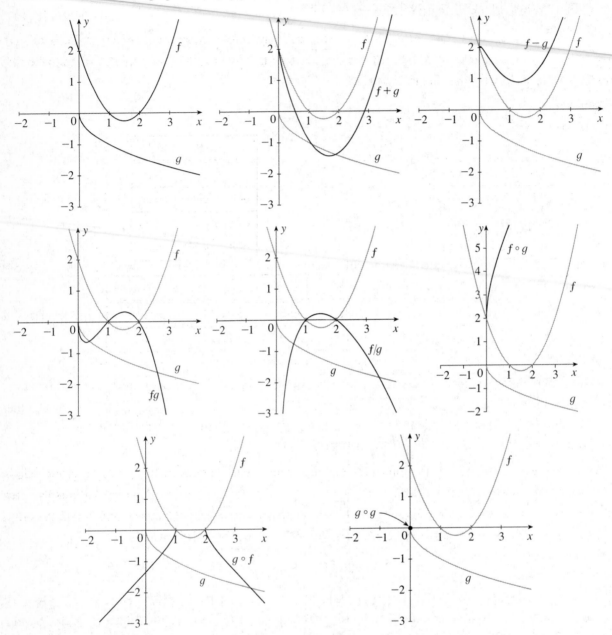

■ Group Work 1: Transformation of Plane Figures

This tries to remove the composition idea from the numerical context, and introduces the notion of symmetry groups. It is a longer activity than it seems, and can lead to an interesting class discussion of this topic.

Answers:

1. (a) $f\left(\ulcorner\right) = \urcorner$ (b) $g\left(\urcorner\right) = \ulcorner$ (c) $f\left(f\left(\llcorner\right)\right) = \urcorner$ (d) $g\left(g\left(\urcorner\right)\right) = \urcorner$

2. This is false. For example, $(f \circ g)\left(\llcorner\right) = \llcorner$, but $(g \circ f)\left(\llcorner\right) = \urcorner$.

3. It is true: reversing something thrice in a mirror gives the same result as reversing it once.

4. It rotates the shape $270°$ clockwise or, equivalently, $90°$ counterclockwise.

■ Group Work 2: Odds and Evens

This is an extension of Exercise 66 in the text. Students may find the third problem very difficult to start. You may want to give selected table entries on the board first, before handing the activity out, to make sure students understand what they are trying to do.

Answers:

1.

a	b	$a+b$
even	even	even
odd	even	odd
even	odd	odd
odd	odd	even

2.

a	b	$a \cdot b$
even	even	even
odd	even	even
even	odd	even
odd	odd	odd

3.

f	g	$f+g$	fg	$f \circ g$	$g \circ f$
even	even	even	even	even	even
even	odd	neither	odd	even	even
odd	even	neither	odd	even	even
odd	odd	odd	even	odd	odd
neither	neither	unknown	unknown	unknown	unknown

■ Group Work 3: It's More Fun to Compute

Each group gets one copy of the graph. During each round, one representative from each group stands, and one of the questions below is asked. The representatives write their answer down, and all display their answers at the same time. Each representative has the choice of consulting with their group or not. A correct solo answer is worth two points, and a correct answer after a consult is worth one point.

1. $(f \circ g)(5)$ **5.** $(g \circ g)(5)$ **9.** $(g \circ f)(1)$

2. $(g \circ f)(5)$ **6.** $(g \circ g)(-3)$ **10.** $(f \circ f \circ g)(4)$

3. $(f \circ g)(0)$ **7.** $(g \circ g)(-1)$ **11.** $(g \circ f \circ f)(4)$

4. $(f \circ f)(5)$ **8.** $(f \circ g)(1)$ **12.** $(f \circ g \circ f)(4)$

Answers: 1. 0 **2.** 0 **3.** 1 **4.** 5 **5.** 1 **6.** 1 **7.** 1 **8.** 0 **9.** 2 **10.** 1 **11.** 1 **12.** 1

■ Homework Problems

Core Exercises: 5, 15, 21, 35, 41, 45, 49, 63

Sample Assignment: 3, 4, 5, 6, 10, 15, 16, 21, 22, 25, 30, 31, 35, 41, 42, 45, 49, 51, 54, 62, 63, 64, 67

GROUP WORK 1, SECTION 3.6
Transformation of Plane Figures

So far, when we have been talking about functions, we have been assuming that their domains and ranges have been sets of numbers. This is not necessarily the case. For example, look at this figure:

Let's let our domain be all the different ways we can move this figure around, including flipping it over:

$$D = \left\{ \text{L}, \text{Γ}, \text{7}, \text{⌐}, \text{J}, \text{L}, \text{Γ}, \text{7} \right\}$$

Now let f be the function that rotates the shape $90°$ clockwise: $f\left(\text{L}\right) = \text{Γ}$. Let g be the function that

flips the shape over a vertical line drawn through the center: $g\left(\text{L}\right) = \text{J}$

1. Find the following:

(a) $f\left(\text{Γ}\right)$ (b) $g\left(\text{7}\right)$ (c) $f\left(f\left(\text{L}\right)\right)$ (d) $g\left(g\left(\text{7}\right)\right)$

2. Is it true that $f \circ g = g \circ f$? Why or why not?

3. Is it true that $g \circ g \circ g = g$? Why or why not?

4. Write, in words, what the function $f \circ f \circ f$ does to a shape.

GROUP WORK 2, SECTION 3.6
Odds and Evens

1. Let a be an odd number, and b be an even number. Fill in the following table (the first row is done for you).

a	b	$a+b$
even	even	even
odd	even	
even	odd	
odd	odd	

2. We can also multiply numbers together. Fill in the corresponding multiplication table:

a	b	$a \cdot b$
even	even	
odd	even	
even	odd	
odd	odd	

3. Now we let f and g be (nonzero) functions, not numbers. We are going to think about what happens when we combine these functions. When you fill in the table, you can write "unknown" if the result can be odd *or* even, depending on the functions. You can solve this problem by drawing some pictures, or by using the definition of odd and even functions.

f	g	$f+g$	fg	$f \circ g$	$g \circ f$
even	even				
even	odd				
odd	even				
odd	odd				
neither	neither				

143

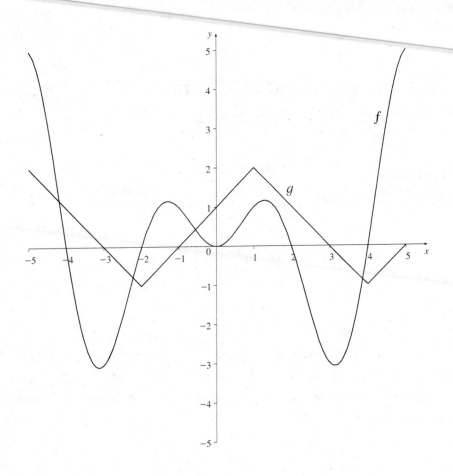

■ Suggested Time and Emphasis

$1-1\frac{1}{2}$ classes. Essential material.

■ Points to Stress

1. One-to-one functions: their definition and the Horizontal Line Test.

2. Algebraic and geometric properties of inverse functions.

3. Finding inverse functions.

■ Sample Questions

• **Text Question:** Sketch the inverse function of the function graphed below.

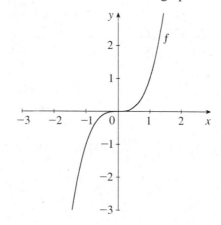

Answer:

• **Drill Question:** If $f(-2) = 4$, $f(-1) = 3$, $f(0) = 2$, $f(1) = 1$ and $f(2) = 3$, what is $f^{-1}(2)$?

Answer: 0

■ In-Class Materials

• Make sure students understand the notation: f^{-1} is not the same thing as $\dfrac{1}{f}$.

• Starting with $f(x) = \sqrt[3]{x - 4}$ compute $f^{-1}(-2)$ and $f^{-1}(0)$. Then use algebra to find a formula for $f^{-1}(x)$. Have the class try to repeat the process with $g(x) = x^3 + x - 2$. Note that facts such as $g^{-1}(-2) = 0$, $g^{-1}(0) = 1$, and and $g^{-1}(8) = 2$ can be found by looking at a table of values for $g(x)$ but that algebra fails to give us a general formula for $g^{-1}(x)$. Finally, draw graphs of f, f^{-1}, g, and g^{-1}.

- Pose the question: If f is always increasing, is f^{-1} always increasing? Give students time to try prove their answer.

  Answer: This is true. Proofs may involve diagrams and reflections about $y = x$, or you may try to get them to be more rigorous. This is an excellent opportunity to discuss concavity, noting that if f is concave up and increasing, then f^{-1} is concave down and increasing.

- Point out that the idea of "reversing input and output" permeates the idea of inverse functions, in all four representations of "function". When finding inverse functions algebraically, we explicitly reverse x and y. When drawing the inverse function of a graph, by reflecting across the line $y = x$ we are reversing the y- and x-axes. If $c(x)$ is the cost (in dollars) to make x fruit roll-ups, then $c^{-1}(x)$ is the number of fruit roll-ups that could be made for x dollars—again reversing the input and the output. Finally, show the class how to find the inverse of a function given a numeric data table, and note that again the inputs and outputs are reversed.

x	$f(x)$
1	3
2	4.2
3	5.7
4	8

x	$f^{-1}(x)$
3	1
4.2	2
5.7	3
8	4

- Make sure to discuss units carefully: when comparing $y = f(x)$ to $y = f^{-1}(x)$, the units of y and x trade places.

▨ Example

The graph of a complicated function and its inverse:

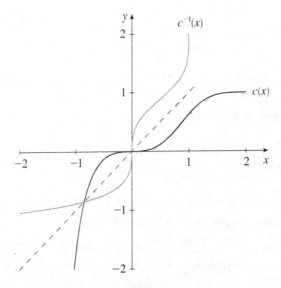

■ Group Work 1: Inverse Functions: Domains and Ranges

While discussing the domains and ranges of inverse functions, this exercise foreshadows later excursions into the maximum and minimum values of functions.

If a group finishes early, ask them this question:

"Now consider the graph of $f(x) = \sqrt{2x-3} + 2$. What are the domain and range of $f(x)$? Try to figure out the domain and range of $f^{-1}(x)$ by looking at the graph of f. In general, what information do you need to be able to compute the domain and range of $f^{-1}(x)$ from the graph of a function f?"

Answers:

1. It is one-to-one, because the problem says it climbs steadily.
2. a^{-1} is the time in minutes at which the plane achieves a given altitude.
3. Reverse the data columns in the given table to get the table for the inverse function. The domain and range of a are $0 \le t \le 30$ and $0 \le a \le 29{,}000$, so the domain and range of a^{-1} are $0 \le x \le 29{,}000$ and $0 \le a^{-1} \le 30$.
4. You can expect to turn on your computer after about 8.5 minutes.
5. a is no longer 1-1, because heights are now achieved more than once.

Bonus The domain of f^{-1} is the set of all y-values on the graph of f, and the range of f^{-1} is the set of all x-values on the graph of f.

■ Group Work 2: The Column of Liquid

If students need a hint, you can mention that the liquid used in the drugstore is mercury.

Answers:

1. The liquid is 1 cm high when the temperature is $32°$ F.
2. The liquid is 10 cm high when the temperature is $212°$ F
3. The inverse function takes a height in cm, and gives the temperature. So it is a device for measuring temperature.
4. A thermometer

■ Group Work 3: Functions in the Classroom Revisited

This activity starts the same as Group Work 2: Functions in the Classroom, in Section 3.2 At this point, students have learned about one-to-one functions, and they are able to explore this activity in more depth.

Answers:

Chairs: Function, one-to-one, bijection (if all chairs are occupied). If one-to-one, the inverse assigns a chair to a person.

Eye color: Function, not one-to-one

Mom & Dad's birthplace: Not a function; mom and dad could have been born in different places

Molecules:

Function, one-to-one (with nearly 100% probability); inverse assigns a number of molecules to the appropriate student.

Spleens: Function, one-to-one, bijection. Inverse assigns each spleen to its owner.

147

Pencils: Not a function; some people may have more than one or (horrors!) none.

Social Security Number: Function, one-to-one; inverse assigns each number to its owner.

February birthday: Not a function; not defined for someone born on February 29.

Birthday: Function, perhaps one-to-one. If one-to-one, the inverse assigns a day to a person.

Cars: Not a function; some have none, some have more than one.

Cash: Function, perhaps one-to-one. If one-to-one, the inverse assigns an amount of money to a person.

Middle names: Not a function; some have none, some have more than one.

Identity: Function, one-to-one, bijection. Inverse is the same as the function.

Algebra instructor: Function, not one-to-one.

Homework Problems

Core Exercises: 11, 13, 15, 21, 27, 35, 47, 57

Sample Assignment: 4, 6, 8, 11, 13, 15, 19, 21, 26, 27, 35, 41, 42, 47, 51, 57, 67, 75, 79

GROUP WORK 1, SECTION 3.7
Inverse Functions: Domains and Ranges

Let $a(t)$ be the altitude in feet of a plane that climbs steadily from takeoff until it reaches its cruising altitude after 30 minutes. We don't have a formula for a, but extensive research has given us the following table of values:

t	$a(t)$
0.1	50
0.5	150
1	500
3	2000
7	8000
10	12,000
20	21,000
25	27,000
30	29,000

1. Is $a(t)$ a one-to-one function? How do you know?

2. What does the function a^{-1} measure in real terms? Your answer should be descriptive, similar to the way $a(t)$ was described above.

3. We are interested in computing values of a^{-1}. Fill in the following table for as many values of x as you can. What quantity does x represent?

x	$a^{-1}(x)$

What are the domain and range of a? What are the domain and range of a^{-1}?

4. You are allowed to turn on electronic equipment after the plane has reached 10,000 feet. Approximately when can you expect to turn on your laptop computer after taking off?

5. Suppose we consider $a(t)$ from the time of takeoff to the time of touchdown. Is $a(t)$ still one-to-one?

GROUP WORK 2, SECTION 3.7
The Column of Liquid

It is a fact that if you take a tube and fill it partway with liquid, the liquid will rise and fall based on the temperature. Assume that we have a tube of liquid, and we have a function $h(T)$, where h is the height of the liquid in cm at temperature T in °F.

1. It is true that $h(32) = 1$. What does that mean in physical terms?

2. It is true that $h(212) = 10$. What does that mean in physical terms?

3. Describe the inverse function h^{-1}. What are its inputs? What are its outputs? What does it measure?

4. There is a device, currently available at your local drugstore, that measures the function h^{-1}. What is the name of this device?

GROUP WORK 3, SECTION 3.7
Functions in the Classroom Revisited

Which of the following are functions? Of the ones that are functions, which are one-to-one functions? Describe what the inverses tell you.

Domain	Function Values	Function
All the people in your classroom	Chairs	f (person) = his or her chair
All the people in your classroom	The set {blue, brown, green, hazel}	f (person) = his or her eye color
All the people in your classroom	Cities	f (person) = birthplace of their mom and dad
All the people in your classroom	$\mathbb{R}$, the real numbers	f (person) = number of molecules in their body
All the people in your classroom	Spleens	f (person) = his or her own spleen
All the people in your classroom	Pencils	f (person) = his or her pencil
All the people in the United States	Integers from 0–999999999	f (person) = his or her Social Security number
All the living people born in February	Days in February, 2007	f (person) = his or her birthday in February 2007
All the people in your classroom	Days of the year	f (person) = his or her birthday
All the people in your classroom	Cars	f (person) = his or her car
All the people in your classroom	$\mathbb{R}$, the real numbers	f (person) = how much cash he or she has
All the people in your college	Names	f (person) = his or her middle name
All the people in your classroom	People	f (person) = himself or herself
All the people in your classroom	People	f (person) = his or her algebra instructor

CHAPTER 4   Polynomial and Rational Functions

4.1 | Quadratic Functions and Models

■ Suggested Time and Emphasis

1 class. Essential material.

■ Points to Stress

1. Graphing quadratic functions, including obtaining the exact coordinates of the vertex by completing the square.

■ Sample Questions

- **Text Question:** If $f(x) = 4x^2 + 16x + 5$, why would it be useful to complete the square?

  Answer: Completing the square would reveal the zeros of the function.

- **Drill Question:** Find the vertex of the quadratic function $f(x) = -x^2 + 9x + 2$.

  Answer: $\left(\frac{9}{2}, \frac{89}{4}\right)$

■ In-Class Materials

- A straightforward way to demonstrate the utility of quadratic functions is to demonstrate how thrown objects follow parabolic paths. Physically throw an actual ball (perhaps trying to get it into the wastebasket) and have the class observe the shape of the path. Note that not only can thrown objects' paths be modeled by parabolas, their height as a function of time can (on Earth) be modeled by quadratic functions of the form $f(x) = -16t^2 + v_0 t + s_0$, where t is in seconds, f is in feet, v_0 is initial velocity, and s_0 is initial height.

- Show students how quadratic functions can come up in an applied context. If a demand function is linear then the revenue will be quadratic. For example, if the number of shoes you can sell is given by $10000 - 3c$, where c is the cost per shoe, then the revenue is $R = c(10000 - 3c)$. If we are thinking of costs in a narrow possible range, we can usually approximate revenue in such a way.

- Having covered quadratic functions, it is not a big leap to talk about quadratic inequalities. After graphing $f(x) = x^2 + 4x - 5$, find the intervals described by $x^2 + 4x + 5 > 0$, $x^2 + 4x + 5 \geq 0$, $x^2 + 4x + 5 < 0$, and $x^2 + 4x + 5 \leq 0$.

■ Example

A quadratic function that can be graphed by hand: $f(x) = -2x^2 + 12x - 13 = -2(x-3)^2 + 5$

■ Group Work 1: The Penny Drop

This is a classic type of physics problem with the differentiation omitted.

Answers:

1. $t = \frac{5}{16} = 0.3125$ s

2. $t = \frac{5}{16} = 0.3125$ s

3. $\frac{4825}{16} \approx 301.56$ ft

153

4. $\frac{5}{16}\left(1 + \sqrt{193}\right) \approx 4.654$ s

5. It is moving at 138.9 ft/s downward.

▪ Homework Problems

Core Exercises: 13, 25, 27, 33, 35, 67

Sample Assignment: 3, 7, 13, 17, 18, 25, 27, 28, 33, 35, 37, 42, 54, 58, 59, 67, 69, 76

GROUP WORK 1, SECTION 4.1
The Penny Drop

Suppose we are standing on top of a 300-ft tower and we are holding a shiny new penny. We do not hurl it down, for that would be wrong. We toss it *up* at a velocity of 10 feet per second, and then when it comes down, it happens to plummet to the ground below.

At a time t seconds after the toss, the velocity is given by $v(t) = -32t + 10$. (Note that positive velocity corresponds to the penny moving up, as it does initially, and negative velocity corresponds to it moving down, as it does eventually.) The distance from the sidewalk, in feet, is given by $p(t) = -16t^2 + 10t + 300$.

1. At what time is the penny's velocity zero?

2. When is the penny at its highest point?

3. What is the maximum height achieved by the penny?

4. How long is the penny in the air?

5. How fast is it going when it hits the ground?

■ Suggested Time and Emphasis

$\frac{1}{2}$ – 1 class. Essential material.

■ Points to Stress

1. The terminology and notation associated with polynomial functions.

2. Characteristics of polynomial graphs: smoothness, continuity, end behavior, and boundaries on the number of local maxima and minima.

3. Graphing polynomials using the zeros (taking into account multiplicity) and end behavior.

■ Sample Questions

- **Text Question:** Which of the following are polynomial functions?

    (a) $f(x) = -x^3 + 2x + 4$

    (b) $f(x) = (\sqrt{x})^3 - 2(\sqrt{x})^2 + 5(\sqrt{x}) - 1$

    (c) $f(x) = (x - 2)(x - 1)(x + 4)^2$

    (d) $f(x) = \dfrac{x^2 + 2}{x^2 - 2}$

    Answer: (a) and (c)

- **Drill Question:** Sketch the graph of the polynomial $f(x) = x^3 + 5x^2 + 6x$.

    Answer:

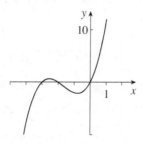

■ In-Class Materials

- Point out the strengths and limitations of their current state of knowledge of graphing polynomials. On the positive end, they can now sketch the graph of a polynomial function like $f(x) = (x - 1)(x - 2)^2(x - 3)$ relatively quickly, and understand its shape. However, they still cannot find the precise coordinates of the two local minima, nor could they tell how fast the function is increasing as x gets large, compared to other polynomials. Point out that "for now" they have a good method of getting a general idea of the shape of a polynomial, and more precision will come with calculus.

- This is one application of the Intermediate Value Theorem for Polynomials: Consider $f(x) = 90x^3 + 100x^2 + 10x + 1$ and $g(x) = 91x^3 - 60x^2$. Have students graph each on their calculator, if they can find a good window. It will be tough. After giving them some time, put some graphs on the board.

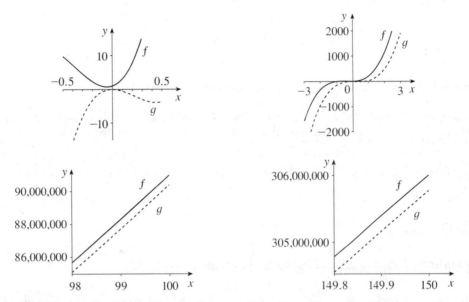

It certainly looks like these two curves never cross. One way to prove that they do would be to actually find the crossing point—to solve $f(x) - g(x) = 0$. But a much quicker way is to use the intermediate value property. Let $h(x) = f(x) - g(x)$. We know $g(x)$ will cross $f(x)$ when $h(x) = 0$. Now $h(0)$ is positive, and $h(1000)$ is negative. We don't *need* to go hunting for the value of x that makes $h(x) = 0$; we can simply invoke the intermediate value property to prove that such an x does exist.

- Explore, using technology, the concept of families of functions. Take, for example, the easy-to-graph curve $y = x^3 - x$. Add in a constant: $y = x^3 - x + 1$, $y = x^3 - x + 2$, $y = x^3 - x - 1$. Using material from Chapter 3, students should be able to predict what these graphs look like. Now add in a quadratic term: $y = x^3 + \frac{1}{2}x^2 - x$, $y = x^3 + x^2 - x$, $y = x^3 + 8x^2 - x$, $y = x^3 + -x^2 - x$. By graphing these curves on the same axes, have students attempt to put into words the effect that an x^2 term has on this cubic function.

- When discussing local extrema, make sure that students understand that just because a fifth-degree polynomial (for example) *can* have four local extrema, doesn't mean it *must* have four local extrema. Have students graph $f(x) = x^5$ as a quick example, and then $f(x) = x^5 - x^3$ as an example of a fifth-degree polynomial with two local extrema. Have students try to come up with a proof that there can't be a fifth-degree polynomial with exactly one or three local extrema.

Examples

- A polynomial function with zeros of various multiplicities:

$$f(x) = x^6 + x^5 - x^4 - x^3 = (x-1)\,x^3\,(x+1)^2$$

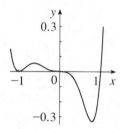

- Two sixth-degree polynomial functions that look very similar, but have different numbers of extrema: $f(x) = x^6 - 3x^3$ has one local minimum and a flat spot at $x = 0$. $f(x) = x^6 - 3.0x^3 - 0.015x^4 + 0.09x$ has two local minima and one local maximum — an obvious local minimum at $x \approx 1.145$, and two very subtle extrema at $x \approx \pm 0.1$.

Group Work 1: The Waste-Free Box

The first problem is a classic, and appears in the Focus on Modeling section of the text. The second two problems are original variants with surprising results. The global maximum for the second problem occurs at an endpoint, and the third one, which seems identical to the second, has its global maximum at a local maximum. The students don't need to know about global and local extrema to solve this problem—they just have to understand what they are doing when they are modeling the phenomenon, and looking for an extreme value.

Set up the activity by actually building a box for students out of an $8.5'' \times 11''$ sheet of paper, so they can see exactly what is going on before they try to construct a mathematical model.

This activity also appears in Section 2.7.

Answers:

1. $V(x) = x\,(8.5 - 2x)\,(11 - 2x)$

2. The domain is $0 \le x \le 4.25$.

3. The maximum $V \approx 66.148$ occurs when $x \approx 1.585$.

4. $V(x) = x(8.5 - 2x)(11 - 2x) + x^3$. Domain: $0 \le x \le 4.25$

The maximum $V \approx 76.766$ occurs when $x = 4.25$.

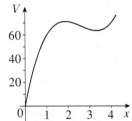

5. There is no open topped box. We cut the biggest squares we can and then throw away the scrap. Because the box needs a bottom, it is a less efficient user of materials than the handsome pen-and-pencil holder.

6. In the $6'' \times 10''$ case, $V(x) = x(6 - 2x)(10 - 2x) + x^3$. Domain: $0 \le x \le 3$

The maximum $V \approx 35$ occurs when $x \approx 1.39096$.

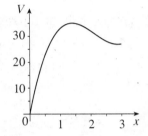

▪ Group Work 2: My Mother's Gifts

This exercise is primarily about taking a verbal description of a problem and translating it into a (polynomial) function. It also explores some large growth rates.

Answers:

1. 396 cm^3

2. 4940 cm^3

3. $V(x) = x(x + 9)(x + 16) = x^3 + 25x^2 + 144x$

4. 512 cm^2

5. 1888 cm^2

6. $A(x) = 2x(x + 9) + 2x(x + 16) + 2(x + 9)(x + 16) = 6x^2 + 100x + 288$

7. Solving $6x^2 + 100x + 288 = 11,000$, we find that $x \approx 34.7338$, so according to his claim, I will be 34 when he makes his last one. But he will never stop!

8. 73,100 cm^3 or about $2\frac{1}{2}$ cubic feet

▪ Homework Problems

Core Exercises: 5, 11, 17, 25, 27, 31, 33, 41, 59, 61, 71

Sample Assignment: 3, 4, 5, 9, 10, 11, 12, 13, 14, 17, 18, 21, 23, 25, 27, 31, 33, 37, 38, 41, 46, 49, 50, 54, 59, 61, 71, 73, 83

The Waste-Free Box

Assume we take a sheet of standard $8.5'' \times 11''$ typing or "notebook" paper. We can transform it into a box by cutting identical squares of side length x from each corner, and folding up the sides, like so:

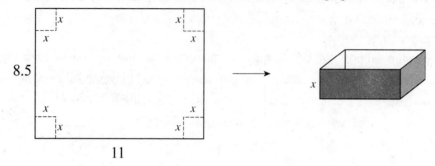

1. Express the volume V of the box as a function of x.

2. What is the domain of V?

3. Draw a graph of the function V and use it to estimate the maximum volume for such a box.

The previous problem is a classic problem often given to calculus students. People have been doing this problem for centuries, never caring about those four squares, those cast-off pieces of paper. What is to be their fate? They are often thrown out—sometimes (cruel irony!) in the very box that they helped to create! Should we stand for this waste of paper? The answer is "No!", particularly since we can use the four squares to make a handsome pen-and-pencil holder, by taping them together to form their own box. This new box will have neither top nor bottom, but it still can be used to hold pens and pencils.

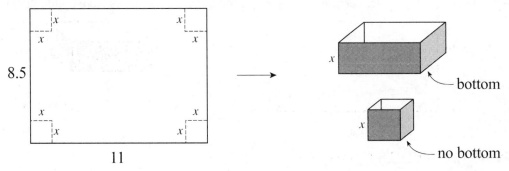

4. What is the maximum possible combined volume of an open-topped box plus a handsome pen-and-pencil holder that can be made by cutting four squares from an $8.5'' \times 11''$ sheet of paper?

5. Describe the open-topped box that results from this maximal case. Intuitively, why do we get the result that we do?

6. Repeat this problem for a $6'' \times 10''$ piece of paper.

GROUP WORK 2, SECTION 4.2
My Mother's Gifts

I have a brother who is sixteen years older than I am, and a sister who is nine years older. Every Mother's Day, since I was two, my father (who is a competent woodworker) has made the same gift for my mother. He gives her a box whose length, width and height (in centimeters) are my brother's, my sister's, and my age, respectively. The first couple were just silly, but as time goes on, the boxes have gotten larger and more useful.

1. What was the volume of the first box he made?

2. What was the volume of the box he made when I was ten?

3. Write a formula that gives the volume of the box he will make when I am x years old.

Dad doesn't just give her the box unadorned. He always puts a gift in the box, and wraps it up in wrapping paper. He then draws a mortar-and-pestle on it (Mom was a pharmacist) and tapes on a stick of gum (don't ask).

4. How much wrapping paper did he have to use for that first box? Give your answer in cm^2.

5. How much wrapping paper did he have to use when I was ten?

6. Write a formula that gives the amount of wrapping paper he will have to use when I am x years old.

7. A standard roll of wrapping paper has an area of about $11,000$ cm^2. Dad has said he is going to stop building these boxes when they take more than a roll to wrap up. How old will I be when he makes his last box? Do you think he will really stop?

8. What will be the volume of that "final" box?

■ Suggested Time and Emphasis

$\frac{1}{2} - 1$ class. Essential material. Can be combined with Section 4.4.

■ Points to Stress

1. The division algorithm for polynomials.

2. Synthetic division.

3. The Remainder and Factor Theorems.

■ Sample Questions

- **Text Question:** It is a fact that $x^3 + 2x^2 - 3x + 1 = (x + 2)(x^2 + 1) + (-4x - 1)$. Fill in the blanks:

  Remainder:

  $$x^2 + 1 \enclose{longdiv}{x^3 + 2x^2 - 3x + 1}$$

Answers: $x + 2$, $-4x - 1$

- **Drill Question:** Divide $x^3 + 2x^2 - 3x + 1$ by $x + 2$.

Answer: $\dfrac{x^3 + 2x^2 - 3x + 1}{x + 2} = x^2 - 3 + \dfrac{7}{x + 2}$ or "$x^2 - 3$, remainder 7"

■ In-Class Materials

- At this time, the teaching of long division in elementary schools is inconsistent. It will save time, in the long run, to do an integer long division problem for students, cautioning them to remind themselves of every step in the process, because you are going to be extending it to polynomials. For example, divide 31,673 by 5 using the long division algorithm. Then show how the answer can be written as $\dfrac{31,673}{5} = 6334 + \dfrac{3}{5}$ or 6334 R 3. They will not be used to writing the result this way: $31673 = 5(6334) + 3$. It is important that they understand the form

$$\text{dividend} = \text{divisor} \cdot \text{quotient} + \text{remainder}$$

because that is the form in which the division algorithm is presented, both in this course, and any future math course involving generalized division. If students don't seem to understand (or start moving their lips as if beginning the process of rote memorization) it may even be worth the time to write out a very simple example, such as $35 = 3(11) + 2$, just so students are very clear how this is a trivial restatement of $\dfrac{35}{3} = 11$ R 2.

- After doing a routine example, such as $\dfrac{x^4 + 3x^3 - x^2 - x + 3}{x^2 + 2x - 1} = x^2 + x - 2 + \dfrac{1 + 4x}{x^2 + 2x - 1}$, verify the answer by having students go through the multiplication. In other words, write $\left(x^2 + 2x - 1\right)\left(x^2 + x - 2\right) + \left(4x + 1\right)$ and multiply it out to verify that the result is $x^4 + 3x^3 - x^2 - x + 3$.

- Students often miss the crucial idea that synthetic division is a technique that only works for divisors of the form $x - c$. They also tend to believe that synthetic division is a magic process that has nothing to do with the long division that they have just learned. They should be disabused of both notions. For example, divide the polynomial $x^3 - x^2 + x - 1$ by $x - 2$ using both methods, showing all work, and then have students point out the similarities between the two computations. They should see that both processes are essentially the same, the only difference being that synthetic division minimizes the amount of writing and thinking.

- One important application of polynomial division is finding asymptotes for rational functions. This is a good time to introduce the concept of a horizontal asymptote. This idea is explored in Group Work 1: Asymptology. A good example to discuss with students are $f(x) = \dfrac{2x^2 + 3x + 5}{x^2 - 4x + 2}$. Use long division to write this as $f(x) = 2 + \dfrac{11x + 1}{x^2 - 4x + 2}$. Now note what happens to the second term for large values of x. (If students have calculators, they can go ahead and try $x = 100$, $x = 100{,}000$, and $x = 1{,}000{,}000{,}000$. Show how, graphically, this corresponds to a horizontal asymptote. Now point out that the 2 came from only the highest-degree term in the numerator and the highest-degree term in the denominator. Now discuss the possibilities for horizontal asymptotes in the rational functions $\dfrac{x^2 + 2x + 2}{3x^2 + 2x + 2}$, $\dfrac{x^2 + 2x + 2}{x - 7}$, and $\dfrac{x^2 + 2x + 2}{x^5 - x + 4}$. In all cases, go ahead and do the long division, so the students see the possibilities. (The second one has no horizontal asymptote. The idea of an oblique asymptote is covered in Group Work 1.)

Examples

- Fourth-degree polynomial functions with zeros at $x = -3$, 1, and 2:
$$f(x) = (x + 3)^2 (x - 1)(x - 2) = x^4 + 3x^3 - 7x^2 - 15x + 18$$
$$f(x) = (x + 3)(x - 1)^2 (x - 2) = x^4 - x^3 - 7x^2 + 13x - 6$$
$$f(x) = (x + 3)(x - 1)(x - 2)^2 = x^4 - 2x^3 - 7x^2 + 20x - 12$$

- An example to use in demonstrating the remainder and factor theorems: $f(x) = x^3 - x^2 - 14x + 24$ has zeros $x = -4$, 2, and 3; $f(0) = 24$, $f(1) = 10$, and $f(-1) = 36$.

▪ Group Work: Asymptology

In addition to encouraging practice with polynomial functions, this activity uses concepts that every economics student will have to learn.

It is not necessary to do all three parts of this activity. Depending on time pressure, you may want to stop after Part 1 or after Part 2. It will take at least one full class period to do all three parts.

Stress to students that this activity involves what happens to a function in the long run, as opposed to what they have been thinking about so far, which is what happens for relatively small values of x. Perhaps put a figure like this on the board:

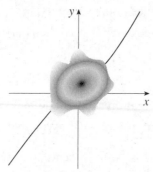

The first part will lead students to discover the idea of a horizontal asymptote. When all (or most) of students are done with this page, regain the attention of the class, and discuss this concept with them, perhaps doing another example. Make sure to be picky on their use of "=" and "≈" here, because the distinction is a major idea in this context. Take the time to give them a good understanding of what they have discovered. The second part leads students to the idea of an oblique asymptote, and the third page talks of quadratic asymptotes. (If you wish, you can generalize this idea with your students.)

The last problem on each part is intended to be used with graphing technology; the other problems do not need it.

Answers:

1. (a) 0.0568   (b) 0.000510   (c) 5×10^{-10}

  (d) $n(x)$ is getting closer and closer to zero. It is incorrect to say that $n(x) = 0$.

  (e) $n(x)$ is getting closer and closer to zero. It is incorrect to say that $n(x) = 0$.

2. (a) $3x^2 - 6x + 29 = (x^2 - 2x + 8)3 + 5$ (b) $f(x) = 3 + \dfrac{5}{x^2 - 2x + 8}$

  (c) $f(x)$ gets close to 3.   (d)

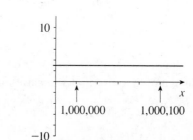

3.

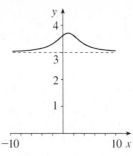

4. (a) $n(x)$ is getting closer and closer to zero. It is incorrect to say that $n(x) = 0$.

(b) $n(x)$ is getting closer and closer to zero. It is incorrect to say that $n(x) = 0$.

5. $f(x) = \left(-\frac{1}{2}x + 2\right) + \dfrac{-6x + 26}{2x^2 + 4x - 6}$

6. $f(x)$ gets close to $-\frac{1}{2}x + 2$.

Students should notice that the curves are nearly identical. If they are not using a calculator, they should not be able to distinguish between them.

7.

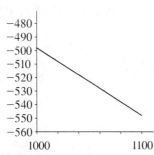

8.

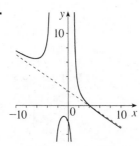

9. (a) $f(x) = x^2 + \dfrac{4}{x^2 + 3x - 5}$

(b) $f(x)$ resembles x^2.

(c)

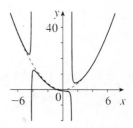

▪ Homework Problems

Core Exercises: 3, 7, 25, 39, 53, 57, 59

Sample Assignment: 1, 2, 3, 6, 7, 18, 20, 21, 25, 27, 30, 36, 39, 44, 45, 53, 57, 59, 60, 61, 69

Asymptology

1. As a warm-up, we are going to look at the function $n(x) = \dfrac{5}{x^2 - 2x + 8}$. Approximate the following to three significant figures:

(a) $n(10)$ (b) $n(100)$ (c) $n(100{,}000)$

(d) What is happening to $n(x)$ as x gets very large?

(e) We call numbers like $-1{,}000{,}000$ "large and negative" What is happening to $n(x)$ when x gets very large and negative?

2. Now we are going to consider $f(x) = \dfrac{3x^2 - 6x + 29}{x^2 - 2x + 8}$.

(a) Use polynomial division to write $3x^2 - 6x + 29$ in the form $\left(x^2 - 2x + 8\right) Q(x) + R(x)$, where $Q(x)$ and $R(x)$ are polynomials.

(b) Use your answer to part (a) to write $f(x)$ in the form $f(x) = Q(x) + \dfrac{R(x)}{x^2 - 2x + 8}$.

(c) Now use what you learned in Question 1 to figure out what is happening to $f(x)$ when x is very large.

(d) Without using a calculator, sketch an approximate graph of $f(x)$ for $1{,}000{,}000 \le x \le 1{,}000{,}100$.

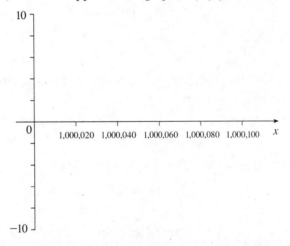

3. If you have a graphing calculator, graph both $f(x)$ and the curve $y = 3$ on the same axes, on the interval $-10 \le x \le 10$. What do you notice?

4. We now consider $f(x) = \dfrac{-x^3 + 2x^2 + 5x + 14}{2x^2 + 4x - 6}$. Again we are going to warm up by looking at a simpler

rational function, $n(x) = \dfrac{-6x + 26}{2x^2 + 4x - 6}$.

(a) What is happening to $n(x)$ as x gets very large and positive?

(b) What is happening to $n(x)$ as x gets very large and negative?

5. Now use polynomial division to write $f(x)$ in the form $f(x) = Q(x) + \dfrac{R(x)}{2x^2 + 4x + 6}$.

6. Use your answers to Questions 4 and 5 to figure out what is happening to $f(x)$ as x gets large. This will require more thought than it did on the previous page, but go ahead and put it into words.

7. We are now going to sketch some graphs without using a calculator.

(a) Graph the line $y = -\frac{1}{2}x + 2$ (in the range $1000 \leq x \leq 1100$) on the axes below.

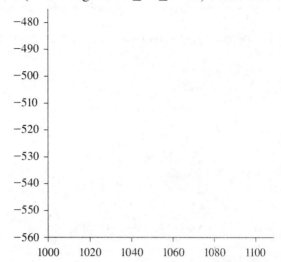

(b) Using your answer to Question 6, add a sketch of $f(x)$ to your graph. Plot a few points of $f(x)$ afterwards, to confirm that your sketch is reasonable.

8. If you have a graphing calculator, graph both $f(x)$ and the curve $y = -\frac{1}{2}x + 2$ on the same axes, on the interval $-10 \leq x \leq 10$. What do you notice?

9. We now consider the function $f(x) = \dfrac{x^4 + 3x^3 - 5x^2 + 4}{x^2 + 3x - 5}$.

(a) We will dispense with the warm-ups. Use polynomial division to write $f(x)$ in the form $f(x) = Q(x) + \dfrac{R(x)}{D(x)}$, where Q, R and D are appropriate polynomial functions.

(b) When x gets large, what polynomial function will $f(x)$ most closely resemble? Why?

(c) If you have a graphing calculator, graph $f(x)$ and your answer to part (b) on the axes below.

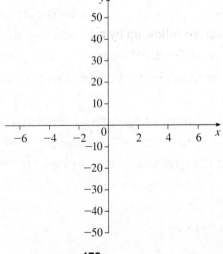

Suggested Time and Emphasis

$\frac{1}{2}$ – 1 class. Essential material. Can be combined with Section 4.2.

Points to Stress

1. The Rational Zeros Theorem: The rational zeros of a polynomial function are always quotients of factors of the constant and the leading terms.
2. Factoring large polynomials using the Rational Zeros Theorem and the quadratic formula.
3. Bounding the number and size of zeros of a polynomial function.

Sample Questions

• **Text Question:** Consider $f(x) = x^6 - 2x^5 - x^4 + 4x^3 - x^2 - 2x + 1$.

   (a) According to the Rational Zeros Theorem, how many possible rational zeros can this polynomial have?

   (b) List all the rational zeros of $f(x)$. Ignore multiplicities and show your work.

   Answer:

   (a) 2

   (b) Both 1 and -1 are zeros of f. This can be shown by manually calculating $f(1)$ and $f(-1)$.

• **Drill Question:** Factor $f(x) = x^3 - 6x + 4$.
   Answer: $f(x) = (x - 2)\left(x + 1 + \sqrt{3}\right)\left(x + 1 - \sqrt{3}\right)$

In-Class Materials

• Students often misinterpret the Rational Zeros Theorem in two ways. Some believe that it classifies *all* the real zeros of a polynomial function, not just the rational ones. Others believe that it apples to *all* polynomial functions, not just the ones with integer coefficients.

   Start with the simple quadratic $p(x) = x^2 - 2$, pointing out that the candidates for rational zeros are ± 1 and ± 2. None of these candidates are zeros of $p(x)$, but it is simple to find that there are two real zeros: $x = \pm\sqrt{2}$. Then move to a polynomial with one real zero and two irrational ones, such as the one in the Drill Question: $p(x) = x^3 - 6x + 4$. Ask students if they can come up with a polynomial with three real, irrational zeros. One example is $p(x) = x^3 - 3x - \sqrt{2}$ (the zeros are $-\sqrt{2}$ and $\frac{1}{2}\sqrt{2} \pm \frac{1}{2}\sqrt{6}$). This might be perceived as a bit of a cheat, so follow up by asking them if they can come up with a polynomial with integer coefficients and three real, irrational zeros ($x^3 - 5x + 1$ works, for example). The fact that there are three real roots can be determined from a graph, the fact that none are rational can be determined using the Rational Zeros Theorem.

• Ask students why we do not advocate using synthetic division to find the roots of a polynomial such as $p(x) = x^2 + 9x + 20$, $p(x) = x^2 + 9x - 7$, or even $p(x) = x^2 + \pi x - \sqrt[5]{2}$. Hopefully, you will arrive at the conclusion that the quadratic formula is easier to use and will find all the zeros, not just the rational ones. Point out that there actually is such a formula for third-degree polynomials, but that it is much harder to use. (For those interested, this formula is included below as a bonus.) There is one for fourth-degree polynomials as well. It has been proved that there is no such formula for arbitrary fifth-degree polynomials. In other words, we can find the exact roots for any polynomial up through a fourth-degree polynomial, but there are some polynomials, fifth-degree and higher, whose roots we can only approximate. See Exercise 101 in the text.

- Point out that being able to find the zeros of a polynomial allows us to solve many types of problems. The text gives several examples of applied problems (and there are many more, of course). For example, we can now find the intersection points between two polynomial curves [if $f(x) = g(x)$, then $f(x) - g(x) = 0$]. If $p(x)$ is a polynomial with an inverse, we can find $p^{-1}(k)$ for a specific k by solving $p(x) - k = 0$. In addition, being able to factor polynomials is very important. For example, the graph of $f(x) = \dfrac{x^3 - 4x}{x^3 + 6x^2 + 11x + 6}$ has a hole at $x = -2$, vertical asymptotes at $x = -1$ and $x = -3$, and x-intercepts at $(2,0)$ and $(0,0)$. This information is easily obtained if we write $f(x)$ as $\dfrac{(x+2)(x-2)x}{(x+1)(x+2)(x+3)}$.

Examples

- A polynomial with many rational zeros:

$$f(x) = 6x^5 + 17x^4 - 40x^3 - 45x^2 + 14x + 8$$

Factored form: $(2x-1)(3x+1)(x+4)(x+1)(x-2)$

Zeros: $x = \frac{1}{2}, -\frac{1}{3}, -4, -1$, and 2

- A polynomial with one rational zero, and four irrational zeros that can be found by elementary methods:

$$f(x) = 2x^5 - 10x^3 + 12x - x^4 + 5x^2 - 6 = (2x-1)(x^2-2)(x^2-3)$$

Zeros: $x = \frac{1}{2}, \pm\sqrt{2}$, and $\pm\sqrt{3}$

Bonus: Solving a Cubic Equation

As you know, given an equation of the form $ax^2 + bx + c = 0$ we have a formula that will give us all possible solutions:

$$x = \frac{-b \pm \sqrt{b^2 - 4ac}}{2a}$$

Notice that this gives us the exact solutions, not approximations.

We now solve $ax^3 + bx^2 + cx + d = 0$. First, we "depress the cubic". This does not involve telling the cubic that its favorite band has broken up, its favorite television show has been cancelled, and that nobody has ever really loved it. It means finding a way to remove the coefficient of the x^2 term. (This is done in Exercise 94 of your text, and was first done by Nicolo Fontana Tartaglia in the 1500s.) We make the substitution $x = s - \dfrac{b}{3a}$. In other words we are going to solve

$$a\left(s - \frac{b}{3a}\right)^3 + b\left(s - \frac{b}{3a}\right)^2 + c\left(s - \frac{b}{3a}\right) + d = 0$$

for the variable s, and after we have done so we will use $x = s - \dfrac{b}{3a}$ to find x. Why does this help us?

Because after all the arithmetic, the above equation will simplify to

$$s^3 + ps + q = 0$$

for some p and q.

Exercise 95 points out that one solution to this cubic is

$$s = \sqrt[3]{\frac{-q}{2} + \sqrt{\frac{q^2}{4} + \frac{p^3}{27}}} + \sqrt[3]{\frac{-q}{2} - \sqrt{\frac{q^2}{4} + \frac{p^3}{27}}}$$

So after you depress your cubic, you can find one solution s using this formula. You can then subtract $\dfrac{b}{3a}$ to get a solution x to the original equation. Then synthetic division gives you a quadratic to solve to get the other two solutions.

Note that if the original equation has three real roots, then this equation will be very difficult to use, because you will have to deal with some nasty complex numbers and take care to take correct square roots.

▪ Group Work 1: Supply and Demand

Answers:

1. 10,000 people would take a treat (or one person would take 10,000 of them). We could not afford to make any.

2. We could afford to make 1,509,200 treats if we charged such an exorbitant price, but nobody would buy one.

3. $S(x) - D(x) = 0$. This happens when $x = 2$. We should charge \$2 per treat.

▪ Group Work 2: Sketch the Graph

This is a straightforward activity, where students use the zeros of a polynomial function to sketch its graph.

Answers:

$f(x) = (4x - 3)^2 (x - 2)(x + 1)^2$, which has roots $x = \frac{3}{4}$, 2, and -1.

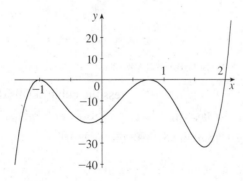

▪ Homework Problems

Core Exercises: 15, 29, 45, 55, 65, 69, 77, 91, 97

Sample Assignment: 3, 6, 8, 9, 12, 14, 15, 19, 20, 21, 29, 36, 41, 45, 51, 52, 55, 60, 61, 65, 69, 77, 82, 91, 97, 100, 103

GROUP WORK 1, SECTION 4.4
Supply and Demand

Assume that we are in the business of making and selling tacky, deluxe 10 ounce cat treats in the likenesses of fading celebrities. Economists tell us that there is a function $D(x)$ that tells us how many treats consumers will buy at a price x. They also tell us that there is a function $S(x)$ that tells us how many we can afford to make if we are selling them at a price x. Therefore, they say, we should set our price at the point where $S(x) = D(x)$. They also tell us that we can assume a completely rational consumer, that cat treats never go bad, that there is no international treat cartel that we have to deal with, and that price-fixing and tariffs do not exist. The economists live in a very nice world; speak quietly so as not to frighten them.

Anyway, assume that for $0 \le x \le 100$, $S(x) = x^3 + 3x^2 + 4792x$. (This is due to economies of scale. If we are charging \$100 for a cat treat, we can afford to make a heck of a lot of them.) And also assume that for $0 \le x \le 100$, $D(x) = x^2 - 200x + 10{,}000$. (In the given interval, this model says that the more we charge, the fewer people are willing to buy a cat treat.)

1. If we give away the treats for free, how many people would be willing to take a treat? How many could we afford to make if we were giving them away for free?

2. If we were charging \$100 per treat, how many people would buy them? How many could we afford to make if we were selling them at \$100 per treat?

3. According to the economists, what should we charge for a treat?

GROUP WORK 2, SECTION 4.4
Sketch the Graph

Sketch the graph of $f(x) = 16x^5 - 24x^4 - 39x^3 + 40x^2 + 21x - 18$. First plot the intercepts, then plot some points between the intercepts, and finally sketch the whole graph.

■ Suggested Time and Emphasis

$\frac{1}{2}$ class. Essential material.

■ Points to Stress

1. The Complete Factorization Theorem.

2. The Conjugate Zeros Theorem.

3. The Linear and Quadratic Factors Theorem

■ Sample Questions

- **Text Question:** Let $f(x) = x^3 + ax^2 + bx + c$.

  (a) What is the maximum number of zeros this polynomial function can have?

  (b) What is the minimum number of real zeros this polynomial function can have?

  Answer: (a) 3   (b) 1

- **Drill Question:** Consider the polynomial $f(x) = x^5 - 2x^4 + 16x^3 + 8x^2 + 20x + 200$. It is a fact that -2 is a zero of this polynomial, and that $(x - 1 - 3i)^2$ is a factor of this polynomial. Using this information, factor the polynomial completely.

  Answer: $f(x) = (x - 1 - 3i)^2 (x - 1 + 3i)^2 (x + 2)$

■ In-Class Materials

- Stress the power of the Complete Factorization Theorem, and how it dovetails with the Linear and Quadratic Factors Theorem. Once we allow complex numbers, we can view *all* polynomial functions as functions of the form $f(x) = a(x - c_1)(x - c_2) \dots (x - c_n)$; simple products of linear factors. If we don't want to allow complex numbers (the preference of many students), we still can write all polynomials almost as simply, as the product of linear and (irreducible) quadratic factors.

- Point out that when graphing $y = f(x)$, the real zeros appear as x-intercepts, as expected. Remind students how the multiplicities of the real zeros can be seen. A multiplicity of 1 crosses the x-axis, an even multiplicity touches the x-axis, and an odd multiplicity greater than one crosses the x-axis and is flat there. (See Section 2.1.) Note that the complex zeros don't appear on real plane.

- Exercise 70 discusses roots of unity—the zeros of polynomials of the form $f(x) = x^n - 1$ or, equivalently, the solutions of $x^n = 1$. It is easy to find the real solutions, 1 if n is odd and ± 1 if n is even. Exercise 70 prompts students to solve $x^n = 1$ for $n = 2, 3$, and 4. If your students have been exposed to trigonometric functions, then you can show them the general formula: $x^n = 1 \Leftrightarrow x = \cos\left(\dfrac{2\pi k}{n}\right) + i\sin\left(\dfrac{2\pi k}{n}\right)$ for $k = 0, \dots, n$.

Interestingly enough, if you plot the solutions in the complex plane, there is a wonderful amount of symmetry. Even if you don't want to discuss the general formula, you can show your students where the roots of unity live.

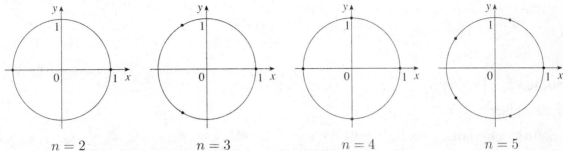

$$n = 2 \qquad\qquad n = 3 \qquad\qquad n = 4 \qquad\qquad n = 5$$

The complex roots of unity can be thought of as points that are evenly distributed around the unit circle.

- It is possible to use the techniques of the previous sections to solve polynomials with nonreal coefficients. If you want to demonstrate this fact, consider the polynomial $f(z) = z^3 + (2 - 3i) z^2 + (-3 - 6i) + 9i$, and use synthetic division to obtain $f(z) = (z - 1)(z + 3)(z - 3i)$

▪ Examples

- A polynomial that is the product of two irreducible quadratic terms:

$$f(x) = x^4 + 2x^3 + 9x^2 + 2x + 8 = (x^2 + 1)(x^2 + 2x + 8)$$

This can be factored by noting that $x = i$ is a zero, and therefore $x = -i$ is a zero, and then dividing by $(x^2 + 1)$.

- A polynomial that is the product of two linear terms and an irreducible quadratic term:

$$f(x) = x^4 + 5x^3 + 10x^2 + 16x - 32 = (x^2 + 2x + 8)(x - 1)(x + 4)$$

▪ Group Work: Complex Roots

Students should, at this point, be able to factor a polynomial by dividing out linear factors (found by the Rational Roots Theorem) and then using the quadratic formula, if necessary, on what is left. This technique only works if there are at most two nonrational roots. This activity allows them to explore a quartic function with four complex roots.

Allow students to puzzle over Question 3, but give them the Hint Sheet if it doesn't look like their puzzling is getting anywhere.

Answers:

1. $\pm 1, \pm 2, \pm 4, \pm 5, \pm 10, \pm 20$

2. This polynomial has no real zero. This can be determined by evaluating f at each of the 12 possible zeros, by synthetic division and use of bounding theorems, or by graphing f.

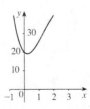

3. $(x - i)(x + i)[x - (4 + 2i)][x - (4 - 2i)]$

Answers (Hint Sheet)

1. Synthetic division works here.
2. $x = -i$ is a zero.
3. $x^2 + 1$
4. $f(x) = (x^2 + 1)(x^2 - 8x + 20)$
5. $\pm i, 4 \pm 2i$

■ Homework Problems

Core Exercises: 5, 19, 25, 35, 39, 45, 65

Sample Assignment: 2, 5, 9, 15, 19, 24, 25, 32, 33, 35, 37, 39, 40, 42, 45, 46, 47, 52, 53, 56, 63, 65, 69, 73

GROUP WORK, SECTION 4.5
Complex Roots

Consider the polynomial function $f(x) = x^4 - 8x^3 + 21x^2 - 8x + 20$.

1. According to the Rational Zeros Theorem, what are the possible rational zeros of this polynomial?

2. Which of the possible rational zeros are, in fact, zeros of f?

3. Factor this polynomial.

GROUP WORK, SECTION 4.5
Complex Roots (Hint Sheet)

1. Factoring $f(x) = x^4 - 8x^3 + 21x^2 - 8x + 20$ looks like it is going to be difficult, eh? Well, here is a hint. The imaginary number i is a zero of the polynomial. Verify that this is correct.

2. According to the Conjugate Zeros Theorem, the fact that $x = i$ is one zero of this polynomial informs you of another zero of this polynomial. What is that zero?

3. Use your answer to the previous parts to come up with an irreducible quadratic that is a factor of f.

4. Factor f into irreducible quadratic factors.

5. What are all the zeros of f?

182

Suggested Time and Emphasis

1 class. Essential material.

Points to Stress

1. Various kinds of asymptotes and end behavior of functions, particularly rational functions.

2. Graphing rational functions.

Sample Questions

- **Text Question:** What is a slant asymptote?

  Answer: Answers will vary

- **Drill Question:** Find all the asymptotes of the rational function $f(x) = \dfrac{x^2 + 1}{2x^2 - 5x - 3}$.

  Answer: Horizontal asymptote at $y = \frac{1}{2}$, vertical asymptotes at $x = -\frac{1}{2}$ and $x = 3$

In-Class Materials

- This is a good time to remind students of parameters. For example, give each section of the class a different value of c and have them sketch $f(x) = \dfrac{x}{x^2 - c}$.

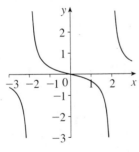

$c = 4$

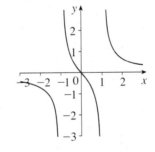

$c = 1$

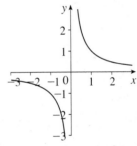

$c = 0$

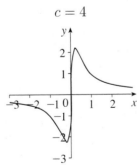

$c = -0.05$

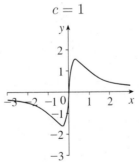

$c = -0.1$

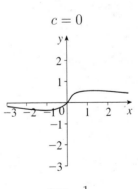

$c = -1$

  Note that when c is positive, there is a middle piece which disappears when $c = 0$ (the two vertical asymptotes become one). Note how the curve still gets large at $x = 0$ when c is small and negative.

- If the group work "Asymptology" from Section 3.2 was assigned, it should be reviewed at this point, because it lays the groundwork for this section's discussion of asymptotes. Students should see how the concepts they have previously discovered are described in the text.

- A bit of care should be exercised when checking vertical asymptotes. For example, have students examine $f(x) = \dfrac{x^2 + 3x + 2}{x^2 - 1}$. If they are alert, they will notice an apparent x-intercept at $x = -1$, making it impossible to follow the text's dictum: "When choosing test values, we must make sure that there is no x-intercept between the test point and the vertical asymptote." The reason is that there is not a vertical asymptote at $x = -1$ is that there is a hole there, as seen when f is factored: $f(x) = \dfrac{(x+1)(x+2)}{(x+1)(x-1)}$. See Exercise 75 in the text.

- A good example to do with students is $f(x) = \dfrac{1}{x^2 + 1}$. A curve of this type is called a *Witch of Agnesi*. Its history may amuse your students. Italian mathematician Maria Agnesi (1718–1799) was a scholar whose first paper was published when she was nine years old. She called a particular curve *versiera* or "turning curve". John Colson from Cambridge confused the word with *avversiera* or "wife of the devil", and translated it "witch".

Examples

- A rational function with a slant asymptote:

$$f(x) = \frac{x^2 + x - 2}{x - 2} = \frac{(x-1)(x+2)}{x - 2}$$

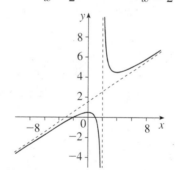

Intercepts: $(1, 0)$, $(-2, 0)$, $(0, 1)$. Asymptotes: $x = 2$, $y = x + \frac{3}{2}$

- A rational function with many asymptotes and intercepts that are hard to find by inspecting a single viewing rectangle:

$$f(x) = \frac{3x^3 + 6x^2 - 3x - 6}{x^3 - 5x^2 + 6x} = \frac{3(x+1)(x-1)(x+2)}{x(x-2)(x-3)}$$

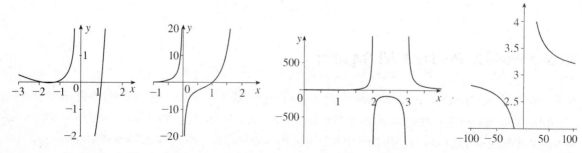

Intercepts: $(1, 0)$, $(-1, 0)$, $(-2, 0)$. Asymptotes: $x = 0$, $x = 2$, $x = 3$, $y = 3$

- A rational function with no asymptote:

$$f(x) = \frac{x^4 + 3x^2 + 2}{x^2 - 4x + 5} = \frac{(x^2 + 1)(x^2 + 2)}{x^2 - 4x + 5}$$

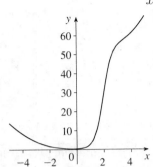 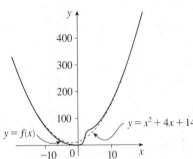

Note that the end behavior of this function is similar to that of $y = x^2 + 4x + 14$.

▓ Group Work 1: Fun with Asymptotes

This activity extends the concepts of this section and reviews the idea of odd and even functions.

Answers:

1. Answers will vary. There should be vertical asymptotes at $x = \pm\frac{1}{2}$ and $x = \pm 1$.

2. Answers will vary. There should be asymptotes at $x = \pm 1$, $x = \pm 2$, and $y = 2$.

3. There are vertical asymptotes at $x = \pm 1.5$. This is not a rational function.

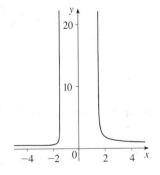

▓ Group Work 2: Putting It All Together

At first, students may just try to put this in their calculators. You may want to give them the hint that it will be very hard to find a viewing window that shows all the features of this graph by trial and error. When they've done some of the mathematical analysis of this graph, they should be encouraged to draw graphs using several windows, given that no one range is completely illustrative.

Answer:

Intercepts: $\left(-\frac{1}{2}, 0\right)$, $\left(\frac{3}{2}, 0\right)$, $(1, 0)$. Asymptotes: $x = 0$, $x = -1$, $y = 4$

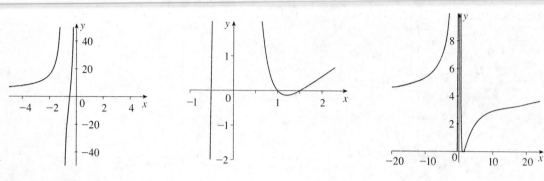

■ Homework Problems

Core Exercises: 23, 25, 31, 35, 39, 53, 55, 57, 65, 73, 83

Sample Assignment: 3, 4, 5, 6, 8, 12, 13, 19, 20, 23, 25, 28, 29, 31, 35, 39, 42, 53, 55, 57, 58, 65, 69, 70, 73, 75, 83, 86, 91

GROUP WORK 1, SECTION 4.6
Fun with Asymptotes

1. Draw an odd function that has the lines $x = \frac{1}{2}$ and $x = -1$ among its vertical asymptotes.

2. Draw an even function that has $x = 1$, $x = -2$, and $y = 2$ among its asymptotes.

3. Analyze the vertical asymptotes of $f(x) = \dfrac{3x^2 + 4x + 5}{\sqrt{16x^4 - 81}}$. Is this a rational function?

Putting It All Together

Sketch the graph of $f(x) = \dfrac{4x^3 - 8x^2 + x + 3}{x^3 + x^2}$.

CHAPTER 5   Exponential and Logarithmic Functions

Suggested Time and Emphasis

$1 - 1\frac{1}{2}$ classes. Essential material.

Points to Stress

1. The definition of an exponential function, including what it means to raise a to an irrational number.
2. The geometry of exponential functions and their transformations.
3. The base e.
4. Periodically and continuously compounded interest.

Sample Questions

- **Text Question:** Sketch a graph of $y = \left(\frac{1}{2}\right)^x$.

  Answer:

  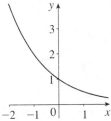

- **Drill Question:** Find the total amount of money in an account after 2 years if $100 is invested at an interest rate of 5.5% per year, compounded continuously.

  Answer: $111.63

In-Class Materials

- Start to draw a graph of $y = 2^x$, using a carefully measured scale of one inch per unit on both axes. Point out that after one foot, the height would be over 100 yards (the length of a football field). After two feet, the height would be 264 miles, after three feet it would be 1,000,000 miles (four times the distance to the moon), after three and a half feet it would be in the heart of the sun. If the graph extended five feet to the right, $x = 60$, then y would be over one light year up.

- Point out this contrast between exponential and linear functions: For equally spaced x-values, linear functions have constant *differences* in y-values, while pure exponential functions have constant *ratios* in y-values. Use this fact to show that the following table describes an exponential function, not a linear one.

x	y
-6.2	0.62000
-2.4	0.65100
1.4	0.68355
5.2	0.71773
9.0	0.75361
12.8	0.79129

- Estimate where $3^x > x^3$ and where $2^x > x^8$ using technology. Notice that exponential functions start by growing *slower* than polynomial functions, and then wind up growing much *faster*. For example, if one were to graph x^2 vs x using one inch per unit, then when $x = 60$, y would be only 100 yards, as opposed to a light year for $y = 2^x$. (The sun is only 8 light minutes from the earth.)

- Have your students fill out the following table, using their calculators, to give them a feel for $y = e^x$.

x	2^x	3^x	e^x
-2	$\frac{1}{4} = 0.25$	$\frac{1}{9} \approx 0.111$	≈ 0.135
-1	$\frac{1}{2} = 0.5$	$\frac{1}{3} \approx 0.333$	≈ 0.368
0	1	1	1
1	2	3	≈ 2.718
2	4	9	≈ 7.389
3	8	27	≈ 20.086

- Anticipate the next section by having students sketch the graphs of the inverse functions of 2^x and e^x by reflecting them across the line $y = x$.

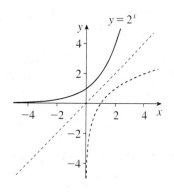
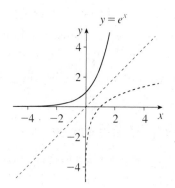

▨ Examples

- A shifted exponential curve:

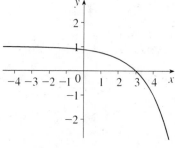

$$f(x) = -2^{x-3} + 1$$

- A comparison of compounding rates: $2000 is put in an IRA that earns 7%. Its worth after 10 years is given in the following table.

Compounded annually	$3934.30
Compounded semi-annually	$3979.58
Compounded monthly	$4019.32
Compounded weekly	$4025.61
Compounded daily	$4027.24
Compounded hourly	$4027.50
Compounded continuously	$4027.51

Note: Most calculators will not be able to determine the amount earned if the interest is compounded, say, every tenth of a second. Underflow errors in the microprocessor will make the computation difficult.

■ Group Work 1: I've Grown Accustomed to Your Growth

Before handing out this activity, it may be prudent to review the rules of exponentiation. This exercise enables students to discover for themselves the equal ratio property of exponential functions.

Answers:

1. Yes ($m = 1$), no, yes ($m \approx 2.08$), yes ($m \approx 2.01$)
2. Equally spaced changes in x-values result in equally spaced changes in y-values
3. Equally spaced changes in x values result in equally proportioned changes in y-values with the same ratio. $b = 2$, $b = 0.9975$, $b = 2.25$, $b = 3$
4. The " $+ C$" gets in the way when taking the ratio. However, the property is close to being true when A and b are large compared to C.

■ Group Work 2: Comparisons

The purpose of this group work is to give students a bit of "picture sense". It is acceptable if they do this by looking at the graphs on their calculators, setting the windows appropriately.

Answers:

1. $0 < x < 1.374$ and $x > 9.940$
2. $0 < x < 1.051$ and $x > 95.7169$
3. $0 < x < 1.17$ and $x > 22.5$
4. $0 < x < 1.34$ and $x > 10.9$
5. $0 < x < 1.077$ and $x > 58.7702$

■ Homework Problems

Core Exercises: 5, 9, 15, 17, 21, 27, 29, 33, 47, 63, 69, 71

Sample Assignment: 2, 5, 8, 9, 13, 14, 15, 17, 21, 23, 24, 27, 29, 31, 32, 33, 43, 47, 52, 60, 61, 63, 69, 71

I've Grown Accustomed to Your Growth

1. Two or three of the following four tables of data have something in common: linear growth. Without trying to find complete equations of lines, determine which of them are linear growth, and determine their rate of change:

x	y
1	2
2	3
3	4
4	5

x	y
21.5	4.32
32.6	4.203
43.7	4.090
54.8	3.980

x	y
−3	1.1
−2.5	2.14
−2	3.18
−1.5	4.25

x	y
1	−5.00
3	−0.98
6	5.05
8	9.07

2. In a sentence, describe a property of linear growth that can be determined from a table of values.

3. The following four tables of data have something in common: exponential growth. Functions of the form $y = Ab^x$ (or Ae^{kx}) have a property in common analogous to the one you stated in Question 2. Find the property, and then find the value of b.

x	y
1	5
2	10
3	20
4	40

x	y
21.5	4.32
32.6	4.203
43.7	4.090
54.8	3.980

x	y
-3	1.1
-2.5	1.65
-2	2.475
-1.5	3.7125

x	y
1	0.8
3	7.2
6	194.4
8	1749.6

4. Unfortunately, the above property does not hold for functions of the form $y = Ab^x + C$. What goes wrong? For what kinds of values of A, b, and C does the property come close to being true?

GROUP WORK 2, SECTION 5.1
Comparisons

You have learned that an exponential function grows faster than a polynomial function. Find the values of $x > 0$ for which

1. $2^x \geq x^3$.

2. $(1.1)^x \geq x^2$.

3. $2^x \geq x^5$.

4. $3^x \geq x^5$.

5. $2^x > x^{10}$.

■ Suggested Time and Emphasis

1 class. Essential material.

■ Points to Stress

1. Definition of the logarithm function as the inverse of the exponential function, from both a numeric and geometric perspective.

2. Properties of the logarithm function, emphasizing the natural and common logarithms.

■ Sample Questions

- **Text Question:** It is a fact that $10^\pi \approx 1385.46$. Is it possible to approximate $\log 1385.46$ without the use of a calculator? If so, then approximate this number. If not, why not?

    Answer: $\log_{10} 1385.46 \approx \pi$

- **Drill Question:** Compute $\log_4 \frac{1}{64}$

    Answer: -3

■ In-Class Materials

- When the logarithm function is graphed on a calculator, it appears to have a horizontal asymptote. Point out that the graph is misleading in that way. Start a graph of $y = \log_{10} x$ on the blackboard, noting the domain and the vertical asymptote. Using the scale of 1 inch = 1 unit (on the x-axis) and 1 foot = 1 unit (on the y-axis), plot some points:

x	0.1	1	2	3	4	5	6	7	8	9	10
$\log_{10} x$	-1	0	0.30	0.47	0.60	0.70	0.78	0.85	0.90	0.95	1

    Now ask how many inches we would have to go out to get up to $y = 2$ feet. (Answer: 100 inches, or $8\frac{1}{3}$ feet.) If the blackboard is large enough, plot the point $(100, 2)$. Then ask how far we would have to go to get up to $y = 5$ feet. (Answer: 1.57 miles.) Note how it turns out to take close to a mile and a half to go from $y = 4$ to $y = 5$, and that (if you graphed it out) it would look a lot like there is a horizontal asymptote. Find the distance from your classroom to a city or landmark in another state, and ask the class to estimate the log of that distance, using the same scale.

- Sketch a graph of $f(x) = 2\log_2(x + 3)$. Sketch the inverse function, then find an algebraic formula for the inverse. Foreshadow the next section by showing that the graph of $f(x)$ is the same as that of $g(x) = \log_2\left((x + 3)^2\right)$.

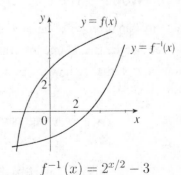

$f^{-1}(x) = 2^{x/2} - 3$

- Ask your students if they have ever had to deal with recharging a battery, for example the battery to a music device or a laptop. Assume that the battery is dead, and it takes an hour to charge it up half way. Ask them how much it will be charged in two hours. (The answer is 75% charged.) They may have noticed that, when charging a laptop battery, it takes a surprisingly long time for the monitor to change from "99% charged" to "100% charged." It turns out that the time it takes to charge the battery to $n\%$ is given by $t = -k \ln \left(1 - \frac{n}{100}\right)$; in our example $k = 1.4427$. Have students compute how long it would take the battery to get a 97% charge, a 98% charge, and a 99% charge. (Remind them that it took only an hour to go from 0% to 50%.) Graph t versus n to demonstrate that the battery will never be fully charged.

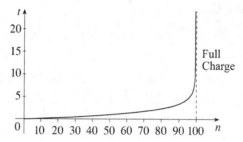

- Show students semilog graph paper (available at university bookstores, from your friendly neighborhood physics teacher, or from websites such as `http://www.csun.edu/science/ref/measurement/data/graph_paper.html`.) Point out how the distance between the y-axis lines is based on the logarithm of the y-coordinate, not on the y-coordinate itself. Have them graph $y = 2^x$ on semilog graph paper.

▪ Example

A shifted logarithmic curve:

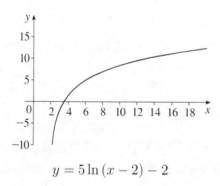

$$y = 5 \ln (x - 2) - 2$$

▪ Group Work 1: The Evan Operation

This activity can be enjoyed on two levels. One level of thought would stop after students used trial and error to discover that the Evan Function concatenates any two numbers. A more challenging level of thought would get students to verbalize how the Evan function works: why it does what it does. An advanced class might be given the goal, and challenged to come up with an expression for the Evan function themselves.

Question 4 can serve as a springboard for discussions of commutativity, associativity, and identity, or it can stand on its own.

In this exercise, $[\![x]\!]$ denotes the greatest integer function.

Answers:

1. (a) 15 (b) $42{,}134$ (c) $5{,}231{,}553$ (d) $8{,}501{,}245$ (e) $4{,}226{,}483{,}173$

2. Evaning is the same as concatenating (writing one next to the other).

3. It is not possible, because negative numbers are outside the domain of the log function

4. (b) and (d) are true, (a) is false, and (c) is not even well-defined.

5. $\llbracket \log_{10} b \rrbracket + 1$ tells us how many digits are in b. We then take a, add that many zeros to its end, and then add b.

■ Group Work 2: Learning Curves

Phrases like "the learning curve is steep" and "the learning curve is shallow" come up occasionally in academia, and many don't know what they mean. This activity will use the idea of a learning curve to play with some of the functions that have been learned thus far. Either start the activity by handing out the worksheet, or by doing the first problem as a class, and then handing out the sheet.

Answers:

1.

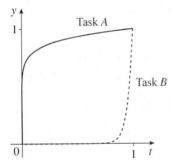

2. Task A. After saying it a couple of times, you pretty much know it.

3. Task B. There is a long period where improvment is slow, and then the learning takes place quickly.

4., 5. Answers will vary. Notice that for most activities of this nature, even though there is no horizontal asymptote, the slope of the learning curve will tend to approach zero (as happens for $y = \ln x$).

6. (a) Make sure students address the horizontal asymptote at $y = 1$ and the concavity change.

    (c) Make sure students address the fact that the y-intercept is not zero.

    (d) Make sure that students address the fact that there is no horizontal asymptote, and that improvement gets slower and slower (perhaps as discussed in Problem 5).

    (f) Make sure students address the periodic "plateaus" in improvement.

    (g) Make sure students address the "dips" where they get worse before they get better. (Games such as darts work like this, where as someone gets better, that person gets less and less lucky "fallout".)

7. It means that improvement is very rapid, implying that the task is easy to learn.

■ Homework Problems

Core Exercises: $5, 7, 9, 19, 25, 39, 49, 51, 53, 59, 65, 79$

Sample Assignment: $4, 5, 7, 8, 9, 12, 13, 17, 19, 22, 23, 25, 31, 32, 35, 36, 38, 39, 47, 49, 51, 53, 59, 65,$ $76, 77, 78, 79, 86, 87, 89$

GROUP WORK 1, SECTION 5.2
The Evan Operation

Consider two positive integers a and b. We know how to compute $a + b$, $a - b$, a/b, and ab. There is another thing we can compute: $a \circledast b$, pronounced "a Evan b". To Evan two numbers together, we perform the following calculation:

$$a \circledast b = a \left(10^{\llbracket \log_{10} b \rrbracket + 1} \right) + b$$

1. Compute the following without the use of a calculator.

(a) $1 \circledast 5$

(b) $42 \circledast 134$

(c) $5231 \circledast 553$

(d) $8 \circledast 501{,}245$

(e) $42{,}264 \circledast 83{,}173$

2. Describe, in words, what it means to Evan two integers together.

3. What happens when we try to Evan negative integers?

4. Which of the following statements are true for arbitrary positive integers a, b, and c?

(a) $a \circledast b = b \circledast a$

(b) $a \circledast (b \circledast c) = (a \circledast b) \circledast c$

(c) $a \circledast 0 = a$

(d) $0 \circledast b = b$

5. Revisit your answer to Question 2. Explain, in words, why $a\left(10^{\llbracket \log_{10} b \rrbracket + 1}\right) + b$ does what you say it does.

GROUP WORK 2, SECTION 5.2
Learning Curves

In psychology, we often graph the amount of material learned as a function of time spent studying or practicing. For example, assume I wanted to learn the capitals of all fifty states in the United States. I know the capitals of five states off the top of my head, and after ten minutes I can probably learn ten more. Ten more minutes will give me ten more, and then I'm going to slow down—I'll start forgetting. But if I put a solid three hours into it, I will know all fifty. If we plot these data on a graph, then I have a "learning curve".

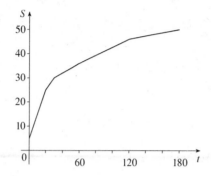

Different types of tasks have different learning curves, and, of course, the learning curves for each person are different. But for some tasks, the overall shape is similar for many people.

Let's look at two activities we are trying to learn how to do. Task A's curve is given by $y = \sqrt[10]{t}$ and Task B's is given by $y = t^{20}$.

1. Sketch both learning curves.

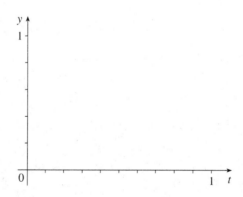

2. One of the tasks is memorizing a five digit number. Is this most likely Task A or Task B? Why?

3. It was interesting watching my five-year-old daughter learn to ride a bicycle. She experienced a period of frustration, where her improvement was slow. She couldn't balance. Suddenly, her mind and body seemed to "click" and she was able to ride perfectly, and started asking me how to pop wheelies, if she could ride to kindergarten by herself, and if unicycles were expensive. Did her learning curve look more like that of Task A or that of Task B? Why?

4. Both of the above tasks stopped at $y = 1$. We can think of $y = 1$ as "knowing the number" and "being able to ride down the street without falling off" Give an example of a task where there is no y-boundary; where one can start learning, and get better and better at the task without limit.

5. Draw the learning curve of the task you described in Question 4.

6. Come up with tasks that fit the following learning curves. Sketching their graphs, starting at $t = 0$, will be helpful.

(a) $L(t) = \dfrac{1}{1 + e^{-t+4}}$

(b) $L(t) = \dfrac{t}{10}$

(c) $L(t) = \dfrac{t}{10} + \dfrac{1}{2}$

(d) $L(t) = \ln(t + 1)$

(e) $L(t) = t^2$ for $0 \le t \le 1$

(f) $L(t) = x + \sin x$ for $0 \le x \le 9.5$

(g) $L(t) = x + 1.25 \sin x$ for $0 \le x \le 9$

7. If someone describes a task to you and says, "The learning curve is steep," what does that mean?

■ Suggested Time and Emphasis

1 – 2 classes. Essential material.

■ Point to Stress

The laws of logarithms, including the change of base formula.

■ Sample Questions

- **Text Question:** Given that $\log_2 3 \approx 1.58496$, approximately what is $\log_2 9$?
  Answer: $\log_2 9 \approx 3.16992$

- **Drill Question:** Express $5 \log (x + 2) - \frac{1}{3} \log x$ as a single logarithm.

  Answer: $\log \left(\dfrac{(x + 2)^5}{\sqrt[3]{x}} \right)$

■ In-Class Materials

- Make sure your students do not neglect the warning after Example 4. Perhaps have them write out all the rules of logarithms they have learned so far, organized this way:

The Equivalence Definition	$y = \log_m x$ is equivalent to $x = m^y$
The Conversion Rule	$\log_m (\text{thing}) = \dfrac{\log_n (\text{thing})}{\log_n (m)}$
The Combining Rules	$\log_m (m^{\text{thing}}) = \text{thing}$ $m^{\log_m (\text{thing})} = \text{thing}$
The Arithmetic Rules	$\log_m 1 = 0$ $\log_m (ab) = \log_m a + \log_m b$ $\log_m \left(\dfrac{a}{b} \right) = \log_m a - \log_m b$ $\log_m (a^b) = b \log_m a$
The Non-Rules	$\log_m (a + b) = \log_m (a + b)$ $\dfrac{\log_m a}{\log_m b} = \dfrac{\log_m a}{\log_m b}$ $(\log_m a)^b = (\log_m a)^b$

Perhaps if your students memorize the non-rules, they will be less likely to indulge in algebraic mischief under exam pressure.

- Note, without necessarily emphasizing, the importance of domains when applying the log rules. For example, $\ln \left(\frac{-5}{-6} \right)$ is not equal to $\ln (-5) - \ln (-6)$.

- Mention how logarithms were used to do calculations before the advent of the calculator. For example, every scientist had a table like this one:

x	$\ln x$		x	$\ln x$
4.4	1.48160		9.8	2.28238
4.5	1.50408		9.9	2.29253
4.6	1.52606		10.0	2.30259
4.7	1.54756		10.1	2.31254
4.8	1.56862		10.2	2.32239

Now let's say a scientist wanted to find $\sqrt[3]{100}$. He would write

$$\sqrt[3]{100} = 10^{2/3}$$
$$\ln\left(\sqrt[3]{100}\right) = \ln\left(10^{2/3}\right)$$
$$= \tfrac{2}{3}\ln(10)$$

Then he would look up $\ln(10)$ from the table to get

$$\ln\left(\sqrt[3]{100}\right) \approx \tfrac{2}{3}(2.30259)$$
$$\approx 1.53506$$

And to find $\sqrt[3]{100}$, he would try to find 1.53506 in the right-hand column of the table. The result is that $\sqrt[3]{100}$ is between 4.6 and 4.7. In practice, the distance between table entries was much closer than 0.1. For a quicker, less accurate estimate, a slide rule was used.

▨ Examples

- A set of logarithms that can be combined:

$$a\ln(b+c) + \frac{3}{4}(\ln a - \ln b) = \ln\left((b+c)^a \sqrt[4]{\left(\frac{a}{b}\right)^3}\right)$$

- A set of logarithms that can be expanded:
  Given $\ln 2 \approx 0.693$ and $\ln 3 \approx 1.099$, compute $\ln\frac{8}{9}\sqrt[5]{6}$.

$$\frac{8}{9}\sqrt[5]{6} = \frac{2^3}{3^2}(2\cdot 3)^{1/5}$$
$$\ln\left(\frac{8}{9}\sqrt[5]{6}\right) = 3\ln 2 - 2\ln 3 + \tfrac{1}{5}(\ln 2 + \ln 3)$$
$$\approx 0.240569$$

▨ Group Work 1: Irrational, Impossible Relations

One of the joys of precalculus is that there are some deep, graduate-level mathematical results that can be explored using nothing more than the techniques of algebra and one's coconut. Start by asking students this true-or-false question:

$$\log_2 3 = \frac{4953}{3125}$$

The answer is, of course, false. Next, review the definitions of rational and irrational numbers, and hand out the first sheet. The hint sheet should be given out only after students have tried to show that $\log_2 3$ is irrational, or at least discussed it enough to understand what they are trying to show. If a group finishes early, have them show that $\log_2 a$ is always irrational if a is an odd integer.

Answers:

1. $-\gamma$ **2.** $-\gamma$ **3.** $\dfrac{\gamma}{2}$ **4.** $\log_2 3 = \dfrac{\ln 3}{\ln 2}$

5. The proof is outlined in the hint sheet.

Answers (Hint Sheet):

1. $2^{a/b} = 3 \;\Rightarrow\; \sqrt[b]{2^a} = 3 \;\Rightarrow\; 2^a = 3^b$

2. If $a = b = 0$, then $\log_2 3 = 0/0$, which is undefined.

3. $2^a = 2 \cdot 2 \cdots \cdot 2$, and $3^b = 3 \cdot 3 \cdots \cdot 3$, so these numbers can never be equal, because the left is always divisible by two, and the right never is (unless $b = 0$).

4. It is irrational because it cannot be written as a ratio of two integers.

■ Group Work 2: The Slide Rule

If possible, give each group a slide rule. If you don't happen to have a lot of real slide rules around, a slide rule cutout is provided. Teach the students how to use the slide rule to multiply:

To multiply a times b, move the 1 on the top over the a on the bottom. Then locate the b on the top, and right below it will be ab. Below is an example, where we multiply 6 by 8 to get 48.

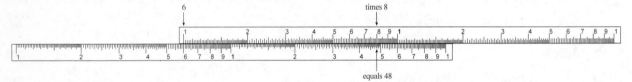

Accuracy isn't the main issue here (real slide rules have a very thin guide that slides perpendicular to the rules, with an embedded hair to ensure accuracy.) The idea is to see how it works.

After students have learned to multiply, hand out the activity sheet.

Answers:

Answers: 1–5 are trivial. Note that Question 5 can be done by multiplying 8×1.2 and remembering to multiply the answer by 10.

6. The numbers are not equally spaced. In fact, they are spaced based on the log of the number. In other words, the 2 is $\log 2$ units from the 1, the 3 is $\log 3$ units from the 1, the 4 is $\log 4$ units from the 1, etc. That is why the numbers get closer and closer together. When you slide the top, you are in effect *adding* the two logarithms. So when we move the slide over the six, and look at the eight, we are adding $\log 6 + \log 8$ The total distance is then $\log (6 \times 8) = \log 48$. And when we look below the 8, we see the number that is $\log 48$ units from the 1, which is 48. In short: We are adding logs, which in effect multiplies the numbers.

■ Homework Problems

Core Exercises: 7, 9, 11, 19, 21, 33, 47, 49, 55, 57, 63, 69

Sample Assignment: 5, 7, 9, 10, 11, 18, 19, 21, 33, 34, 38, 40, 44, 46, 47, 48, 49, 55, 57, 63, 69, 71, 73

GROUP WORK 1, SECTION 5.3
Irrational, Impossible Relations

1. If $\log_2 x = \gamma$, then what is $\log_{1/2} x$?

2. If $\log_b x = \gamma$, then what is $\log_{1/b} x$ (assuming $b > 1$)?

3. If $\log_b x = \gamma$, then what is $\log_{b^2} x$?

4. We are going to estimate $\log_2 3$. Of course, in fifth grade, you memorized that $\log_2 3 \approx 1.584962501$. Suppose you didn't have this fact memorized. There is no $\log_2 3$ button on your calculator! How would you compute it?

5. Unfortunately, the calculator gives us only a finite number of digits. If $\log_2 3$ were a rational number, we would be able to express it as a fraction, giving us perfect accuracy. Do you think it is rational or irrational? Try to prove your result.

GROUP WORK 1, SECTION 5.3
Irrational, Impossible Relations (Hint Sheet)

So, you realize that it's not easy to determine whether $\log_2 3$ is rational!

One way to attempt to show that $\log_2 3$ is rational is to assume that it is, and try to find integers a and b such that $\log_2 3 = \dfrac{a}{b}$. If we can show that there are no such a and b, then $\log_2 3$ *cannot* be rational.

1. Assume that $\log_2 3 = \dfrac{a}{b}$. Show that a and b must then satisfy $2^a = 3^b$

2. Notice that $a = 0$, $b = 0$ satisfies $2^a = 3^b$. Show that this fact doesn't help us.

3. Find $a \neq 0$ and $b \neq 0$ that satisfy $2^a = 3^b$, or show that no such $\{a, b\}$ exists.

4. Is $\log_2 3$ rational or irrational? Why?

GROUP WORK 2, SECTION 5.3
The Slide Rule

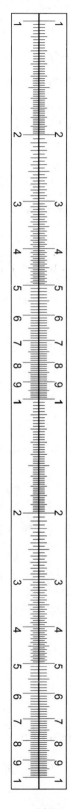

Before we ask the million-dollar question, it is important that you are familiar with the operation of a slide rule. Use your slide rule to do the following computations. (We are aware that you don't *need* a slide rule to do them, the idea here is to learn how a slide rule works.)

1. $2 \times 4 =$

2. $5 \times 5 =$

3. $1.3 \times 8 =$

4. $6 \times 8 =$

5. $8 \times 12 =$

And now, the big question:

6. Why does the slide rule work? What is this magical property it possesses that allows us to multiply in this way?

   Hint: It has something to do with the section you have just covered in class.

Suggested Time and Emphasis

$\frac{1}{2}$ – 1 class. Essential material. Can be combined with Section 5.5.

Point to Stress

Solving equations involving exponential and logarithmic functions, algebraically and graphically.

Sample Questions

- **Text Question:** Solve the equation $4 + 3 \log (2x) = 16$.

  Answer: $x = 5000$

- **Drill Question:** If I invest $2000 at an annual interest rate of 3%, compounded continuously, how long will it take the investment to double?

  Answer: $\dfrac{\ln 2}{0.03} \approx 23$ years

In-Class Materials

- At this point students know the algebraic rules for working with exponential and logarithmic functions. Stress that if these rules do not suffice to solve an equation, there is a good chance that they cannot find an exact solution. Give students an equation such as $x^2 = 2 \ln (x + 2)$ (Example 9) and have them try to solve it algebraically. The correct answer is that students cannot do so, but you will find that many make up rules and somehow wind up with a solution.

- Review the concept of inverse functions. Have students find the inverse of functions such as $f(x) = 2^{x^3 + 1}$ and $f(x) = \ln (x - 5) + e^3$.

- Build up some tough problems from simple ones. For example, first have students solve $x^2 + 2x - 15 = 0$. Then have them solve $(e^x - 1)^2 + 2(e^x - 1) - 15 = 0$. One can even belabor the point with $\ln \left((e^x - 1)^2 + 2(e^x - 1) - 14 \right) = 0$.

Examples

- Solve $\log (x^2 - 1) - \log (x + 1) = 3$.

  Answer: $x = 1001$

- Solve $(\ln x - 2)^3 - 4(\ln x - 2) = 0$.

  Answer: $x = 1, e^2, e^4$

Group Work 1: The Rule of 72

If a group finishes early or has trouble with Question 7, have them redo Questions 1–5 for annual compounding. Another good continuation is the following: is it true that the length of time it will take an investment to quadruple is always twice the amount that it will take the money to double? Prove your answer or provide a counterexample. The proofs that the students write may surprise you with their quality and use of the properties of exponents and logarithms.

Answers:

1. 13.86 years

2. The doubling time is not affected by changes in principal. Algebraically, the P_0 drops out of the exponential growth equation. Intuitively, the doubling time is a property of the ratio of two numbers, not a property of the numbers themselves.

3. Estimate: 14.4 years, a 3.90% error.

4.

Interest Rate	Actual Doubling Time	Estimated Doubling Time	Error
3%	23.1 years	24 years	3.90%
8%	8.66 years	9 years	3.92%
12%	5.78 years	6 years	3.81%
18%	3.85 years	4 years	3.90%

The Rule of 72 is accurate to within 4% for the given range of interest rates.

5. If r is the interest rate (as a number, not a percentage), then the doubling time is $D = \dfrac{\ln 2}{r}$.

6. $100 \ln 2 \approx 69$. This estimate gives a doubling time of 13.8, for an error of 0.4%.

7. If the compounding is assumed to be annual, 72 works best for values of r between 3% and 15%. For example, 10% compounded annually doubles every 7.2735 years. The rule of 72 gives 7.2, a good approximation, and the rule of 69 gives 6.9, a bad one.

▪ Group Work 2: Every Nest Egg Needs a Bird

This activity involves some repetitive calculation. Stress that part of working in a group effectively is to figure out how best to divide up the work.

Answers:

1. $2000e^{(0.07)47} + 2000e^{(0.07)46} + 2000e^{(0.07)45} + 2000e^{(0.07)44} + 2000e^{(0.07)43} + 2000e^{(0.07)42}$
$$+ 2000e^{(0.07)41} + 2000e^{(0.07)40} + 2000e^{(0.07)39} + 2000e^{(0.07)38} = \$399{,}759.00$$

2. $\sum\limits_{n=0}^{37} 2000e^{(0.07)n} = \$366{,}753.00$

3. Most people are surprised by this fact.

▪ Homework Problems

Core Exercises: 7, 9, 11, 29, 33, 37, 41, 43, 49, 59, 71, 73, 77, 83

Sample Assignment: 2, 7, 9, 11, 13, 14, 26, 29, 33, 37, 41, 43, 46, 49, 50, 53, 59, 60, 71, 73, 77, 83, 84, 86

GROUP WORK 1, SECTION 5.4
The Rule of 72

In this exercise, we attempt to answer the question asked by many investors: "How long is it going to take for me to double my money?"

1. Consider an investment of $100 invested at 5%, compounded continuously. How long would it take for the investor to have $200?

2. What would the doubling time be if the initial investment were $1,000? $10,000? What effect does changing the principal have on the doubling time, and why?

One of the first things that is taught in an economics class is the Rule of 72. It can be summarized thusly:

> "The number of years it takes an investment to double
> is equal to 72 divided by the annual percentage interest rate."

3. What would the Rule of 72 say the doubling time of a 5% investment is? Is it a good estimate?

4. Repeat Problems 1 and 3 for investments of 3%, 8%, 12% and 18%. What can you say about the accuracy of the Rule of 72?

5. Derive a precise formula for the time T to double an initial investment.

6. There is an integer that gives a more accurate answer for continuous or nearly continuous compounding than the Rule of 72. What is this number? Check your answer by using it to estimate the doubling time of a 5% investment.

7. It turns out that there is a reason that we use the number 72 in the Rule. It has to do with one of the assumptions we made. Why do economists use the Rule of 72?

GROUP WORK 2, SECTION 5.4
Every Nest Egg Needs a Bird

Johnny and Jenny had a crazy dream. They wanted to retire wealthy, or at least comfortable.

1. Johnny started saving at age 20. Every year, for simplicity assume January 1 of every year, Johnny put $2000 into a type of personal retirement savings account called an IRA. Again, for simplicity, let's assume that the IRA made 7% interest per year. Ten years later, Johnny gave up saving for retirement, and never put any money away again. How much money did Johnny have when he was 67 years old?

2. Jenny spent most of her twenties reading magazines and watching movies, and didn't start saving until she was 30. At that point she started putting $2000 a year into her IRA (again, let's assume it makes 7% per year and she put it away on January 1). When she was 40 she continued to save, and at 50 she continued to save. In fact, she put in $2000 per year until she was 67, when she also retired. How much money did Jenny have when she was 67?

3. Which of the two had more money? Is that the result you expected?

5.5 | Modeling with Exponential and Logarithmic Functions

■ Suggested Time and Emphasis

$\frac{1}{2}$ – 1 class. Recommended material. Can be combined with Section 5.4.

■ Points to Stress

1. Translating verbal descriptions of problems into mathematical models, and solving the problems using the models.

2. Certain standard types of problems such as those dealing with exponential growth and decay and logarithmic scales.

■ Sample Questions

- **Text Question:** Recall that Newton's Law of Cooling is given by

$$T(t) = T_s + D_0 e^{-kt}$$

Which of the constants in this law correspond to surrounding temperature? Which represents the initial difference between the object and its surroundings? How do you know?

Answer: T_s, D_0. There is a horizontal asymptote at T_s, which would have to correspond to the surrounding temperature, because things cool off to the surrounding temperature. Their initial difference is D_0, because when $t = 0$ we know that $T = T_s + D_0$.

- **Drill Question:** Recall that the pH of a substance is given by $-\log\left[\text{H}^+\right]$, where H^+ is the concentration of hydrogen ions measured in moles per liter. Also recall that solutions with a pH of 7 are neutral, those with pH > 7 are basic, and those with pH < 7 are acidic.

  (a) If a sample of rebulon was measured to have hydrogen concentration of $\left[\text{H}^+\right] = 4 \times 10^{-8}$ M, what would the pH be?

  (b) What is the hydrogen ion concentration in a neutral substance?

  Answer: (a) 7.4   (b) 10^{-7}

■ In-Class Materials

- Show that the expression $y = e^{kt}$ can be written as $y = a^t$ and vice versa. Add that e^{kt+c} is equivalent to Ae^{kt}.

- One way to measure the growth of the Internet is to measure the number of Internet hosts. The following data show the number of Internet hosts over time. Try to determine with students if this is exponential growth. (Note: Do not show the student the third column right away. Let them come up with the idea of finding growth rates between data points.)

Month	Hosts	Growth	Month	Hosts	Growth
Aug 1981	213	–	Jan 1993	1,313,000	1.7762
May 1982	235	1.1404	Apr 1993	1,486,000	1.6520
Aug 1983	562	2.0065	Jul 1993	1,776,000	2.0443
Oct 1984	1024	1.6701	Oct 1993	2,056,000	1.7875
Oct 1985	1961	1.9150	Jan 1994	2,217,000	1.3487
Feb 1986	2308	1.6217	Jul 1994	3,212,000	2.1120
Nov 1986	5089	2.8782	Oct 1994	3,864,000	2.0818
Dec 1987	28,174	4.8615	Jan 1995	4,852,000	2.4618
Jul 1988	33,000	1.3112	Jul 1995	6,642,000	1.8739
Oct 1988	56,000	8.1509	Jan 1996	9,472,000	2.0357
Jan 1989	80,000	4.1168	Jul 1996	12,881,000	1.8525
Jul 1989	130,000	2.6620	Jan 1997	16,146,000	1.5654
Oct 1989	159,000	2.2231	Jul 1997	19,540,000	1.4692
Oct 1990	313,000	1.9686	Jan 1998	29,670,000	2.2900
Jan 1991	376,000	2.0824	Jul 1998	36,739,000	1.5387
Jul 1991	535,000	2.0364	Jan 1999	43,230,000	1.3809
Oct 1991	617,000	1.7608	Jul 1999	56,218,000	1.6985
Jan 1992	727,000	1.9172	Jan 2000	72,398,092	1.6516
Apr 1992	890,000	2.2511	Jul 2000	93,047,785	1.6541
Jul 1992	992,000	1.5453	Jan 2001	109,574,429	1.3831
Oct 1992	1,136,000	1.7122			

Answer: We can graph the data, and get a curve that looks like exponential growth. We can also graph growth rate and see (except for two spikes in the late 1980s) a more-or-less constant growth rate.

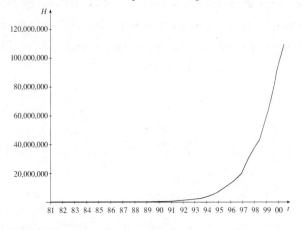
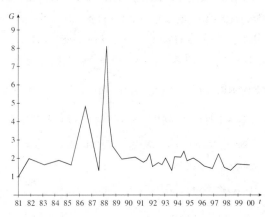

- In 1985 there were 15,948 diagnosed cases of AIDS in the United States. In 1990 there were 156,024. Scientists said that if there was no research done, the disease would grow exponentially. Compute the number of cases this model predicts for the year 2000. The actual number was 774,467. Discuss possible flaws in the model with students, and point out the dangers of extrapolation.

- Discuss the logistic growth model $P = \dfrac{M}{1 + Ae^{-kt}}$. Have students graph a few of these curves with different values of M and k. This model assumes that an environment has a carrying capacity M. It assumes that when a population is much less than M, a population's growth will look like exponential growth, but that when the population approaches M, the population growth gets very slow, asymptotically approaching M. If the population starts out greater than M, then it will decay, exponentially, to M.

- Go over Examples 9 and 10, the Richter scale. Ask students the open-ended question, "How much worse is an earthquake that measures 7 on the Richter scale than an earthquake that measures 6?" and discuss the issue.

Example

Exponential decay: we know that the half-life of carbon-14 is 5,730 years. In 1988, the Vatican consented to give a few fibers to scientists to carbon date the Shroud of Turin, an ancient artifact. They found that the fibers had 92% of the original ^{14}C left. Discuss what this implies about the age of the shroud.

Group Work 1: The Coffee Window

In physics and chemistry, people often refer to "Newton's Law of Cooling" and "Newton's Law of Heating". After completing this exercise, students should have discovered that these are the same law, the only difference being the relative temperatures of the substance being studied and its surroundings. The proper names have been taken from *The Hitch Hiker's Guide to the Galaxy* by Douglas Adams. The temperatures were determined by painful experimentation.

This activity can also launch a discussion of how mathematical models are simplifications of reality. For example, in Newton's Law of Cooling, we assume that the temperature of the cup's surroundings is constant. But of course, that isn't exactly true. In fact, one could argue that as the coffee cools, the energy from the coffee heats up the surroundings by a fraction, and that isn't taken into account in our model. No mathematical model will ever take into account every effect on every molecule of the universe. The question to ask isn't whether a model is true or false, but whether it is accurate enough to be useful.

Answers:

1. The coffee cools down over time; it does not heat up.

2. The thermos is better. A smaller value of k corresponds to a smaller rate of change of the coffee's temperature.

3. $T = \left(118e^{-0.03t} + 42\right)°$ 4. $t \approx 6.19$ minutes

5. $t \approx 20.92$ minutes   6. $t \approx 14.73$ minutes   7. $t \approx 34.82$ minutes

8. It will never cool down to drinking temperature.

9.

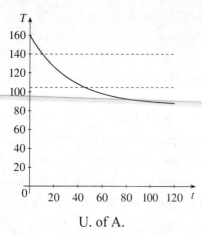

U. of A.

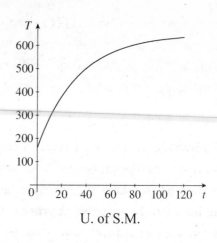

U. of S.M.

They would probably call it "Zaglor's Law of Heating".

■ Group Work 2: Earthquake

This activity is based on Exercises 34 and 35 from the text.

Answers:

1. Approximately 2500 times as intense

2. Approximately twice as intense

3. When the magnitude of an earthquake increases by 0.3 on the Richter scale, its intensity doubles.

■ Homework Problems

Core Exercises: 1, 3, 5, 9, 11, 15, 23, 27, 33, 35, 39

Sample Assignment: 1, 2, 3, 5, 6, 9, 11, 15, 17, 23, 24, 27, 33, 34, 35, 39

GROUP WORK 1, SECTION 5.5
The Coffee Window

(Written with John Hall)

Dr. Tricia MacMillan has a problem. Every day she leaves her apartment in London at the crack of dawn and heads for Milliway's, where she purchases a delicious cup of piping hot coffee. She drinks this coffee while walking to her office. The problem is that sometimes she burns her tongue badly with her first sip, while other times she waits too long and her coffee gets cold. The latter case is the worst, because besides doing a pretty bad job of keeping you warm, cold coffee tastes terrible. As it drops below a certain temperature, coffee undergoes a chemical reaction which turns even the most expensive brand into something that tastes absolutely filthy.

Being a mathematician, Dr. MacMillan doesn't just get mad, she gets more coffee and does an experiment. She wants to figure out exactly when she can take her first sip without burning herself, and from that point, how much time she has before the coffee turns bad. Every one of her mornings for the next week is spent in Milliway's with an oven thermometer and a cup of fresh coffee.

After much painful experimentation, Dr. MacMillan determines that if the temperature of the coffee is above $140°$ F, it burns her tongue. If the temperature drops below $105°$, the coffee undergoes the reaction and becomes undrinkable (unless she's already burnt her tongue so badly in the first experiment that she can't taste a thing).

Just like every other substance in the universe, coffee obeys Newton's Law of Cooling. Its temperature as a function of time is given by

$$T(t) = T_s + D_0 e^{-kt}$$

Note that there are three parameters in this equation. One is the outside temperature, and one depends on the initial temperature of the coffee. For a typical Styrofoam cup, $k \approx 0.05$, if t is measured in minutes.

1. Why is this constant positive?

Dr. MacMillan scoffs at Styrofoam. She is the proud owner of a Sirius Cybernetics Corporation thermos (only 35% asbestos!) For this thermos the constant is $k = 0.03$.

2. Which does a better job of keeping the coffee warm, the Styrofoam cup or the thermos? How does knowing the value of k allow you to figure out the answer?

The next day, Dr. MacMillan leaves Milliway's with a thermos full of coffee at $160°$ F. It is 8:30 A.M., and the outside temperature is $42°$.

3. Find T_s and D_0, and rewrite $T(t) = T_s + D_0 e^{-kt}$ with the appropriate constants for this situation. (Let the time t be measured in minutes, and let $t = 0$ stand for 8:30 A.M.)

4. How long must she wait before she is able to drink the coffee?

5. At what time will the coffee fall below $105°$ and become undrinkable?

6. How much time does Dr. MacMillan have to drink her coffee?

7. What would the answer to Problem 6 be if Dr. MacMillan were teaching at the University of Arizona, where the outside temperature is 86°?

8. What would the answer to Problem 6 be if she were teaching at the University of Southern Mercury (outside temperature 650° in winter)?

9. Draw a graph of coffee temperature versus time for the University of Arizona and the University of Southern Mercury. Why do they look different? What would students at the University of Southern Mercury call Newton's "Law of Cooling" (if they spoke English)?

GROUP WORK 2, SECTION 5.5
Earthquake

1. The devastating 1906 earthquake in San Francisco had a magnitude of 8.3 on the Richter scale. At the same time, in Japan, an earthquake with magnitude 4.9 caused only minor damage. How many times more intense was the San Francisco earthquake than the Japanese earthquake?

2. The Alaska earthquake of 1964 had a magnitude of 8.6 on the Richter scale. How many times more intense was this than the 1906 San Francisco earthquake?

3. Fill in the blank: When the magnitude of an Earthquake goes up by _____ on the Richter scale, its intensity doubles.

CHAPTER 6

Systems of Equations and Inequalities

6.1 | Systems of Equations

■ Suggested Time and Emphasis

$\frac{1}{2}$–1 class. Essential material. Can be combined with Section 6.2.

■ Point to Stress

Solving systems of equations with two variables, using the methods of substitution, elimination, and graphing.

■ Sample Questions

- **Text Question:** The textbook says that given the system

$$3x + 2y = 14$$
$$x - 2y = 2$$

we can add the equations to eliminate y, obtaining $4x = 16$, and thus determining $x = 4$ and $y = 1$. Could this system be solved using the substitution method? If not, why not? If so, would the answers be the same?

Answer: It could, and the answers would be the same.

- **Drill Question:** Solve this system of equations

$$x + y = 2$$
$$4x - 2y = -1$$

Answer: $x = \frac{1}{2}$, $y = \frac{3}{2}$

■ In-Class Materials

- Many students will want to just learn one method of solving systems of equations, and stick with it. It is important that they are familiar with all three. One reason is that some systems are easier to solve with one method than another. Another reason is that if they take mathematics classes in the future, their teachers will use their own favorite method in class.

Either have the students try to come up with three sample systems, each lending itself to a different method, or use these:

$$y = 3x + 2$$
$$\sqrt{y^2 - 8x^2 - 12x - 4} = 4$$

Substitution easiest

$$3x + \tfrac{5}{11}y = 2$$
$$-3x + \tfrac{6}{11}y = 3$$

Elimination easiest

$$y = x^3 - x$$
$$y = e^x$$

Exact solution impossible—a graph can give an approximation

- Solving systems of equations is the soul of applied mathematics. Here is one example of many: Populations with an initial population P_0 grow according the logistic growth model

$$P = \frac{K}{1 + Ae^{-ct}}$$

where A, K and c are constants. $A = \dfrac{K - P_0}{P_0}$ and K is the "carrying capacity" of the environment. Draw a few sample graphs for the students:

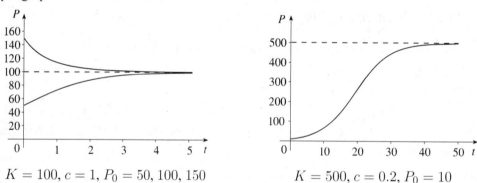

$K = 100, c = 1, P_0 = 50, 100, 150$ $K = 500, c = 0.2, P_0 = 10$

Assume that we want to find out the carrying capacity of an environment ("How many trout will Big Island Lake support?"). We can find (or estimate) P_0, and then measure the population at two times (say, at $t = 1$ and $t = 6$ months). Now we have a system of two equations with two unknowns, and we are able to find K and c.

- This may be a good time to point out that a system of equations can have zero, one, more than one, or infinitely many solutions. The students will be able to solve systems that have one or more than one solution:

$$2x + y = 3$$
$$-2x + 3y = 3$$

$$x^2 = y$$
$$-x^2 + 8 = y$$

$$y = x^3 - x^2 - 4x$$
$$y = 4$$

When demonstrating these systems, it is important to show the graphical solution as well as an analytic solution. Then have the students show, graphically, a system of equations with no solutions and then one with infinitely many solutions.

▩ Examples

- A non-linear system with an integer solution:

$$x^3 - y^2 = 23$$
$$2x - 3y = 0$$

Answer: $x = 3$, $y = 2$

- A non-linear system with a transcendental solution:

$$e^x + 2y = 5$$
$$-e^x + 5y = 2$$

Answer: $x = \ln 3$, $y = 1$

- A straightforward word problem:
  Retaining bricks for gardens are usually either 6 inches or 12 inches long. A 6-inch brick costs eighty cents and a 12-inch brick costs \$1.20. Assume we have a garden with an 8-foot perimeter and we spend \$10.80. How many bricks of each type did we buy?
  Answer: 6 small bricks, and 5 large ones

▩ Group Work 1: Area and Perimeter

Do not start out by reminding students of the relevant formulas—let them look them up. This should partially be a review of area and perimeter formulas. Notice that the rectangle referred to in Problem 1 is the very piece of paper that the students are writing on!

Answers:

1. 8.5 inches and 11 inches

2. 5 inches, 5 inches, and 6 inches

▩ Group Work 2: Intersection Points

The first three problems are routine. The fourth also involves solving a system, but requires some thought.

Answers:

1. $(1, 3), (-2, -6), (-3, -21)$

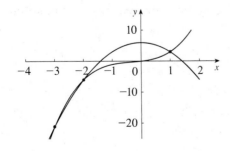

2. $(2, 4 + \ln 2) \approx (2, 4.693)$

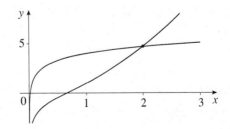

3.   There is no solution.

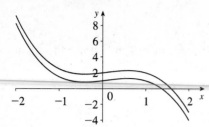

4. $\{2 = a - b + 2, 2 = a + b\}; a = 1, b = 1$

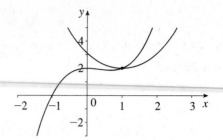

■ Homework Problems

Core Exercises: 5, 11, 15, 21, 47, 51

Sample Assignment: 4, 5, 8, 10, 11, 13, 15, 18, 19, 20, 21, 24, 28, 36, 37, 38, 47, 48, 51, 61

GROUP WORK 1, SECTION 6.1
Area and Perimeter

1. The area of a rectangle is 93.5 square inches and its perimeter is 39 inches. What are the dimensions of the rectangle?

2. The surface area of a box with a square base is 170 square inches and its volume is 150 cubic inches. What are the dimensions of the box?

Intersection Points

Graph the following pairs of curves, and then find each pair's point(s) of intersection.

1. $y = x^3 + x^2 + x$, $y = -3x^2 + 6$

2. $y = \ln x + 4$, $y = \ln x + x^2$

3. $y = 2^x - x^3$, $y = 2^x - x^3 + 1$

4. $y = ax^3 - bx^2 + 2$, $y = ae^{x-1} + be^{-x+1}$ [Find a and b that make these curves intersect at the point $(1, 2)$.]

■ Suggested Time and Emphasis

$\frac{1}{2}$–1 class. Essential material. Can be combined with Section 6.1.

■ Points to Stress

1. Solving systems of linear equations.

2. Inconsistent and dependent systems.

3. Using the modeling process to solve applied problems.

■ Sample Questions

- **Text Question:** Why does the dependent system $x + y = 2$, $2x + 2y = 4$ have infinitely many solutions?
  Answer: For any given x, there is a y that satisfies both equations.

- **Drill Question:** A woman rows a boat upstream from one point on a river to another point 4 miles away in 3 hours. The return trip, traveling with the current, takes 2 hours. How fast does she row relative to the water, and at what speed is the current flowing?
  Answer: She rows at $\frac{5}{3}$ mi/h and the current flows at $\frac{1}{3}$ mi/h.

■ In-Class Materials

- Most graphing calculators can solve systems of linear equations. If your students are all using the same or similar calculators, it may be worth using some class time to teach them how to use this feature. It will enable you to construct and discuss problems without worrying whether the numbers are "nice," and will be an asset to the students in their future science courses and projects.

- The text has shown examples of systems of linear equations with 0, 1, and infinitely many solutions. Ask the students to try to come up with an example of a system with a different outcome, or to explain why it is not possible. Discussing graphical solutions to these systems will not only make the answer apparent, but it will also reinforce the nomenclature "linear equation".

- Complex arithmetic can be reviewed at this time. Ask the students if this is a system of linear equations in two variables and (if so) to solve it:

$$(2 - i)\, x + 4y = 5$$
$$(4 - 3i)\, x - 2y = 3 + i$$

- Notice that some systems that are not technically linear can be solved by similar means. For example, given

$$\sqrt{x} + 2^y = 10$$
$$5\sqrt{x} - 3\left(2^y\right) = -14$$

one can use elimination to obtain $\sqrt{x} = 2$, $2^y = 8 \quad \Rightarrow \quad x = 4, y = 3$.

▪ Examples

- A system of linear equations:

$$2x - 3y = 10$$
$$x - 5y = 12$$

Answer: $x = 2, y = -2$

- A "mixture problem": Peanuts cost \$4.00 per pound and cashews cost \$7.50 per pound. If I buy a 5-pound bag consisting of peanuts and cashews, and I pay \$23.50 for the bag, how many pounds of cashews are in it?

Answer: 1 lb cashews, 4 lb peanuts

▪ Group Work 1: The Goniff Problem

This problem can be done as two variables in two unknowns, but some students will find a way to boil it down to a one-variable problem.

Answer: 12

▪ Group Work 2: Driving to Minneapolis

This is in the genre of "distance-rate-time" problems, with a bit of a twist. If a group finishes early, ask them to explain why the answer to Problem 2 is not 3 hours (the figure cited in the problem). Notice that the numbers are a bit messy, but the data are accurate. The beautiful thing is that we see that a five-minute swing in driving time (based on who is driving for how long) stems from a radical difference in driving speeds.

Answers:

1. I drive at 67.66 mi/h and she drives at 80.34 mi/h.

2. 3.022 hours, or 3 hours, 1 minute, 20 seconds. This is slightly longer than each person driving the same amount of time because the slow driver winds up driving for more time under this scheme.

▪ Homework Problems

Core Exercises: 11, 23, 25, 51, 53

Sample Assignment: 2, 5, 6, 7, 11, 12, 13, 23, 24, 25, 39, 43, 47, 48, 51, 53, 55, 56, 58

GROUP WORK 1, SECTION 6.2
The Goniff Problem

A group of people have breakfast together before going to work. They calculate the tip to be $9.60, and from that figure out each person's individual share. Everyone counts the money, and tosses it in.

But it comes up short! One reason is that the boss did not contribute to the tip, because he paid for breakfast. Another reason is that one of the group, Mr. P., refuses to tip because he doesn't believe in it. To cover the two non-contributors, everyone else has to put in an additional sixteen cents.

How many people ate breakfast?

GROUP WORK 2, SECTION 6.2
Driving to Minneapolis

Once a month, my girlfriend and I drive to Minneapolis, Minnesota to visit her mother and sister. The distance between the Cedar Falls, Iowa gas station and her mother's house is 222 miles. (Yes, I checked.) We used to switch off driving fairly often—we each drove half the time. When we did that, the trip took precisely 3 hours. Once I learned how to grade papers while she was driving, I started to drive less during these trips. She started driving for two-thirds of the time. When this happened, the trip took 2 hours 55 minutes.

1. What is my average driving speed? What is my girlfriend's average driving speed?

2. If we decided to share the driving by distance (I drive 111 mi, then she drives the remaining 111 mi) how long would the trip take?

6.3 | Systems of Linear Equations in Several Variables

■ Suggested Time and Emphasis

1 class. Essential material.

■ Points to Stress

1. Solving systems of linear equations using Gaussian elimination.
2. Using linear systems to solve applied problems.

■ Sample Questions

- **Text Question:** Consider this system of three equations:

$$x - 2y + 3z = 1$$
$$x + 2y - z = 13$$
$$3x + 2y - 5z = 3$$

Is the following system equivalent to the first one? Why or why not?

$$x - 2y + 3z = 1$$
$$100x + 200y - 100z = 1300$$
$$3x + 2y - 5z = 3$$

Answer: It is. The second equation was simply multiplied by a nonzero constant.

- **Drill Question:** Solve this system using Gaussian elimination:

$$x - 2y + z = 1$$
$$-x + y - z = 4$$
$$-x + 2y - 4z = 8$$

Answer: $x = -6$, $y = -5$, $z = -3$

■ In-Class Materials

- If students have learned to use their calculators to solve linear systems, they may not realize the calculator's limitations. Have them attempt to solve a 5×5 system using their calculators, and record the length of time that it takes. Then have them attempt a 10×10 system. It turns out that the length of time required to solve an arbitrary linear system grows very quickly with the number of variables involved. When doing a system by hand, it is possible to take advantage of properties of the particular system in question. For example, show them this system:

$$-v \qquad\qquad -2y + z = 1$$
$$v \qquad\qquad + 2y \qquad = 3$$
$$v + w - x + 2y \qquad = 2$$
$$-v \qquad + x - 2y \qquad = 7$$
$$v + w + x + y + z = 26$$

One can go through the traditional algorithm (or have a calculator do it), and it will take some time. (The time it takes to enter it into a calculator counts!) But, by looking at the individual equations, one can get w, x and z instantly (add equations 1 and 2, 2 and 4, and 3 and 4) and then v and y come easily as well.

- One can discuss the geometry of systems of three variables as an extension of the geometry of two variables, replacing lines by planes. Ask the class how they could think of a four-variable system. This is not a trivial question. We are looking at the intersection of three hyperplanes in four dimensional space. Even though you may not get a satisfactory answer (but then again, you may) there is value in trying to come up with visual interpretations for complex, abstract mathematical concepts.

- Have the students go over the applied problems from their homework. Ask them to try to come up with similar problems involving three or four variables. For example, Exercise 60 can be expanded this way:

> A woman keeps fit by bicycling, running, and swimming every day. On Monday she spends $\frac{1}{2}$ hour at each activity, covering a total of 14.25 mi. On Tuesday she runs for 12 minutes, cycles for 45 minutes, and swims for 30 minutes, covering a total of 15.45 miles. On Wednesday she runs for 30 minutes, cycles for 10 minutes, and swims for 30 minutes, covering a total of 9.25 miles. Assuming her running and cycling speeds don't change from day to day, find these speeds.

Make sure to point out that, for the problem to be solvable, they now need three pieces of information instead of two (that is, if there is a Monday and a Tuesday in the problem, we now need a Wednesday). Also, they need to make sure that their problem has a solution. In two dimensions, it is very easy to get a consistent system, using random numbers. In three dimensions, it is a bit tougher.

- Foreshadow Section 6.5 by reading through a few of the modeling problems in the assignments for this and the previous section. Notice that, while some of them are clearly realistic (Exercise 53 in this section, dealing with animal nutrition, for example) some of them are using "exactly" when most people would use "at least". (For example Exercise 38 in this section, in which an investor wants a total annual return of $6700—and not a penny more!) Try to get the students to suggest that inequalities are often more appropriate in applied problems.

▪ Examples

- A consistent 3×3 system:

$$
\begin{aligned}
3x + 2y + z &= 4 \\
x - y - z &= 1 \\
2x - 4y - z &= -1
\end{aligned}
$$

Answer: $x = 1$, $y = 1$, $z = -1$

- An inconsistent 3×3 system:

$$
\begin{aligned}
x - y + z &= 3 \\
2x - y + 2z &= 4 \\
3x - 2y + 3z &= 8
\end{aligned}
$$

• A dependent 3×3 system:

$$x + 5y - z = 4$$
$$2x + 3y + 4z = 0$$
$$3x + 8y + 3z = 4$$

▩ Group Work 1: Curve Fitting

This activity can be extended, having students write systems that fit points to a variety of curves.

Answers:

1. $k = \ln \frac{23}{20} \approx 0.1398$, $A = \frac{800,000}{12,167} \approx 65.752$

2.

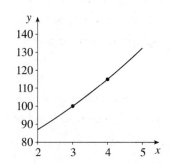

3. $y = -2x^2 + 10x + 3$

4. There is no solution, because parabolas are functions, and these three points fail the Vertical Line Test.

▩ Group Work 2: Earthquake

Although this problem seems to have two pieces of data, it actually winds up requiring students to solve three equations in three unknowns. Given the unfamiliar nature of this problem, some groups may be tempted to give up too soon. Offer words of encouragement, but try to delay giving actual hints until the class has had time to discuss the problem and try to figure out a strategy.

If you need to give a hint, tell the class that the three unknowns here are t_1, the time it took the first wave to arrive, t_2, the time it took the second wave to arrive, and s, the distance from Otisville to the epicenter.

Answer:

$$6t_1 = s$$
$$3t_2 = s$$
$$t_2 - t_1 = 4$$

So $s = 24$ km.

■ Group Work 3: Find the Triangles

This is a exercise involves solving a nonlinear 3×3 system. Students may have the wrong idea that all systems of three equations and three unknowns are linear. This problem will disabuse them of that notion, while still being tractable.

Answers: 1. $3, 4, 5$ **2.** $4, 7, \sqrt{65}$

■ Homework Problems

Core Exercises: 7, 17, 25, 27, 37

Sample Assignment: 1, 2, 7, 14, 17, 18, 25, 27, 31, 32, 36, 37, 40, 44

GROUP WORK 1, SECTION 6.3
Curve Fitting

In science, we often know the general shape of a curve, and then find the curve by making measurements to find data points and fitting them to the curve. For example, we know that if a quantity decays exponentially (like the number of C_{14} atoms in a sample or the rate of CD sales from a one-hit wonder) its graph can be described as $y = Ae^{kt}$, where t is a variable representing time, and A and k are constants.

1. Assume that when $t = 3$, $y = 100$ and when $t = 4$, $y = 115$. Find A and k.

2. Here is another way to ask the previous question: Assume that a graph is of the form $y = Ae^{kt}$. Find A and k so that $(3, 100)$ and $(4, 115)$ are on the graph. Go ahead and graph your answer to Problem 1, and make sure that the points $(3, 100)$ and $(4, 115)$ do indeed lie on the graph.

3. Now let's assume that we know a particular graph is a parabola. (For example, if an object is thrown upward on the surface of a planet, the graph of its height versus time will be very close to a parabola). We know its equation is of the form $y = ax^2 + bx + c$. Find the equation of the parabola that goes through the points $(-1, -9)$, $(1, 11)$, and $(2, 15)$.

4. Now find the equation of the parabola that goes through the points $(-1, 9)$, $(1, 11)$, and $(1, 13)$. Explain your results.

GROUP WORK 2, SECTION 6.3
Earthquake

If you have ever been in an earthquake, you already know what an aftershock is. An earthquake causes two types of waves through the earth to be created, a primary wave and a secondary wave. (Actually, there are more than two, but these are the main types.) The primary wave travels faster than the secondary wave does. So if you are, say, thirty miles from the epicenter of an earthquake, you would first feel the primary wave shake you up, and then, a short time later, you would feel another shaking as the second wave hits. This second shake-up is called an aftershock.

Assume that, in the western United States, a primary wave travels at 6 km/s and a secondary wave travels at 3 km/s. You live in the town of Otisville, and you are awakened by a jolt. Earthquake! Four seconds later you feel an aftershock. How far are you from the epicenter of the quake?

GROUP WORK 3, SECTION 6.3
Find the Triangles

1. The area of a right triangle is 6 square inches and its perimeter is 12 inches. What are the side lengths of the triangle?

2. The area of a right triangle is 14 square inches, and its perimeter is $11 + \sqrt{65}$ inches. What are the side lengths of the triangle?

■ **Suggested Time and Emphasis**

$\frac{1}{2}$–1 class. Optional material.

■ **Point to Stress**

Decomposing a rational function into partial fractions.

■ **Sample Questions**

- **Text Question:** What does it mean to express a rational expression as partial fractions?

  Answer: : It means to write the expression as a sum of fractions with simpler denominators.

- **Drill Question:** Express $\dfrac{2}{x^2 - 1}$ as a sum of partial fractions.

  Answer: $\dfrac{2}{x^2 - 1} = \dfrac{1}{x - 1} - \dfrac{1}{x + 1}$

■ **In-Class Materials**

- It is possible to cover this section without covering every single case. For example, one might just cover the idea of linear factors (Cases 1 and 2) and mention that it is also possible to work with irreducible quadratic factors. Notice that just because every rational expression can be decomposed in theory doesn't mean it is always possible in practice, because there is no closed-form formula for factoring a polynomial of degree 5 or higher.

- Remind students of the process of polynomial division, perhaps by rewriting $\dfrac{2x^3 + 3x^2 + 7x + 4}{2x + 1}$ as $x^2 + x + 3 + \dfrac{1}{2x + 1}$. Be sure to indicate that, in order to use partial fractions, the degree of the numerator has to be less than the degree of the denominator.

- Find the coefficients for the partial fraction decomposition for $\dfrac{x + 3}{(x - 2)(x - 1)}$ in two different ways: first using two linear equations, and then using the method of creating zeros [setting $x = 1$ and then $x = -2$ in $x + 3 = A(x + 2) + B(x - 1)$].

- Point out that the quadratic in the denominator of $f(x) = \dfrac{1}{x^2 + x - 6}$ is not irreducible. It can be factored into the two linear terms $x - 2$ and $x + 3$, and so the partial fraction decomposition is found by writing $\dfrac{1}{x^2 + x - 6} = \dfrac{A}{x + 2} + \dfrac{B}{x - 3}$ and solving for A and B. Therefore it is important, when factoring the denominator, to make sure all quadratics are irreducible.

- Show the class how a complicated partial fractions problem would be set up, without trying to solve it. An example is $\dfrac{5x + 3}{x^3(x + 1)(x^2 + x + 4)(x^2 + 3)^2}$.

▨ Examples

- Case 1:

$$\frac{x-7}{(x-2)(x+3)} = \frac{-1}{x-2} + \frac{2}{x+3}$$

- Case 2:

$$\frac{3x^2 - x - 3}{x^2(x+1)} = \frac{1}{x+1} + \frac{2}{x} - \frac{3}{x^2}$$

- Case 3:

$$\frac{3}{(x-1)(x^2+2)} = \frac{1}{x-1} - \frac{x+1}{x^2+2}$$

- Case 4:

$$\frac{1}{(x^2+1)^2 x} = \frac{1}{x} - \frac{x}{x^2+1} - \frac{x}{(x^2+1)^2}$$

▨ Group Work: Partial Fraction Practice

Four problems are given, each dealing with a different case. Feel free to pick and choose which problems to assign, depending on what skills you want to emphasize. You may decide to allow the students to solve the linear systems on their calculators, or to stop at setting up the systems.

Answers:

1. (a) $x^3 - x^2 - 4x + 4 = (x-1)(x+2)(x-2)$

(b) $\dfrac{2x^2 + 3x - 8}{(x-1)(x+2)(x-2)} = \dfrac{1}{x-1} - \dfrac{1}{2(x+2)} + \dfrac{3}{2(x-2)}$

(c) $\dfrac{3x^5 - 3x^4 - 12x^3 + 16x^2 - 16 + 6x}{(x-1)(x+2)(x-2)} = 3x^2 + \dfrac{2}{x-1} - \dfrac{1}{x+2} + \dfrac{3}{x-2}$

2. (a) $x^3 - 3x + 2 = (x-1)^2(x+2)$

(b) $\dfrac{5x^2 - 5x - 3}{x^3 - 3x + 2} = \dfrac{2}{x-1} - \dfrac{1}{(x-1)^2} + \dfrac{3}{x+2}$

(c) $\dfrac{x^5 - 3x^3 + 7x^2 - 5x - 3}{(x-1)^2(x+2)} = x^2 + \dfrac{2}{x-1} - \dfrac{1}{(x-1)^2} + \dfrac{3}{x+2}$

3. (a) $x^3 + 3x^2 + 4x = x(x^2 + 3x + 4)$

(b) $\dfrac{x^2 + 13x + 16}{x^3 + 3x^2 + 4x} = \dfrac{4}{x} - \dfrac{3x-1}{x^2+3x+4}$

4. (a) $x^4 + 2x^2 + 1 = (x^2+1)^2$

(b) $\dfrac{3x^3 - x^2 + 3x + 3}{x^4 + 2x^2 + 1} = \dfrac{3x-1}{(x^2+1)} + \dfrac{4}{(x^2+1)^2}$

▨ Homework Problems

Core Exercises: 3, 5, 7, 11, 13, 27, 37, 41, 43

Sample Assignment: 1, 2, 3, 5, 7, 11, 13, 14, 15, 16, 27, 30, 31, 37, 41, 43

GROUP WORK, SECTION 6.4
Partial Fraction Practice

1. (a) Factor $x^3 - x^2 - 4x + 4$.

    (b) Write $\dfrac{2x^2 + 3x - 8}{x^3 - x^2 - 4x + 4}$ as a sum of partial fractions.

    (c) Write $\dfrac{3x^5 - 3x^4 - 12x^3 + 16x^2 - 16 + 6x}{x^3 - x^2 - 4x + 4}$ as a sum of partial fractions.

2. (a) Factor $x^3 - 3x + 2$.

    (b) Write $\dfrac{5x^2 - 5x - 3}{x^3 - 3x + 2}$ as a sum of partial fractions.

    (c) Write $\dfrac{x^5 - 3x^3 + 7x^2 - 5x - 3}{x^3 - 3x + 2}$ as a sum of partial fractions.

3. (a) Factor $x^3 + 3x^2 + 4x$.

    (b) Write $\dfrac{x^2 + 13x + 16}{x^3 + 3x^2 + 4x}$ as a sum of partial fractions.

4. (a) Factor $x^4 + 2x^2 + 1$.

    (b) Write $\dfrac{3x^3 - x^2 + 3x + 3}{x^4 + 2x^2 + 1}$ as a sum of partial fractions.

▪ Suggested Time and Emphasis

1 class. Recommended material.

▪ Point to Stress

Graphing inequalities and systems of inequalities by graphing the border and testing points in the defined regions.

▪ Sample Questions

- **Text Question:** Consider the system of inequalities

$$x^2 + y^2 < 25$$
$$x + 2y \geq 5$$

Which of the following are true:

1. The solution set of this system is all the points that satisfy at least one of these inequalities.

2. The solution set of this system is all the points that satisfy exactly one of these inequalities.

3. The solution set of this system is all the points that satisfy both of these inequalities.

Answer: Only 3 is true.

- **Drill Question:** Graph the solution set of the system of inequalities

$$-\tfrac{1}{2}x^2 + y \geq -2$$
$$x - y < 0$$

Answer:

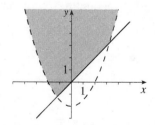

▪ In-Class Materials

- Surprisingly, many students are not able to correctly answer this question: "True or false: If $a < b$ then $a \leq b$." Perhaps take a minute or two to remind the students of the basics of inequalities. From straightforward statements involving inequalities, make the transition to some very simple regions such as $x > 2$, $y \leq 3$, etc. The idea is to make sure that the students are crystal-clear on the objects they are working with before working with them.

- This section allows one to foreshadow the concept of area. For example, students should be able to compute the area of the regions defined by the following systems:

$$\{x \geq 1, x \leq 3, y \leq 2, y \geq 0\}$$

$$\{y \geq 2, x \geq 1, y + 2x \geq 0\}$$

$$\left\{y \geq 2x, (x-3)^2 + (y-6)^2 \leq 4\right\}$$

- If areas are discussed, then the idea of infinite regions with finite areas can be discussed. It is interesting that these regions have finite area:

$$x \geq 1$$
$$x \geq 1$$
$$x \geq 1$$
$$y \leq e^{-x}$$
$$y \leq \frac{1}{x^2}$$
$$y \leq \frac{1}{x^{1.05}}$$

while these do not:

$$x \geq 1$$
$$x \geq 1$$
$$x \geq 1$$
$$y \leq \frac{1}{x}$$
$$y \leq \frac{1}{x \ln(x+1)}$$
$$y \leq \frac{x}{100(x^2 + x)}$$

- Have the students come up with examples of systems of two cubic inequalities with varying numbers of separate solution spaces.

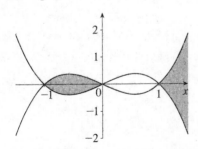

$\{y \leq x^3 - x, y \geq -x^3 + x\}$, two solution spaces

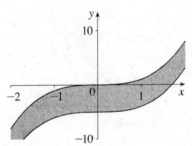

$\{y \leq x^3, y \geq x^3 - 5\}$, one solution space

■ Examples

- $\{5x - 3y < 3, x - 2y > 4, x + y \leq 1\}$

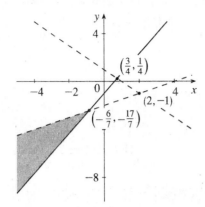

- $\{y > x^2 - 4, y \leq 4 - x^2\}$

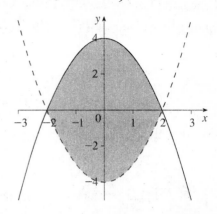

■ Group Work: Describe the Region

The students should warm up by trying a few examples of graphing solution sets of inequalities and systems of inequalities, as in the above examples and in the homework. This activity asks them to reverse the process, to describe a region of interest. If students find this very difficult, the solutions to one or two of them could be given out of order, and this could start out as a matching activity.

Answers:

1. $y < 3x + 2$

2. $y \leq \sqrt[3]{x}$
$y \geq x^2$

3. $x^2 + y^2 > 1$
$x^2 + y^2 \leq 9$

4. $x^2 + y^2 \geq 9$

5. $y \leq 2x$
$y \geq -x + 6$
$y \geq x$

6. $y \leq 3 + \sqrt{4 - x^2}$
$y \geq 0$

■ Homework Problems

Core Exercises: 7, 15, 33, 39, 47, 51

Sample Assignment: 2, 7, 10, 15, 16, 19, 20, 24, 25, 32, 33, 36, 39, 47, 51, 54

GROUP WORK, SECTION 6.5
Describe the Region

Write inequalities or systems of inequalities that describe the following regions.

1.

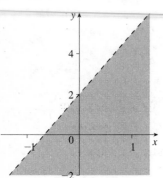

2.

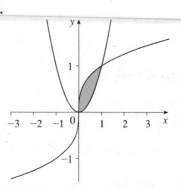

3.

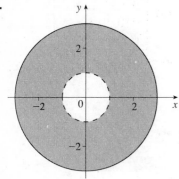

4.

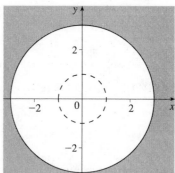

5.

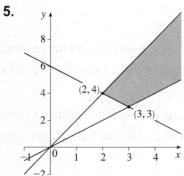

6.

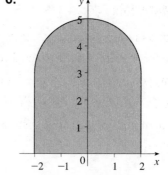

CHAPTER 7

Matrices and Determinants

| Matrices and Systems of Linear Equations

■ **Suggested Time and Emphasis**

2 classes. Recommended material.

■ **Points to Stress**

1. Definitions: Matrix, dimension, row, column, row-echelon form, reduced row-echelon form

2. Finding the augmented matrix of a linear system, and manipulating it using row operations.

3. Gaussian and Gauss-Jordan elimination, including inconsistent and dependent systems.

■ **Sample Questions**

- **Text Question:** Which of the following matrices are in row-echelon form? Which are in reduced row echelon form?

  (a) $\begin{bmatrix} 1 & 4 & 0 & 0 & 0 \\ 0 & 0 & 1 & 0 & -5 \\ 0 & 0 & 0 & 1 & \pi \\ 0 & 0 & 0 & 0 & 0 \end{bmatrix}$
  (b) $\begin{bmatrix} 1 & 0 & 0 & 0 & 0 \\ 0 & 0 & 1 & 0 & 0 \\ 0 & 1 & 0 & 1 & 0 \\ 0 & 1 & 0 & 0 & 1 \end{bmatrix}$
  (c) $\begin{bmatrix} 1 & 4 & 3 & 0 & 5 \\ 0 & 0 & 1 & 2 & -5 \\ 0 & 0 & 0 & 1 & \pi \\ 0 & 0 & 0 & 0 & 0 \end{bmatrix}$

  Answer: (a) and (c) are in row-echelon form, (a) is in reduced row-echelon form.

- **Drill Question:** Consider this system of equations:

$$x + y = -1$$
$$2x - 3y = 8$$

  (a) Find the augmented matrix of this system.

  (b) Put the matrix in reduced row-echelon form.

  Answers: $\begin{bmatrix} 1 & 1 & -1 \\ 2 & -3 & 8 \end{bmatrix}$, $\begin{bmatrix} 1 & 0 & 1 \\ 0 & 1 & -2 \end{bmatrix}$

■ **In-Class Materials**

- Point out that as noted in the text, the row-echelon form of a given matrix is not unique, but the reduced row-echelon form is unique. In fact, it can be shown that if two matrices have the same reduced row-echelon form, you can transform one into the other via elementary row operations.

- It is possible to introduce the concept of homogeneous systems as a way of getting the students to think about dependent and inconsistent systems. Define a homogenous system as one where the equations are all equal to zero:

$$3x - 2y - z = 0$$
$$4x + 5y - 4z = 0$$
$$2x - 8y - z = 0$$

Start by asking the class some simple questions: Are homogeneous systems easier or harder to solve than arbitrary systems and why? Then ask them to find and solve a dependent homogenous system, a homogeneous system with a unique solution, and finally one with no solution. (Give them some time to do this—a lot of learning will take place while they go through the process of creating and solving problems both forward and backward.) When students or groups of students finish early, ask them to articulate why there cannot be an inconsistent homogeneous system.

After the students have thought about this type of system, bring them all together. Point out that it is clear that $x = 0$, $y = 0$, $z = 0$ is always a solution to a homogeneous system, and so there cannot be an inconsistent one. The only possible solutions sets are $(0, 0, 0)$ and a set with infinitely many points, one of which is $(0, 0, 0)$.

- Point out that the techniques in this section are extensible in a way that some ad hoc techniques are not. One can solve an 8×8 or even a 100×100 system (in theory) using this method. If you want to pursue this line earlier, it is interesting to estimate the complexity of using this technique. Have the students solve a 2×2 system, keeping track of every multiplication they do, and every addition, Then have them do the same for a 3×3. They can then do the same for a 4×4—not necessarily bothering to actually do all the additions and multiplications, just doing the count. Notice that the increase in complexity grows faster than a linear function.

▧ Examples

- Word problems

  1. I have $6.50 in nickels, dimes and quarters. I have twice as many nickels as dimes. That's a lot of nickels. In fact, if you add the number of dimes I have to twice the number of quarters I have, you get the number of nickels I have. How many nickels do I have?
  Answer:

  $$5n + 10d + 25q = 650$$
  $$n - 2d + 0q = 0$$
  $$-n + d + 2q = 0$$

  40 nickels, 20 dimes, 10 quarters

  2. A pet-shop has 100 puppies, kittens, and turtles. A puppy costs $30, a kitten costs $20, and a turtle costs $5. If there are twice as many kittens as puppies, and if the stock is worth $1050, how many of each type of animal is there?
  Answer:

  $$p + k + t = 100$$
  $$30p + 20k + 5t = 1050$$
  $$2p - k + 0t = 0$$

  10 puppies, 20 kittens, 70 turtles

- A system with infinitely many solutions:

$$x + 2y - 3z = 12$$
$$-2x + y + 4z = 2$$
$$x + 7y - 5z = 38$$

Answer: $x = \frac{11}{5}t + \frac{8}{5}, y = \frac{2}{5}t + \frac{26}{5}, z = t$. Note: the representation of this set of solutions is not unique.

▤ Group Work 1: Finding the k

This activity can stand on its own, or it can dovetail with a discussion of homogeneous systems, as discussed in the in-class materials. The idea is for the students to realize that, since $(0, 0, 0)$ is a solution of the system, the only way there can be another one is to make a dependent system. Once they realize this, finding $k = 9$ is straightforward. This activity can be made more challenging by using the system

$$x + 2y + 3z = 0$$
$$x + 6y + kz = 0$$
$$x + 4z = 0$$

Answer: $k = 9$ for the system in the group work, $k = 1$ for the more challenging system given above.

▤ Group Work 2: The Lemonade Trick

Students tend to find the "mixture problems" from Section 1.2 difficult. This will serve as a review and extension of those problems. If a group finishes early, ask them to show that, regardless of how many liters she winds up with, the proportions of the final recipe will be the same.

Answer:

1.5 liters of her father's, 2 liters of the store-bought, and 2.5 liters of Grandma's.

A table, such as the one used in Example 8, can be very helpful in problems like these:

	Lemon	Sugar	Water	Amount
Father	$(0.26)\,f$	$(0.12)\,f$	$(0.62)\,f$	f
Store	$(0.10)\,s$	$(0.31)\,s$	$(0.59)\,s$	s
Grandma	$(0.10)\,g$	$(0.10)\,g$	$(0.80)\,g$	g
Total	$(0.14)\,6$	$(0.175)\,6$	$(0.685)\,6$	6

$$f + s + g = 6$$
$$0.26f + 0.1s + 0.1g = (0.14)\,6$$
$$0.12f + 0.31s + 0.1g = (0.175)\,6$$

▤ Homework Problems

Core Exercises: 2, 19, 21, 23, 29, 31, 51, 55

Sample Assignment: 2, 3, 19, 20, 21, 23, 25, 26, 29, 31, 39, 40, 45, 46, 51, 55, 56, 57, 61

GROUP WORK 1, SECTION 7.1
Finding the k

Consider the following system:

$$x + 2y + 3z = 0$$
$$3x + 6y + kz = 0$$
$$x + 4z = 0$$

Convince yourself that, regardless of the value of k, $x = 0$, $y = 0$, $z = 0$ is a solution of this system. We call this solution the *trivial solution*.

Find a value of k to ensure that this system has a nontrivial solution.

The Lemonade Trick

A college student is dissatisfied with her lemonade options, and decides to mix three kinds of lemonade in her glorious quest to find the perfect cup. She mixes some of her father's sour lemonade (which turns out to be 26% lemon juice, 12% sugar, and 62% water), some store-bought supersweet lemonade (10% lemon juice, 31% sugar, 59% water) and some of her grandmothers watery lemonade (10% lemon juice, 10% sugar, 80% water with an insignificant dash of Worcestershire sauce for "color"). When she is finished, she has six liters of lemonade that contains a nice mix of 14% lemon juice and 17.5% sugar.

How many liters of each kind has she used?

■ Suggested Time and Emphasis

1 class. Recommended material.

■ Points to Stress

1. Matrix addition
2. Scalar and matrix multiplication

■ Sample Questions

• **Text Question:** True or false:

(a) $\begin{bmatrix} 3 & 4 \\ 1 & 2 \end{bmatrix} \begin{bmatrix} -1 & 5 \\ 1 & 0 \end{bmatrix} = \begin{bmatrix} -3 & 20 \\ 1 & 0 \end{bmatrix}$

(b) $\begin{bmatrix} 3 & 4 \\ 1 & 2 \end{bmatrix} + \begin{bmatrix} -1 & 5 \\ 1 & 0 \end{bmatrix} = \begin{bmatrix} 2 & 9 \\ 2 & 2 \end{bmatrix}$

Answer: (a) False   (b) True

• **Drill Question:** Compute $\begin{bmatrix} 5 & 9 & 2 \\ 6 & 5 & 3 \end{bmatrix} \begin{bmatrix} 5 \\ -1 \\ 1 \end{bmatrix}$.

Answer: $\begin{bmatrix} 18 \\ 28 \end{bmatrix}$

■ In-Class Materials

• The text describes which properties of real number addition and multiplication carry over to matrix addition, matrix multiplication, and scalar multiplication. Discuss how some of their consequences carry over as well. Ask the students if they believe that $(A + B)(A + B) = AA + 2AB + BB$. Let them discuss and argue. It turns out that this is false, because of commutativity. It *is* true that $(A + B)(A + B) = AA + AB + BA + BB$. Have the class look at $(A + B)(A - B)$ next.

• Let A and B be 2×2 matrices. Although AB may not be equal to BA, there are special matrices for which $AB = BA$. One necessary (but not sufficient) condition for this to happen is that $a_{12}b_{21} = a_{21}b_{12}$. It is relatively simple to show this condition, by explicitly multiplying out AB and BA. After demonstrating this condition, challenge the students to find a pair of distinct matrices, without zero elements, such that $AB = BA$. The process of searching for them will give students good practice multiplying matrices. One example that works is $A = \begin{bmatrix} 1 & 2 \\ 3 & 4 \end{bmatrix}, B = \begin{bmatrix} -1 & 2 \\ 3 & 2 \end{bmatrix}$.

• This is a good time to discuss permutation matrices. A permutation matrix is a matrix that is all zeros except for a single 1 in each row and each column.

$$\begin{bmatrix} 0 & 0 & 1 & 0 & 0 \\ 1 & 0 & 0 & 0 & 0 \\ 0 & 0 & 0 & 1 & 0 \\ 0 & 1 & 0 & 0 & 0 \\ 0 & 0 & 0 & 0 & 1 \end{bmatrix}$$

Have the class figure out if the sum of two permutation matrices must always be a permutation matrix (no) and if the product of two permutation matrices must always be a permutation matrix (yes). Finally, have the students multiply arbitrary matrices by permutation matrices, to see what happens to them (the rows or columns get rearranged, depending on whether the permutation matrix was multiplied on the left or on the right). There is a group work about this topic in the next section.

- Foreshadow the next section by having students compute $\begin{bmatrix} 2 & 5 & 1 \\ 4 & 2 & 1 \\ 5 & 3 & 1 \end{bmatrix} \begin{bmatrix} x \\ y \\ z \end{bmatrix}$.

■ Examples

Let $A = \begin{bmatrix} 3 & 1 \\ -1 & 0 \\ 3 & 2 \end{bmatrix}$, $B = \begin{bmatrix} 5 & 1 \\ 1 & 2 \\ -6 & -1 \end{bmatrix}$, and $C = \begin{bmatrix} 3 & 1 \\ 2 & 5 \end{bmatrix}$.

$$A + B = \begin{bmatrix} 8 & 2 \\ 0 & 2 \\ -3 & 1 \end{bmatrix} \qquad B - A = \begin{bmatrix} 2 & 0 \\ 2 & 2 \\ -9 & -3 \end{bmatrix} \qquad AC = \begin{bmatrix} 11 & 8 \\ -3 & -1 \\ 13 & 13 \end{bmatrix}$$

$$BC = \begin{bmatrix} 17 & 10 \\ 7 & 11 \\ -20 & -11 \end{bmatrix} \qquad (A+B)C = \begin{bmatrix} 28 & 18 \\ 4 & 10 \\ -7 & 2 \end{bmatrix}$$

If using these examples, occasionally throw in an undefined operation such as $A + C$ or AB.

■ Group Work: Quest for the Unknown

This activity is a fairly straightforward chance for students to practice matrix operations.

Answers:

1. $a = 5$ **2.** $a = 2$ **3.** $a = \frac{5}{7}, b = -\frac{1}{7}, c = -\frac{3}{7}, d = \frac{2}{7}$

4. $a = \frac{5}{7}, b = -\frac{1}{7}, c = -\frac{3}{7}, d = \frac{2}{7}$ **5.** $a = -1, b = \frac{7}{2}, c = -2$

■ Homework Problems

Core Exercises: 5, 15, 21, 23, 25, 27, 39, 45

Sample Assignment: 3, 5, 7, 8, 9, 10, 12, 13, 14, 15, 18, 19, 20, 21, 23, 25, 27, 28, 29, 30, 39, 45, 49, 53

GROUP WORK, SECTION 7.2
Quest for the Unknown

For each of the following computations, find the unknowns

1. $\begin{bmatrix} 1 & 5 & 3 & 1 \\ -2 & -5 & 0 & 1 \end{bmatrix} + 2\begin{bmatrix} -1 & 1 & -3 & 5 \\ -2 & a & 3 & 1 \end{bmatrix} = \begin{bmatrix} -1 & 7 & -3 & 11 \\ -6 & 5 & 6 & 3 \end{bmatrix}$

2. $\begin{bmatrix} 1 & -2 & 1 & -2 \\ -3 & 3 & -3 & 7 \\ 0 & -1 & 2 & -5 \\ -2 & 3 & -1 & 0 \end{bmatrix}\begin{bmatrix} 1 & 2 & 3 & 4 \\ -4 & -3 & -2 & -1 \\ 0 & 1 & 0 & -1 \\ 3 & 1 & a & 4 \end{bmatrix} = \begin{bmatrix} 3 & 7 & 3 & -3 \\ 6 & -11 & -1 & 16 \\ -11 & 0 & -8 & -21 \\ -14 & -14 & -12 & -10 \end{bmatrix}$

3. $\begin{bmatrix} 2 & 1 \\ 3 & 5 \end{bmatrix}\begin{bmatrix} a & b \\ c & d \end{bmatrix} = \begin{bmatrix} 1 & 0 \\ 0 & 1 \end{bmatrix}$

4. $\begin{bmatrix} a & b \\ c & d \end{bmatrix}\begin{bmatrix} 2 & 1 \\ 3 & 5 \end{bmatrix} = \begin{bmatrix} 1 & 0 \\ 0 & 1 \end{bmatrix}$

5. $\begin{bmatrix} -6 & 2 & 1 \\ -4 & 2 & 0 \\ -1 & 1 & -1 \end{bmatrix}\begin{bmatrix} a & \frac{3}{2} & -1 \\ -2 & b & -2 \\ -1 & 2 & c \end{bmatrix} = \begin{bmatrix} 1 & 0 & 0 \\ 0 & 1 & 0 \\ 0 & 0 & 1 \end{bmatrix}$

7.3 | Inverses of Matrices and Matrix Equations

■ Suggested Time and Emphasis

1 class. Recommended material.

■ Points to Stress

1. The identity matrix.

2. Definition and computation of the inverse of a matrix.

■ Sample Questions

- **Text Question:** If $AB = I$, where I is the identity matrix, is it necessarily true that $BA = I$?

  Answer: Yes

- **Drill Question:** Find the inverse of the matrix $\begin{bmatrix} 3 & 0 \\ 0 & -\frac{5}{8} \end{bmatrix}$.

  Answer: $\begin{bmatrix} \frac{1}{3} & 0 \\ 0 & -\frac{8}{5} \end{bmatrix}$

■ In-Class Materials

- Example 7 is particularly important, because Section 7.1 presented a straightforward method of solving an $n \times n$ system. The advantage of finding the inverse matrix really kicks in when solving a series of systems with the same coefficient matrix.

- Perhaps take this opportunity to talk about the inverse of a complex number: how do we find $\dfrac{1}{3+4i}$? The technique, multiplying by $\dfrac{3-4i}{3-4i}$, is not as important as the concept that given a real, complex, or matrix quantity it is often possible to find an inverse that will reduce it to unity. One can also add "inverse functions" to this discussion—in this case $f(x) = x$ is the identity function, so-called because it leaves inputs unchanged (analogous to multiplying by 1). Try to get the students to see the conceptual similarities in solving the three following equations:

$$3x = 2$$
$$(3+i)x = 2 - 4i$$
$$\begin{bmatrix} 2 & 1 \\ 3 & -4 \end{bmatrix} \begin{bmatrix} x \\ y \end{bmatrix} = \begin{bmatrix} 3 \\ 1 \end{bmatrix}$$

- After doing a standard example or two, throw a singular matrix on the board before defining singularity. "Unexpectedly" run into trouble and thus discover, with your class, that not every matrix has an inverse. Examples of singular matrices are given in the Examples section.

253

- It is straightforward to demonstrate that $\left(A^{-1}\right)^{-1} = A$ for specific 2×2 or 3×3 matrices. Students can pick up why it should be true, given the definition of inverse. A general algebraic proof is a little messy:

$$\left(A^{-1}\right)^{-1} = \begin{bmatrix} \dfrac{d}{ad-bc} & -\dfrac{b}{ad-bc} \\ -\dfrac{c}{ad-bc} & \dfrac{a}{ad-bc} \end{bmatrix}^{-1}$$

$$= \dfrac{1}{\left(\dfrac{a}{ad-bc}\right)\left(\dfrac{d}{ad-bc}\right) - \left(\dfrac{b}{ad-bc}\right)\left(\dfrac{c}{ad-bc}\right)} \begin{bmatrix} \dfrac{a}{ad-bc} & \dfrac{b}{ad-bc} \\ \dfrac{c}{ad-bc} & \dfrac{d}{ad-bc} \end{bmatrix}$$

$$= \dfrac{1}{1/\left(ad-bc\right)} \cdot \dfrac{1}{ad-bc} \cdot \begin{bmatrix} a & b \\ c & d \end{bmatrix} = \begin{bmatrix} a & b \\ c & d \end{bmatrix} = A$$

- Note that there is a formula for 3×3 inverses, just as there is one for 2×2 inverses. Unfortunately, it is so complicated that it is easier to do 3×3 inverses manually than to use a formula.

$$\begin{bmatrix} a & b & c \\ d & e & f \\ g & h & i \end{bmatrix}^{-1} = \dfrac{1}{afh - aei + bdi - bfg + ceg - cdh} \begin{bmatrix} fh - ei & bi - ch & ce - bf \\ di - fg & cg - ai & af - cd \\ eg - dh & ah - bg & bd - ae \end{bmatrix}$$

■ Examples

- Nonsingular real matrices

$$\begin{bmatrix} -2 & 1 \\ 3 & 3 \end{bmatrix}^{-1} = \begin{bmatrix} -\frac{1}{3} & \frac{1}{3} \\ \frac{1}{3} & \frac{2}{9} \end{bmatrix} \qquad \begin{bmatrix} -1 & 1 & 1 \\ 4 & -1 & 1 \\ 4 & 2 & 1 \end{bmatrix}^{-1} = \begin{bmatrix} -\frac{1}{5} & \frac{1}{15} & \frac{2}{15} \\ 0 & -\frac{1}{3} & \frac{1}{3} \\ \frac{4}{5} & \frac{2}{5} & -\frac{1}{5} \end{bmatrix}$$

$$\begin{bmatrix} 0 & 2 & 0 & 0 \\ 2 & 0 & 0 & 0 \\ 0 & 0 & 5 & 0 \\ 0 & 1 & 0 & 6 \end{bmatrix}^{-1} = \begin{bmatrix} 0 & \frac{1}{2} & 0 & 0 \\ \frac{1}{2} & 0 & 0 & 0 \\ 0 & 0 & \frac{1}{5} & 0 \\ -\frac{1}{12} & 0 & 0 & \frac{1}{6} \end{bmatrix}$$

- Singular real matrices

$$\begin{bmatrix} 5 & 4 \\ 15 & 12 \end{bmatrix}$$

$$\begin{bmatrix} 1 & 2 & 3 \\ -1 & 3 & -2 \\ -1 & 8 & -1 \end{bmatrix}$$

$$\begin{bmatrix} 8 & 3 & 5 & -8 \\ -7 & 6 & 0 & -6 \\ -5 & -3 & 7 & 9 \\ -4 & 6 & 12 & -5 \end{bmatrix}$$

- A complex matrix and its inverse

$$\begin{bmatrix} 1 & 2i \\ 1-i & 1 \end{bmatrix}^{-1} = \dfrac{1}{-1-2i}\begin{bmatrix} 1 & -2i \\ -1+i & 1 \end{bmatrix} = \begin{bmatrix} -\frac{1}{5}+\frac{2}{5}i & \frac{4}{5}+\frac{2}{5}i \\ -\frac{1}{5}-\frac{3}{5}i & -\frac{1}{5}+\frac{2}{5}i \end{bmatrix}$$

▪ Group Work: Some Special Kinds of Matrices

This activity uses various types of special matrices as a way of getting students to think about inverses, and to introduce them to some of the vocabulary of matrix algebra, such as the word "idempotent" meaning a matrix with the property $A^2 = A$. Before handing out the sheet, start by defining a diagonal matrix, one for which $a_{ij} = 0$ whenever $i \neq j$ such as $\begin{bmatrix} 1 & 0 & 0 \\ 0 & 2 & 0 \\ 0 & 0 & 3 \end{bmatrix}$. Ask the students to figure out the inverse of $\begin{bmatrix} 1 & 0 \\ 0 & 2 \end{bmatrix}$, $\begin{bmatrix} 1 & 0 & 0 \\ 0 & 2 & 0 \\ 0 & 0 & 3 \end{bmatrix}$,

and then an arbitrary diagonal matrix. They will find that $\begin{bmatrix} a & 0 & 0 \\ 0 & b & 0 \\ 0 & 0 & c \end{bmatrix}^{-1} = \begin{bmatrix} 1/a & 0 & 0 \\ 0 & 1/b & 0 \\ 0 & 0 & 1/c \end{bmatrix}$. Then hand out

the activity which will allow the students to explore more special types of matrices.

Problem 4 hits an important theorem in matrix algebra: that the only nonsingular idempotent matrix is the identity. If the students finish early, follow up on Problem 10 by asking how they could tell, at a glance, if a given permutation matrix is its own inverse. When everyone is done, close the activity by discussing that question. It turns out that if the permutation just swaps pairs of elements, then doing it twice will bring us back to the identity permutation. So all one does is makes sure that if $a_{ij} = 1$ then $a_{ji} = 1$ as well.

Answers:

Answers will vary.

1. $\begin{bmatrix} 1 & 0 & 0 \\ 0 & 1 & 0 \\ 0 & 0 & 0 \end{bmatrix}$
2. $\begin{bmatrix} 1 & 0 & 0 \\ 0 & \frac{1}{2} & \frac{1}{2} \\ 0 & \frac{1}{2} & \frac{1}{2} \end{bmatrix}$ or $\begin{bmatrix} 1 & 0 \\ 2 & 0 \end{bmatrix}$
3. $\begin{bmatrix} 1 & 0 \\ 0 & 1 \end{bmatrix}$

4. Another cannot exist. If $A^2 = A$, then $A^2 A^{-1} = A A^{-1}$ and $A = I$.

5. $\begin{bmatrix} 42 \\ 51 \\ 27 \end{bmatrix}$
6. $\begin{bmatrix} b \\ d \\ a \\ c \\ e \end{bmatrix}$
7. $\begin{bmatrix} c \\ d \\ e \\ a \\ b \end{bmatrix}$

8. They permute the elements of a matrix without changing them.

9. $\begin{bmatrix} 1 & 0 & 0 \\ 0 & 0 & 1 \\ 0 & 1 & 0 \end{bmatrix}$
10. $\begin{bmatrix} 0 & 1 & 0 \\ 0 & 0 & 1 \\ 1 & 0 & 0 \end{bmatrix}$

▪ Homework Problems

Core Exercises: 3, 9, 17, 19, 25, 47

Sample Assignment: 2, 3, 4, 9, 10, 17, 18, 19, 25, 27, 28, 33, 34, 40, 41, 47, 49, 50

GROUP WORK, SECTION 7.3
Some Special Kinds of Matrices

A matrix A is called *idempotent* if $A^2 = A$.

1. Find a 3×3 diagonal idempotent matrix that is not the identity.

2. Find a nondiagonal idempotent matrix.

3. Find a nonsingular idempotent matrix.

4. Find a different nonsingular idempotent matrix, or show why one cannot exist.

A permutation matrix has a single 1 in each row and each column. The rest of the entries are zeros. Here are some permutation matrices:

$$\begin{bmatrix} 0 & 1 & 0 \\ 0 & 0 & 1 \\ 1 & 0 & 0 \end{bmatrix} \qquad \begin{bmatrix} 0 & 1 & 0 & 0 & 0 \\ 0 & 0 & 0 & 1 & 0 \\ 1 & 0 & 0 & 0 & 0 \\ 0 & 0 & 1 & 0 & 0 \\ 0 & 0 & 0 & 0 & 1 \end{bmatrix} \qquad \begin{bmatrix} 0 & 0 & 1 & 0 & 0 \\ 0 & 0 & 0 & 1 & 0 \\ 0 & 0 & 0 & 0 & 1 \\ 1 & 0 & 0 & 0 & 0 \\ 0 & 1 & 0 & 0 & 0 \end{bmatrix}$$

256

5. Compute $\begin{bmatrix} 0 & 1 & 0 \\ 0 & 0 & 1 \\ 1 & 0 & 0 \end{bmatrix} \begin{bmatrix} 27 \\ 42 \\ 51 \end{bmatrix}$.

6. Compute $\begin{bmatrix} 0 & 1 & 0 & 0 & 0 \\ 0 & 0 & 0 & 1 & 0 \\ 1 & 0 & 0 & 0 & 0 \\ 0 & 0 & 1 & 0 & 0 \\ 0 & 0 & 0 & 0 & 1 \end{bmatrix} \begin{bmatrix} a \\ b \\ c \\ d \\ e \end{bmatrix}$.

7. Compute $\begin{bmatrix} 0 & 0 & 1 & 0 & 0 \\ 0 & 0 & 0 & 1 & 0 \\ 0 & 0 & 0 & 0 & 1 \\ 1 & 0 & 0 & 0 & 0 \\ 0 & 1 & 0 & 0 & 0 \end{bmatrix} \begin{bmatrix} a \\ b \\ c \\ d \\ e \end{bmatrix}$.

8. Why are matrices of this type called permutation matrices?

9. Find a permutation matrix $A \neq I$ such that $A^{-1} = A$.

10. Find a permutation matrix $A \neq I$ such that $A^{-1} \neq A$.

▪ Suggested Time and Emphasis

1 class. Recommended material: determinants; optional material: Cramer's Rule.

▪ Points to Stress

1. Definition and computation of determinants, including row operations.
2. The relationship between determinants and singularity.
3. Cramer's Rule.

▪ Sample Questions

- **Text Question:** Name one application of determinants.
  Answers: Determining the singularity of a matrix, solving systems with Cramer's Rule, finding the area of a triangle.

- **Drill Question:** Find $\begin{vmatrix} 2 & 1 & 3 \\ 1 & 0 & 0 \\ 0 & 2 & -1 \end{vmatrix}$.

  Answer: 7

▪ In-Class Materials

- Make sure the students see the fundamentally recursive nature of determinants. Draw a 6×6 matrix on the board and expand by a row, showing how you would then have to compute six 5×5 determinants, which would require the computation of thirty 4×4 determinants, and so forth.

- Discuss computational complexity. If a 2×2 determinant requires 3 arithmetical operations (two multiplications and a subtraction), then a 3×3 determinant requires 12, and a 4×4 requires 52. If we let $f(n)$ be the number of arithmetical operations for an $n \times n$ matrix, we get the formula $f(n) = nf(n-1) + n$: there are n determinants of $(n-1) \times (n-1)$ matrices and n extra multiplications (when expanding by a row). So we can generate the following table:

n	Number of Operations
2	3
3	12
4	52
5	265
6	1596
7	11,179
8	89,440
9	804,969
10	8,049,700
11	88,546,711
⋮	⋮
20	5,396,862,315,159,760,000

Students can observe this rapid growth on their calculators; it will take the calculator ten times as long to do a 10×10 determinant as it takes to do a 9×9. In fact, $f(n)$ grows a little more rapidly than $n!$.

- Determinants have many nice properties. For example, if a row or column consists of all zeros, it is trivial to prove that the determinant is zero. The row/column transformation rule given in the text then lets us conclude that if two rows of a matrix are identical, the determinant is zero. Also, the determinant of a product is the product of the determinants.

- Show the students the "basket" method of computing a 3×3 determinant. Stress that this method does not generalize to higher dimensions. One rewrites the first two columns of the matrix, and then multiplies along the diagonals, adding the top-to-bottom diagonals and subtracting the bottom-to-top ones. In the example below, we calculate the determinant of $\begin{bmatrix} 1 & 4 & 7 \\ 2 & 5 & 8 \\ 3 & 6 & 9 \end{bmatrix}$ to be $105 + 48 + 72 - (45 + 96 + 84) = 0$.

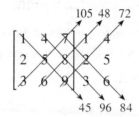

- When solving a single $n \times n$ system, Cramer's Rule doesn't have much of an advantage over Gaussian elimination. There are, however, some circumstances when Cramer's Rule is vastly superior. One such situation is when there is a large system (say 100 equations with 100 unknowns) and we are interested in only one variable. Gaussian elimination requires us to do the work to solve the complete system. Finding the inverse of the matrix also requires us to do all the work necessary to find all the variables. Cramer's Rule, however, allows us to find two (admittedly large) determinants to get our answer.

  Another situation is when the coefficient matrix is sparse—a large percentage of the entries are zero. It is usually very quick to find determinants of sparse matrices, and in that case Cramer's Rule can be very quick.

Examples

- A 4×4 determinant:

$$\begin{vmatrix} 1 & 1 & 1 & 1 \\ 2 & -1 & 0 & 5 \\ 0 & 8 & 1 & 2 \\ 0 & 2 & 1 & 3 \end{vmatrix}$$

Expand by Row 3:

$$D = -8 \begin{vmatrix} 1 & 1 & 1 \\ 2 & 0 & 5 \\ 0 & 1 & 3 \end{vmatrix} + \begin{vmatrix} 1 & 1 & 1 \\ 2 & -1 & 5 \\ 0 & 2 & 3 \end{vmatrix} - 2 \begin{vmatrix} 1 & 1 & 1 \\ 2 & -1 & 0 \\ 0 & 2 & 1 \end{vmatrix}$$

$$= -8(-9) + (-15) - 2(1) = 55$$

● Cramer's Rule:

$$x - y + z = 8$$
$$-x - y - z = -9$$
$$x - 2y - 4z = 5$$

$$D = \begin{vmatrix} 1 & -1 & 1 \\ -1 & -1 & -1 \\ 1 & -2 & -4 \end{vmatrix} = 10, \; D_x = \begin{vmatrix} 8 & -1 & 1 \\ -9 & -1 & -1 \\ 5 & -2 & -4 \end{vmatrix} = 80, \; D_y = \begin{vmatrix} 1 & 8 & 1 \\ -1 & -9 & -1 \\ 1 & 5 & -4 \end{vmatrix} = 5, \text{ and}$$

$$D_z = \begin{vmatrix} 1 & -1 & 8 \\ -1 & -1 & -9 \\ 1 & -2 & 5 \end{vmatrix} = 5, \text{ so we have } x = 8, y = \frac{1}{2}, \text{ and } z = \frac{1}{2}.$$

▓ Group Work 1: Determinants and Row Operations

This activity can be given before or after row and column transformations of a determinant are covered. It will enable the students to discover the effect of all three row operations on the determinant of a matrix.

If students finish early, have them try to prove their answers.

Answers:

1. 16

2. Multiplying a row by a multiplies the determinant by a.

3. Oddly enough, adding a scalar multiple of one row to another row does not change the determinant, no matter what the multiple is.

4. Switching rows changes the sign of the determinant.

▓ Group Work 2: Divide and Conquer

This activity is mathematically routine. The idea here is for the students to figure out how to use their groups to do "parallel processing". In other words, if each member of the group tries to do the problem his- or herself, it will be long and boring. However, if they find a way to divide up the work, it will be quick (and boring). Put students in groups of four or five. Start by saying that each group will compute a 5×5 determinant. Give them three minutes to come up with a strategy that will enable their group to compute this determinant (a) quickly and (b) accurately. They may each want to take one of the smaller determinants, or they may want one student to be the "checker" of the others' work. Or they may want to pair up. If a group suggests trading answers with another group, allow that as well. Effective parallel processing is still a major area of research in computer science, and determinants are wonderful for illustrating this principle.

Answer: -3

▓ Homework Problems

Core Exercises: 5, 19, 23, 27, 31, 33, 39, 55

Sample Assignment: 1, 2, 3, 5, 6, 10, 19, 21, 22, 23, 27, 29, 31, 33, 34, 39, 55, 60, 66

GROUP WORK 1, SECTION 7.4
Determinants and Row Operations

1. Find $\begin{vmatrix} 1 & 0 & 1 \\ 0 & 3 & -1 \\ 2 & 4 & 6 \end{vmatrix}$.

Recall that we know three elementary row operations. They are:

    I   Multiplying a row by a nonzero scalar

    II   Adding a scalar multiple of one row to another row

    III   Switching the positions of two rows in the matrix

I would like to say that these row operations have no effect on the determinant of a matrix. I would like to say that, but it would be incorrect. Your job is to figure out the effect that each of these operations has on the matrix.

2. Start with the matrix given above. Now do an operation of type I and see what happens to the determinant. Try a few, and see if you can come up with a theory about what row operation I does.

3. Similarly, find out what effect row operation II has.

4. What effect does row operation III have?

GROUP WORK 2, SECTION 7.4
Divide and Conquer

Find

$$\begin{vmatrix} 1 & 1 & -1 & -1 & 1 \\ 2 & -2 & 1 & 0 & 1 \\ 3 & 0 & 2 & -1 & 1 \\ -1 & 1 & 0 & 2 & -1 \\ 1 & 1 & 1 & 1 & 0 \end{vmatrix}$$

by row expansion.

CHAPTER 8

Conic Sections

| Parabolas

■ Suggested Time and Emphasis

$\frac{1}{2}$ class. Recommended material.

■ Points to Stress

1. The definition and geometry of parabolas.

2. Using the equation of a parabola to find relevant constants.

3. Graphing a parabola given its equation.

■ Sample Questions

- **Text Question:** How can you tell if the axis of a parabola is vertical or horizontal?

  Answer: If there is a y^2 term it is horizontal; if there is an x^2 term it is vertical.

- **Drill Question:** Find the focus and directrix of $y = \frac{1}{16}x^2$ and sketch its graph.

  Answer: Focus $\left(0, \frac{1}{4}\right)$, directrix $y = -\frac{1}{4}$

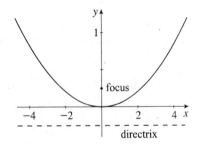

■ In-Class Materials

- Have students sketch a parabola "from scratch." Hand out a sheet of paper with focus and directrix, and hand out rulers. Get the students to just plot points where the distance from the point to the directrix is equal to the distance from the point to the focus. Have them keep plotting points until a parabolic shape emerges.

- Using dental floss and modeling compound (such as clay or playdough) it is easy for the students to make half a cone and slice it. Have the class attempt to do so to get a parabola. Most of them will wind up creating half of a hyperbola. Refer these students to the chapter overview. Make sure that they note a parabola is not as easy to create this way as hyperbolas or ellipses. If the cut is at the wrong angle, even slightly, a hyperbola or an ellipse will be formed instead of a parabola.

- Discuss the reflection properties of parabolas: A beam of light originating at the origin will emerge parallel to the parabola's axis of symmetry, and a beam of light that is parallel to the parabola's axis of symmetry will reflect off of the parabola in a direction that goes through its focus. One nice project is to construct a parabolic pool table or miniature golf hole. The students accurately graph a parabola, and glue erasers or wood along its border, placing the "hole" at the focus. A golf ball or pool ball that is rolled in a direction parallel to the axis will always bounce into the hole.

- As of this writing, it is possible to purchase a parabolic listening device for about \$50 on eBay, or about \$80 new. If this is feasible, many experiments and demonstrations can be done. For example, students can whisper from a long distance away and be heard using the device.

- Make the connection between quadratic functions and parabolas explicit. Point out that any equation of the form $y = ax^2 + bx + c$ can be written as $y = n(x - h)^2 + k$ by completing the square, yielding a (possibly shifted) parabola. The constant n, of course, can be written as $4p$. Note that if $a = 0$ we have a line. So we can call a line a "degenerate parabola".

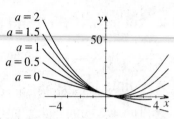

▩ Example

A shifted parabola:

$$
\begin{aligned}
y &= 2x^2 - 8x + 2 \\
&= 2\left(x^2 - 4x\right) + 2 \\
&= 2\left(x^2 - 4x + 4\right) - 6 \\
&= 2\left(x - 2\right)^2 - 6
\end{aligned}
$$

$p = \frac{1}{2}$, focus $\left(0 + 2, \frac{1}{2} - 6\right) = \left(2, -\frac{11}{2}\right)$, directrix $y = -\frac{1}{2} - 6 = -\frac{13}{2}$

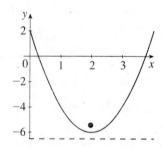

▩ Group Work: The Effect of Gravity

Demonstrate that a tossed object will trace out a parabola. A quick way to do this is, of course, to throw an eraser. A more elaborate way to do it is to darken the room and toss a glow-stick or tiny flashlight. Starting with Problem 5, this activity segues into shifting the parabola, which will be covered in more detail in Section 10.4.

Answers:

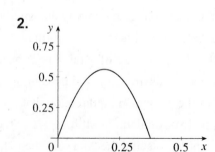

3. The second: it has a higher initial velocity, so its maximum height is greater.

4. The second: it has a higher initial velocity, so it travels upward longer.

5. $h(t) = -16t^2 + v_0 t + 100$

6. $h(t) = -16t^2 + v_0 t + s_0$

7. (a) $0 = -16t^2 + 216 \quad \Rightarrow \quad t \approx 3.674$ s

(b) $0 = -16t^2 + 10t + 216 \quad \Rightarrow \quad t = 4$ s

(c) $h(t) = -16t^2 + 10t + 216 = -16\left(t^2 - \frac{5}{8}t + \frac{25}{256}\right) + 216 + \frac{25}{256} = -16\left(t - \frac{5}{16}\right)^2 + \frac{55,321}{256}$. It reaches its maximum height at $t = \frac{5}{16}$ s.

(d) The maximum height is $\frac{3481}{16} \approx 217.56$ ft.

▩ Homework Problems

Core Exercises: 11, 13, 15, 29, 41, 51, 53

Sample Assignment: 3, 5, 6, 7, 8, 9, 10, 11, 13, 15, 21, 29, 31, 32, 33, 34, 41, 42, 51, 53

GROUP WORK, SECTION 8.1
The Effect of Gravity

If you toss an object upward from the ground, its height at time t (in feet) is given by

$$h(t) = -16t^2 + v_0 t$$

where v_0 (pronounced "vee-naught") is the velocity of the toss in ft/s.

1. Sketch the graph of the height of a ball as a function of time if it is thrown with an initial velocity of 3 ft/s.

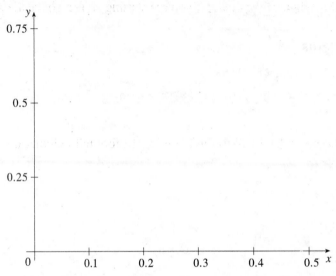

2. Sketch the graph of the height of a ball if it is thrown with an initial velocity of six feet per second.

3. Which of your two graphs has a higher vertex? Physically, why is that the case?

4. Which of your two graphs has a vertex that is farther to the right? Physically, why is that the case?

5. Now assume you are not starting at the ground, but at a height of 100 feet. Find a formula for the height of the object as a function of time.

6. Find a formula for the height of the object if you are starting s_0 feet above the ground.

7. (a) Assume now that you take a ball to the top of a 216 foot tall building and let it drop. When does it reach the ground?

  (b) When would it reach the ground if you tossed it upwards with an initial velocity of 10 ft/s?

  (c) In that case, when would it reach its maximum height?

  (d) What would that maximum height be?

▣ Suggested Time and Emphasis

$\frac{1}{2}$–1 class. Optional material.

▣ Points to Stress

1. The definition and geometry of ellipses.

2. Using the equation of an ellipse to find relevant constants and to graph the ellipse.

3. Eccentricity.

▣ Sample Questions

- **Text Question:** Does $\dfrac{x^2}{5^2} + \dfrac{y^2}{6^2} = 1$ describe a horizontal or a vertical ellipse? How do you know?

  Answer: It is vertical because the denominator of the y^2 term is larger than that of the x^2 term.

- **Drill Question:** Find the vertices and foci of the ellipse $\frac{1}{4}x^2 + y^2 = 1$ and sketch its graph.

  Answer: Vertices $(\pm 2, 0)$, foci $\left(\pm\sqrt{3}, 0\right)$

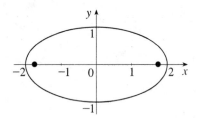

▣ In-Class Materials

- Have students sketch an ellipse with thumbtacks and string, as suggested in the text. Have some use foci that are close together, and some that are farther apart. Make sure they see the connection between this activity and the idea that the summed distance from the foci is a constant.

- As noted in Section 10.1, one can use dental floss and a modeling compound (such as clay or playdough) to make half a cone and slice it. Have the class attempt to do so to get a circle. Note that if their angle is slightly off, they will get an ellipse. Make the analogy that just as a square is a particular kind of rectangle, a circle is a particular kind of ellipse.

- Many representational artists never draw circles, noting that it is rare in nature to see a circle, since we are usually looking at an angle, thus seeing an ellipse. Perhaps have the students bring in photographs of manhole covers and other "circular" objects, noting that if the camera angle is not straight on, the resultant image is elliptical. (Because of the optical illusion of perspective, it makes things easier to draw the outline of the "circle" with a marker to see that it is an ellipse.)

- Discuss the reflection property of an ellipse: a beam of light originating at one focus will reflect off the ellipse and pass through the other focus. One nice project is to construct an elliptical pool table. The students accurately graph an ellipse, and glue erasers or wood along its border, placing the "hole" at one focus and marking the second. A golf ball or pool ball that is placed on the mark and struck in any direction will ricochet into the hole.

- Note that if $a = b$ then we have only one focus, at $(0,0)$. In this case, the geometric definition breaks down, but it is clear from the equation that we have a circle. This is why a circle can be thought of as a "degenerate ellipse".

■ Examples

- A vertical ellipse: $\dfrac{x^2}{16} + \dfrac{y^2}{25} = 1$

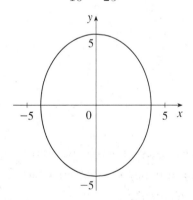

- A horizontal ellipse: $\dfrac{x^2}{9} + 4y^2 = 1$

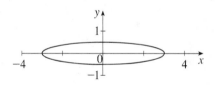

■ Group Work: Ellipses in Nature

As suggested earlier, have the students bring in photographs of circles, either clipped out of magazines or taken by themselves. Have them use a photocopier to make the photograph sufficiently large. Using a photocopier or a transparency, instruct the students to overlay a grid on their photograph, and determine whether the shape in question is a circle or an ellipse. Have the students find the equation of their shape.

■ Homework Problems

Core Exercises: 9, 11, 25, 33, 43

Sample Assignment: 4, 9, 11, 14, 15, 21, 25, 27, 33, 34, 35, 43, 45, 53, 56

8.3 | Hyperbolas

$\frac{1}{2}$ class. Optional material.

■ Points to Stress

1. The definition and geometry of hyperbolas.

2. Using the equation of a hyperbola to find relevant constants.

3. Graphing a hyperbola given its equation.

■ Sample Questions

- **Text Question:** Is $\dfrac{x^2}{5^2} - \dfrac{y^2}{6^2} = 1$ the equation of a horizontal or a vertical hyperbola? How do you know?

  Answer: It is horizontal because the x^2 term is positive.

- **Drill Question:** Find the vertices, foci, and asymptotes of the hyperbola given by $\frac{y^2}{4} - x^2 = 1$. Then graph it.

  Answer: Vertices $(0, \pm 2)$, foci $\left(0, \pm\sqrt{5}\right)$, asymptotes $y = \pm 2x$

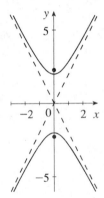

■ In-Class Materials

- Have students sketch a hyperbola "from scratch." Hand out a sheet of paper with two foci, and hand out rulers. Get the students to plot points where the difference of the distances between the points and the foci is 1 inch. Have them keep plotting points until a hyperbolic shape emerges. There is another way to sketch a hyperbola which will be discussed in the Group Work.

- As noted in Section 8.1, one can use dental floss and a modeling compound (such as clay or playdough) to make a half-cone and slice it. Have the students attempt to do so to get a hyperbola. Notice that the slice does not have to be straight up and down, as shown in the prologue to the chapter. As long as the slice would cut the other half of the cone, the resultant curve is a hyperbola.

- Discuss the reflection property of hyperbolas: Take a point between the branches, and aim a beam of light at one of the foci. It will reflect off the hyperbola, and go in a path aimed directly at the other focus. This reflection property is harder to model physically than those of the ellipse and the parabola.

▪ Examples

- A vertical hyperbola: $-\dfrac{x^2}{16} + \dfrac{y^2}{25} = 1$

  Vertices $(0, \pm 5)$, asymptotes $y = \pm\frac{5}{4}x$, foci $\left(0, \pm\sqrt{41}\right)$

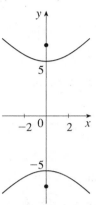

- A horizontal hyperbola: $\dfrac{x^2}{9} - 2y^2 = 1$

  Vertices $(\pm 3, 0)$, asymptotes $y = \pm\frac{1}{3\sqrt{2}}x$, foci $\left(\pm\sqrt{\frac{37}{2}}, 0\right)$

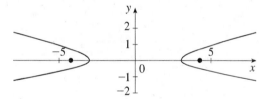

▪ Group Work: Sketching Hyperbolas

This will require students to follow directions very carefully. You may have to model the process for them on an overhead projector. There is a bit of a "knack" to keeping the string in the correct position. The students will need a cardboard ruler or straightedge, a thumbtack, tape or fast-drying glue, string, scissors, a pencil, and patience.

If students finish early, there is another construction they can try: Mark two points A and B on a piece of paper. Draw a circle centered at A with a radius small enough so that B lies outside the circle. Now mark an arbitrary point on the circle and fold the paper so B touches that point. Crease the paper along the fold. Mark a different point on the circle, and crease again. If you do this enough times, the creases will form a filled-in hyperbola. As of this writing, the result of this process can be seen on the web at
http://www.cognitiohk.edu.hk/maths/math/em03con.htm.

Answer:

Let the length of the string be s and the length of the ruler r. Call the unlabeled end of the ruler C. Consider a point on your curve — call it P. (In the figure, the tip of the pencil is at P.)

Then

$$\left| \overline{BP} - \overline{AP} \right| = \left| \overline{BP} - \left(s - \overline{CP} \right) \right|$$
$$= \left| \overline{BP} + \overline{CP} - s \right|$$
$$= \left| r - s \right|$$

Thus $\overline{BP} - \overline{AP}$ is a constant, and so by definition the collection of points P constitutes a hyperbola.

▧ Homework Problems

Core Exercises: 9, 17, 21, 25, 31, 35

Sample Assignment: 2, 5, 6, 7, 8, 9, 10, 17, 19, 21, 23, 25, 31, 34, 35, 43, 50

GROUP WORK, SECTION 8.3
Sketching Hyperbolas

We are going to be constructing the graph of a hyperbola. This method is going to require some patience, and mastering an unnatural motion, but it does work!

1. Mark two points A and B on a piece of paper. They will be the foci of your hyperbola.

2. Cut a piece of string, a bit longer or a bit shorter than your ruler.

3. Attach one end of the string to one end of your ruler, and the other end of the string to A. Attach it firmly—you don't want it to move about.

4. Pin the other end of the ruler to B, so that the ruler is free to rotate around B.

5. Now tighten the string with a pencil, as shown in the diagram, and rotate the ruler. Make sure that the string does not stretch.

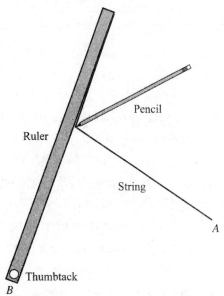

6. To get the other half of the hyperbola, perform the same trick with the end of the ruler tacked to point A and the end of the string attached to point B.

Congratulations! You are now the proud parent of a lovely little hyperbola. Now figure out why this process works.

8.4 | Shifted Conics

■ Suggested Time and Emphasis

1 class. Optional material. May be covered in conjunction with Sections 8.1–8.3.

■ Points to Stress

1. Completing the square in a general equation of a conic in order to apply the techniques of Section 2.2 to graph the conic.
2. Identifying conic sections by the constants in the general equation.
3. Understanding degenerate conic sections.

■ Sample Questions

- **Text Question:** Identify the conic section with equation $9x^2 - 36x + 4y^2 = 0$.

  Answer: Ellipse

- **Drill Question:** Graph the conic section with equation $4x^2 - 16x + 9y^2 - 20 = 0$.

  Answer: $4x^2 - 16x + 9y^2 - 20 = 0 \iff 4(x-2)^2 + 9y^2 = 36 \iff \dfrac{(x-2)^2}{9} + \dfrac{y^2}{4} = 1$

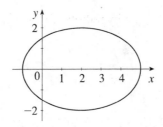

■ In-Class Materials

- Class time can be saved if this section is covered along with Sections 8.1–8.3. For example, after discussing parabolas, immediately do an example of a shifted parabola. Teach ellipses and hyperbolas similarly.
- The text's guide to the general equation of a shifted conic is important, but students should not memorize it blindly. Point out that if they've learned the previous section, these rules of thumb should make perfect sense. Have them look at the three general formulas they have learned, generalizing them to allow for a shift:

$$y = 4p(x-h)^2$$

$$\frac{(x-h)^2}{a^2} + \frac{(y-k)^2}{b^2} = 1$$

$$\frac{(x-h)^2}{a^2} - \frac{(y-k)^2}{b^2} = 1$$

- Help the class recognize the difference between the formulas of conic sections by pointing out that the equation of a parabola has degree 2 in only one variable (which variable it is determines which type of parabola it is). Equations of ellipses and hyperbolas have degree 2 in both variables; for ellipses the second-degree terms have the same sign, and for hyperbolas they have opposite signs.

▨ Examples

- A nondegenerate ellipse:

$$25x^2 + 4y^2 - 150x + 40y + 324 = 0 \quad \Leftrightarrow$$

$$\frac{(x-3)^2}{4} + \frac{(y+5)^2}{25} = 1$$

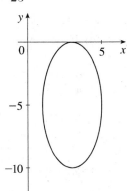

- A degenerate hyperbola:

$$x^2 - y^2 - 4x - 2y + 3 = 0 \quad \Leftrightarrow$$

$$(x-2)^2 - (y+1)^2 = 0$$

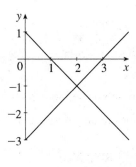

▨ Group Work: It's Easier in Polar

This activity is for classes which have covered polar coordinates.

Answer: The graph is an ellipse if $e < 1$, a hyperbola if $e > 1$, and a parabola when $e = 1$. The directrix is $x = \pm d$ or $y = \pm d$.

▨ Homework Problems

Core Exercises: 7, 9, 13, 23, 25, 31

Sample Assignment: 4, 5, 7, 9, 10, 13, 14, 18, 23, 24, 25, 30, 31, 32, 36, 42

It's Easier in Polar

Consider the polar graph with equation

$$r = \frac{ed}{1 \pm e \sin\theta}$$

It turns out this is always the graph of a (possibly degenerate) conic section. Play with the positive constants d and e. Under what circumstances is the graph an ellipse? A parabola? A hyperbola?

CHAPTER 9 Sequences and Series

▪ Suggested Time and Emphasis

1 class. Optional material.

▪ Points to Stress

1. Definition and notation of sequences.
2. Recursively defined sequences, including the Fibonacci sequence.
3. Partial sums, including summation notation.

▪ Sample Questions

- **Text Question:** Compute $\sum_{k=1}^{5} k$.

  Answer: 15

- **Drill Question:** If we have a sequence defined by $a_1 = 4$, $a_2 = -3$ and $a_n = a_{n-2} + a_{n-1}$ for $n \geq 3$, what is a_4?

  Answer: -2

▪ In-Class Materials

- Students often confuse the idea of a function and a sequence. Have the students graph the function $f(n) = \sin(2\pi n)$, and then the sequence $a_n = \sin(2\pi n)$ to make sure they understand the difference.

- Note that there are many sequences that have no pattern: $1, \pi, 3, e, -27, \dots$. Also point out that not every sequence with a pattern has a rule that is easily written as a formula. For example,

$$3, 1, 4, 1, 5, 9, 2, 6, 5, 3, \dots$$

$$3, 3.1, 3.14, 3.141, 3.1415, \dots$$

$$1, 100, 1000, 2, 99, 1001, 3, 98, 1002, 4, 97, 1003, 5, 96, 1004, \dots$$

$$0, 0.1, 0.12, 0.123, \dots, 0.123456789, 0.12345678910, 0.1234567891011, \dots$$

(The limit of this last sequence is called the Champernowe constant.)

- Have the students try to figure out the pattern of this sequence:

$$3, 3, 5, 4, 4, 3, 5, 5, 4, 3, \dots$$

Answer: It counts the number of letters in the words 'one', 'two', 'three', ...

- Melissa Pfohl's favorite sequence is $a_n = n^2 + (-1)^n n$. Starting with $n = 0$, the sequence goes as follows: $0, 0, 6, 6, 20, 20, 42, 42, \dots$. Note that the formula is far from obvious, and the tantalizing "doubling property" can be proved using elementary methods.

- There are several ways of making the terms of a sequence alternate. The text gives the term $(-1)^n$. Another alternating sequence is $\cos \pi n$. Ask the students to come up with a formula for the following sequence: $0, 1, 0, -1, 0, 1, 0, -1, \dots$. There are several ways to do this, but the cleanest is $\sin\left(\frac{\pi}{2}n\right)$.

- The Fibonacci sequence comes up in many contexts. Group Work 1 gives students several. If this group work is not completely covered, its problems can be used as examples. They can then be called back into service when mathematical induction is covered.

- Have students compute some partial sums that converge quickly to a recognizable number, such as the one associated with $a_n = \dfrac{1}{(n-1)!}$ (with $a_1 = 1$) which converges to e, and $a_n = \left(\frac{3}{4}\right)^n$ which converges to 3. Then have them look at some partial sums that go off to infinity, such as the ones associated with $a_n = 10^n$ and $a_n = n$. Then have them conjecture about the fate of $a_n = \dfrac{1}{n}$, perhaps deferring the answer until Group Work 2.

■ Examples

- A non-obvious telescoping series: Consider the sequence $\frac{1}{2}, \frac{1}{6}, \frac{1}{12}, \frac{1}{20}, \ldots, a_n = \dfrac{1}{n(n+1)}$. This can be rewritten as $a_n = \dfrac{1}{n} - \dfrac{1}{n+1}$. Thus $\sum_{n=1}^{k} a_n = 1 - \dfrac{1}{k+1}$ (as shown in the text).

- A sequence whose values look random: $a_n = \sin\left(n^2\right)$

■ Group Work 1: Finding a Pattern

This activity involves several problems. Divide the students into groups, and give each group a different problem. If a group finishes early, you can have them try to prove their answer, or you can give them a different problem to work on. Have them save their work, because these answers can all be shown by the principle of mathematical induction, which is covered in Section 9.5.

An interesting article about human geneology, related to Form C, can be found at http://www.msnbc.msn.com/id/13621729/.

Answers:

All the questions boil down to finding Fibonacci numbers.

Form A: 165580141

Form B: 165580141

Form C: 1. 5   **2.** 165580141

■ Group Work 2: Using the Notation

The idea of this activity is to familiarize the students with the notation of sequences and series. Perhaps do the first problem with the class, so they get the idea of writing out a general term.

Answers:

1. $5, n, 21$

2. $0.00002, 2 \times 10^{-n}, 0.222222$

3. $0.0002, 20 \times 10^{-n}$ or $2 \times 10^{-n+1}, 2.22222$

4. $12, 2 + 2n, 54$

5. $\dfrac{1}{25}, (-1)^{n+1}\dfrac{1}{n^2}, \dfrac{973}{1200}$

■ **Group Work 3: The Harmonic Series**

This activity was suggested by the Teacher's Guide to AP Calculus published by the College Board. It will allow the students to discover the divergence of the harmonic series for themselves.

Answer:

1. $s_1 = 1$, $s_2 = 1.5$, $s_3 \approx 1.8333$, $s_4 \approx 2.08333$, $s_5 \approx 2.28333$, $s_6 = 2.45$, $s_7 \approx 2.5929$, $s_8 \approx 2.7179$, $s_9 \approx 2.8290$, $s_{10} \approx 2.9290$

2, 4.

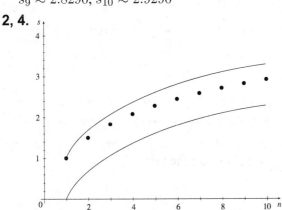

3. The partial sums appear to approach 3.

5. We know $\ln x$ goes to infinity, and the partial sum s_n seems to always be larger than $\ln n$.

6. The guesses will vary, but will almost certainly be overestimates. As of 2008, and continuing through our grandchildren's lives, the answer to five significant digits is 25.967.

■ **Homework Problems**

Core Exercises: 3, 5, 7, 9, 13, 17, 25, 27, 29, 37, 39, 41, 43, 61, 63

Sample Assignment: 2, 3, 5, 6, 7, 11, 12, 13, 15, 16, 17, 25, 26, 27, 28, 29, 37, 38, 39, 41, 43, 47, 48, 61, 62, 63, 64, 69, 75, 77

Sally the Elf likes to climb stairs. She can climb them one step or two steps at a time. The staircase in front of Santa's workshop has four steps. Every day, when she reports to work, Sally tries to climb it a different way. Sometimes she goes one step at a time $(1, 1, 1, 1)$, sometimes two steps at a time $(2, 2)$, sometimes she goes up one step, then two, then one $(1, 2, 1)$, sometimes she goes up one, another, then two $(1, 1, 2)$ or vice versa $(2, 1, 1)$.

So there are a total of five ways she can climb the steps. This suits her fine, because when she reports to work (at 9 A.M., Monday to Friday) she can go up a different way every day of the week.

This will all change in 2008, when Microdweeb acquires Santa's workshop. They are going to make the li'l toy factory into a huge manufacturing megaplex. Poor Sally is going to have to climb a flight of *forty* stairs to get to work every day (at 8 A.M., Monday to Saturday, with no Christmas holidays). The one bright point in her newly sad life is that she will have plenty of ways to climb these stairs.

Your challenge is to compute how many ways Sally can climb this flight of forty steps. There are more than 5,000 of them, so listing them is probably not the way to go on this one.

GROUP WORK 1, SECTION 9.1
Finding a Pattern (Form B)

A sequence of 0s and 1s is called **successor-free** if it does not have two 1s in a row. For example, these sequences are successor-free:

$$00000$$

$$010101$$

$$0100100010001$$

These sequences are not successor-free:

$$0011$$

$$11111111$$

$$0100110001$$

There are five three-element successor-free sequences: 000, 001, 010, 100, and 101.

How many thirty-nine-element successor-free sequences are there? There are more than 5,000 of them, so listing them is probably not the way to go here.

GROUP WORK 1, SECTION 9.1
Finding a Pattern (Form C)

A female bee, or worker, comes from a fertilized egg, laid by the Queen bee. A male bee, or drone, comes from an unfertilized egg, laid by either the Queen bee or a worker bee. In other words:

A female bee has a mother and a father, but a male bee has only a mother.

This makes life strange for bee genealogists. For example, a drone has two grandparents, but a worker has three! Check it out:

Drone Ancestry: One mommy (who has a mommy and a daddy). He has two grandparents.

Worker Ancestry: One mommy (who has a mommy and a daddy) and one daddy (who has a mommy). She has three grandparents.

1. How many great-grandparents does a worker bee have?

2. Assuming all ancestors are distinct, how many great^{37}-grandparents does a worker bee have? (37 "great"s). There are more than 5,000 of them, so listing them is probably not the way to go.

GROUP WORK 2, SECTION 9.1
Using the Notation

Fill in the blanks:

1. $a_1 = 1$, $a_2 = 2$, $a_3 = 3$, $a_4 = 4$, $a_5 =$ _____ , ..., $a_n =$ _____ , $\displaystyle\sum_{n=1}^{6} a_n =$ _____ .

2. $b_1 = 0.2$, $b_2 = 0.02$, $b_3 = 0.002$, $b_4 = 0.0002$, $b_5 =$ _____ , ..., $b_n =$ _____ , $\displaystyle\sum_{n=1}^{6} b_n =$ _____ .

3. $c_1 = 2$, $c_2 = 0.2$, $c_3 = 0.02$, $c_4 = 0.002$, $c_5 =$ _____ , ..., $c_n =$ _____ , $\displaystyle\sum_{n=1}^{6} c_n =$ _____ .

4. $d_1 = 4$, $d_2 = 6$, $d_3 = 8$, $d_4 = 10$, $d_5 =$ _____ , ..., $d_n =$ _____ , $\displaystyle\sum_{n=1}^{6} d_n =$ _____ .

5. $e_1 = 1$, $e_2 = -\frac{1}{4}$, $e_3 = \frac{1}{9}$, $e_4 = -\frac{1}{16}$, $e_5 =$ _____ , ..., $e_n =$ _____ , $\displaystyle\sum_{n=1}^{6} d_n =$ _____ .

GROUP WORK 3, SECTION 9.1
The Harmonic Series

In this exercise, we look at $\displaystyle\sum_{n=1}^{\infty} \frac{1}{n}$.

1. What are the first ten partial sums s_n?

$s_1 =$	$s_6 =$
$s_2 =$	$s_7 =$
$s_3 =$	$s_8 =$
$s_4 =$	$s_9 =$
$s_5 =$	$s_{10} =$

2. The way we will compute $\displaystyle\sum_{n=1}^{\infty} \frac{1}{n}$ (or prove that it goes to infinity) is to compute the limit of its partial sums. Plot the partial sums on the following graph, as accurately as you can.

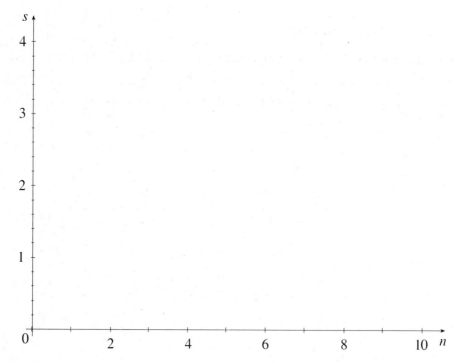

3. The partial sums appear to be approaching a number. What is that number?

4. Now, on the same axes, graph $y = \ln x$ and $y = 1 + \ln x$ for $x \geq 1$. (Both of these graphs, as you know, go to infinity as x gets arbitrarily large.)

5. Using your answer to Problem 4 and your graph, explain why it is reasonable to believe that $\displaystyle\sum_{n=1}^{\infty} \frac{1}{n}$ goes to infinity.

6. Assume that in the year 4000 B.C., you started adding up the terms of the harmonic series, at the rate of, say, one term per second. We know that the sum gets arbitrarily large, but approximately how big would your partial sum be as of now? Go ahead and make a guess, based on your best judgment and intuition.

9.2 | Arithmetic Sequences

■ Suggested Time and Emphasis

$\frac{1}{2}$–1 class. Optional material.

■ Points to Stress

1. Recognizing arithmetic sequences by their formula and by their graph.
2. Finding the first term a and the common difference d of a given arithmetic sequence, and using this information to compute partial sums.

■ Sample Questions

• **Text Question:** What distinguishes an "arithmetic sequence" from a plain ol' arbitrary "sequence"?
  Answer: Successive terms in an arithmetic sequence have a common difference.
• **Drill Question:** Consider the sequence 3, 8, 13, 18, 23, 28, 33, 38, ... Find the 100th partial sum.
  Answer: 25,050

■ In-Class Materials

• The perfect squares 1, 4, 9, 16, . . . can be represented as a square array of dots.

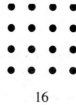

16

• The triangular numbers are those that can be represented by a triangular array of dots: 1, 3, 6, 10, 15, ...

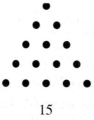

15

Note that the triangular numbers are precisely the partial sums of the sequence 1, 2, 3, 4, ...
• Examine this broader triangular array:

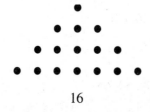

16

Notice we again run into perfect squares! This can be demonstrated by looking at the partial sums of the arithmetic sequence $1 + 2(n - 1)$, or by rearranging the dots of the broader triangle to make a square. (This concept is discussed in more depth in the Discovery Project.)

- Consider the handshaking problem. If n people are in a room, and shake hands, we can ask the question: How many handshakes took place? If, for example, four people (Alfred, Brendel, Claude, and Debussy) all shake hands, a total of 6 shakes take place:

$$
\begin{array}{lll}
A \,\&\, B & B \,\&\, C & C \,\&\, D \\
A \,\&\, C & B \,\&\, D & \\
A \,\&\, D & &
\end{array}
$$

Allow the students to try to figure out how many handshakes take place if 12, or if n people shake hands. It turns out that the answer is $1 + 2 + \cdots + (n-1)$ (as illustrated above), the partial sum of an arithmetic sequence.

- Many phenomena are either linear or locally linear (they look linear when viewing them over a narrow range). For example, assume that a company earns about $120,000 in 2011, $140,000 in 2012, $160,000 in 2013, etc. If it is linear growth over ten years, the total ten-year earning can be found from adding up the terms of an arithmetic sequence.

- Show the students that a constant sequence such as $5, 5, 5, 5, \ldots$ is trivially an arithmetic sequence. Notice that the formula for the partial sum is consistent with what we know about basic arithmetic.

- Have the students try to define an arithmetic sequence recursively. It can be done relatively simply as $a_n = a_{n-1} + d$, but obtaining this formula requires an understanding of arithmetic sequences and recursively defined sequences.

▨ Example

Finding details of an arithmetic sequence given two terms: If an arithmetic sequence has $a_3 = 39$ and $a_{10} = 25$, then we can calculate $a = 43$, $d = -2$. $a_n = 43 - 2(n-1)$, so $a_{100} = -155$ and $\sum_{n=1}^{100} 43 - 2(n-1) = -5600$. Make sure to point out that this trick only works if we *know* ahead of time that this is an arithmetic sequence.

▨ Group Work: Balancing the Budget

This activity gives the students practice with partial sums of arithmetic sequences, and clarifies the differences between terms that are commonly mentioned on the news. After the students have finished the activity, you can discuss the difference between a budget deficit and the national debt.

Answers:

1. $a_n = 50{,}000 - 1250(n-1)$. So $a_{41} = 0$. The deficit will be zero in 2051.

2. $\sum_{n=1}^{41} (50{,}000 - 1250(n-1)) = \$1{,}025{,}000$

▨ Homework Problems

Core Exercises: 5, 9, 13, 27, 37, 43, 49, 59, 65

Sample Assignment: 3, 4, 5, 6, 9, 13, 14, 15, 18, 27, 33, 34, 37, 43, 49, 56, 57, 59, 65, 67

GROUP WORK, SECTION 9.2
Balancing the Budget

The budget deficit of a company or country is the difference between the amount it spends in a year and the amount that it earns. If, for example, a company earns $10,000 and spends $12,000 we say that the budget deficit is $2000. (If a company or country earns more then it spends, we call that a budget surplus).

Assume a company starts out with a budget deficit of $50,000 in the year 2011. The company doesn't want to have a deficit, but it is very hard to erase a budget deficit; it is hard to suddenly reduce costs or increase income. To do this, the company enacts a program to reduce the deficit by $1250 every year. So in the year 2012, for example, the budget deficit will be $48,750.

1. In what year will the deficit be gone?

2. Just because the deficit is gone does not mean the news is all good. Recall that every year from 2011 until the year the deficit goes away, more money is going out than coming in! That amount still has to be made up, and is called (as you would think) debt. What is the total amount of debt the company owes in the year the deficit is eliminate?

▪ Suggested Time and Emphasis

$\frac{1}{2}$–1 class. Optional material.

▪ Points to Stress

1. Definition of geometric series.

2. Definition of infinite series.

3. Formulas for sums of finite and infinite geometric series.

▪ Sample Questions

- **Text Question:** What distinguishes a "geometric sequence" from a plain ol' arbitrary "sequence"?

  Answer: Successive terms in a geometric sequence have a common ratio.

- **Drill Question:** Find the 100th partial sum of the sequence $2, 6, 18, 54, 162, \ldots$.

  Answer: $\dfrac{2\left(1 - 3^{100}\right)}{1 - 3} \approx 5.154 \times 10^{47}$

▪ In-Class Materials

- Represent a geometric series visually. For example, a geometric view of the equation $\displaystyle\sum_{n=1}^{\infty} 1/2^n = 1$ is given below.

An alternative geometric view is given in Group Work 1, Problem 2. If this group work is not assigned, the figure should be shown to the class at this time.

- Introduce the idea that for any two real numbers A and B, the statement $A = B$ is the same as saying that for any integer N, $|A - B| < 1/N$. Now use this idea to show that $0.9999\ldots = 0.\overline{9} = 1$, since

$$\left|1 - 0.\overline{9}\right| < \left|1 - 0.\underbrace{99999\ldots99}_{N \text{ nines}}\right| = 0.\underbrace{00000\ldots0001}_{N-1 \text{ zeros}} = 10^{-N} = \frac{1}{10^N}.$$ Then use the usual approach to

define $0.\overline{9}$ as $\displaystyle\sum_{n=1}^{\infty} 9/10^n$ and show directly that $0.\overline{9} = 1$. Generalize this result by pointing out that *any* repeating decimal ($0.\overline{3}$, $0.\overline{412}$, $0.24\overline{621}$) can be written as a geometric series, and can thus be written as a fraction using the formula for a geometric series. Demonstrate with $0.\overline{412} = \frac{412}{1000}\left(\frac{1}{1 - 1/1000}\right) = \frac{412}{999}$.

- Explore the "middle third" Cantor set with the class: This set is defined as the set of points obtained by taking the interval $[0, 1]$, throwing out the middle third to obtain $\left[0, \frac{1}{3}\right] \cup \left[\frac{2}{3}, 1\right]$, throwing out the middle third of each remaining interval to obtain $\left[0, \frac{1}{9}\right] \cup \left[\frac{2}{9}, \frac{1}{3}\right] \cup \left[\frac{2}{3}, \frac{7}{9}\right] \cup \left[\frac{8}{9}, 1\right]$, and repeating this process *ad infinitum*. Point out that there are infinitely many points left after this process. (If a point winds up as the endpoint of an interval, it never gets removed, and new intervals are created with every step). Now calculate the total length of the sections that were thrown away: $\frac{1}{3} + 2 \cdot \frac{1}{9} + 4 \cdot \frac{1}{27} + \cdots = \displaystyle\sum_{k=0}^{\infty} \frac{2^k}{3^{k+1}} = 1$.

Notice the apparent paradox: We've thrown away a total interval of length 1, but still infinitely many points remain. (See also Exercise 71.)

- Do Exercise 52 (the "St. Ives" problem) with the students. After obtaining the partial sum solution, point out that traditionally people give the answer 1. The problem says "As *I* was going to St. Ives..." So presumably all the other people were going the other way, away from St. Ives!

- One of the consequences of parenthood is it often causes otherwise rational adults to say things like, "If I told you once, I've told you one *hundred* times!" Assume that this was true, and a child was told something on a Friday. The parental rule means that the child was previously told that fact one hundred times, say on Thursday. Thus, on Wednesday, the child must have been told the information 100 times for every time on Thursday, or 10,000 times. Use the methods of this section to determine how many times the child has been told since Monday.

▧ Example

Zeno's Paradox: In order to walk to a wall across the room, you have to first walk halfway to the wall, and in order to do that you have to walk halfway to the halfway point, etc. This process can be viewed as finding the sum of $\frac{1}{2} + \frac{1}{4} + \frac{1}{8} + \cdots$. The sum of this infinite series is 1.

▧ Group Work 1: Made in the Shade

Problem 1 attempts to help the students visualize geometric series. Problem 2 gives a geometric interpretation of the fact that $\frac{1}{2} + \frac{1}{4} + \frac{1}{8} + \frac{1}{16} + \cdots = 1$.

Answers:

1. (a) $a = \frac{1}{2}\pi$, $r = \frac{1}{4}$, $A = \frac{2\pi}{3}$ (b) $a = \frac{1}{4}$, $r = \frac{1}{4}$, $A = \frac{1}{3}$

2. (a) $a_n = \dfrac{1}{2^n}$

  (b) 1. Note that the students may use the geometric series formula to get the answer, but it should be pointed out that the answer is immediate from the diagram.

▧ Group Work 2: An Unusual Series and its Sums

The initial student reaction may be "I have no idea where to start!" One option is to start the problem on the board. Another approach may be to encourage the students to write down the length of the largest dotted line segment (b), then to figure out the length of the next one, which they can get using trigonometry, and keep going as long as they can. Many students still resist the idea of tackling a problem "one step at a time" if it seems difficult.

Answers:

1. $L = b + b\sin\theta + b\sin^2\theta + \cdots$ or $\sum_{n=1}^{\infty} b(\sin\theta)^{n-1}$. Because there are infinitely many terms, we need to write the answer as a series.

2. $L = \dfrac{b}{1 - \sin\theta}$ **3.** L approaches infinity.

4. *Geometrically:* As $\theta \to \frac{\pi}{2}$, the picture breaks down. The easiest way to see this is to have the students try to sketch what happens for θ close to $\frac{\pi}{2}$. The dotted lines become infinitely dense.

  Using infinite sums: $\displaystyle\lim_{\theta \to \pi/2} \dfrac{b}{1 - \sin\theta}$ diverges.

■ Group Work 3: The Popular Organization

This activity dramatizes exponential growth, while at the same time exploring geometric series. After the students have done the assignment, ask them to redo Questions 2 and 4, this time using a time period of 100 years.

Answers:

1. $a_n = 1000 + 100\,(n - 1)$, $a_{10} = 1900$

2. $\sum_{n=1}^{10} (1000 + 100\,(n - 1)) = 14{,}500$

3. $a_n = 1000\,(1.1)^{n-1}$, $a_{10} \approx \$2357.95$

4. $\sum_{n=1}^{10} 1000\,(1.1)^{n-1} \approx \$15{,}937.42$

For 100 years, the arithmetic sequence gives \$595,000 and the geometric sequence gives \$137,796,120.

■ Homework Problems

Core Exercises: 5, 9, 13, 27, 37, 43, 47, 49, 51, 59

Sample Assignment: 2, 3, 5, 6, 9, 10, 13, 16, 20, 22, 26, 27, 31, 36, 37, 40, 43, 47, 49, 51, 53, 54, 57, 59, 61, 64, 67, 77, 78

Made in the Shade

1. Compute the sum of the shaded areas for each figure.

(a)

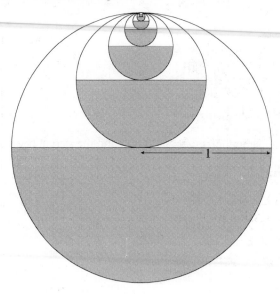

(b)

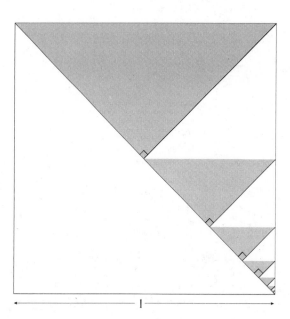

2. Consider the figure below.

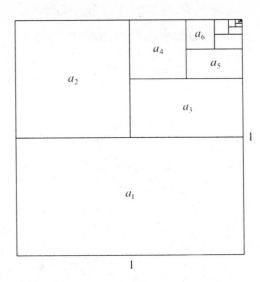

(a) Find an general expression for the area a_n.

(b) What is $\displaystyle\sum_{n=1}^{\infty} a_n$?

An Unusual Series and its Sums

Consider the following right triangle of side length b and base angle θ.

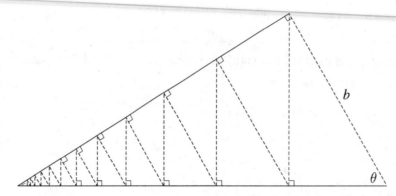

1. Express the total length of the dotted line in the triangle in terms of b and θ. Why should your answer be given in terms of a series?

2. Compute the sum of this series.

3. What happens as $\theta \to \frac{\pi}{2}$?

4. Justify this answer geometrically and using infinite sums.

GROUP WORK 3, SECTION 9.3
The Popular Organization

I have started a wonderful organization, called the Society for the Enhancement of the Lives of certain pro-Fessors (SELF). People can join for an amount of money of their choosing, and it goes to me, to enhance my life. This year hasn't been very good—I made only $1100. But it is better than last year, my first year, when I made $1000.

1. Assume the annual earnings increase as an arithmetic sequence. How much money will people send SELF in year 10?

2. What will be the total earnings after 10 years?

3. Assume the annual earnings increase as a geometric sequence. How much money will people send SELF in year 10?

4. What will be the total earnings after 10 years?

Suggested Time and Emphasis

$\frac{1}{2}$–1 class. Optional material.

Points to Stress

1. The future and present values of an annuity.
2. Calculating the interest rate of an annuity from the size of monthly payments.

Sample Questions

- **Text Question:** What is an annuity?

  Answer: An annuity is a sum of money paid in regular equal payments.

- **Drill Question:** Every year, an investor deposits $2000 in an IRA which earns an interest rate of 6% per year. How much is in the IRA after ten years?

  Answer: $2000\dfrac{(1+0.06)^{10} - 1}{0.06} = 26{,}361.59$

In-Class Materials

The key idea here is that there are many practical examples available to use as illustrations.

- Many states and companies hold lotteries and sweepstakes. The very large ones have options where the winner can chose a large lump sum award, or a larger award paid out over a period of years. Find the data for a local lottery or sweepstakes, and decide which option is the better option from a financial standpoint. For example, in the Midwestern United States Powerball, five white balls are drawn from a set of 53, and one red Powerball is drawn from a set of 42. The payouts are as follows:

Numbers Matched	Payout
All five numbers + Powerball	Jackpot (use $10 million as an example)
All five numbers, without Powerball	$100,000
Four numbers + Powerball	$5000
Four numbers, without Powerball	$100
Three numbers + Powerball	$100
Three numbers without Powerball	$7
Two numbers + Powerball	$7
One number + Powerball	$4
Powerball only	$3

If the grand prize is $10 million, it will be paid over 30 years, or the winner can choose to receive a lump sum payment of $5.8 million.

- A phone call to a cooperative automobile dealership will get a sample monthly payment on a 4-year car loan. Students can figure out the interest rate on cars in their community, and see if it varies based on the cost of the car.

- Students can be assigned to contact mortgage brokers to find the size of payments (and current interest rate) on an average 30 year mortgage on a house near their home or school. They then can explore the effects of making a larger or smaller down payment on the house.

▦ Example

A person borrows $20,000 to buy a car, and wants to pay it off in 4 years. If the interest rate is 8% per year, compounded monthly, what is the amount of each monthly payment?

Answer: $488.26

▦ Group Work: The Double Payment

It is a common myth that if you pay double your first payment on a mortgage, then you will be paid off years earlier. This fact has appeared in newspapers and is often repeated on television. In this activity, your students prove it to be false. It is true, however, that if you make one extra payment *per year* then the mortgage will be paid off significantly faster.

Answers:

1. $1197.55   2. $431,118.00   3. 29 years, 3 months

▦ Homework Problems

Core Exercises: 3, 9, 11, 17, 19, 25

Sample Assignment: 2, 3, 6, 7, 9, 11, 15, 16, 17, 19, 25

GROUP WORK, SECTION 9.4
The Double Payment

I want to buy a $200,000 home, and take a 30 year mortgage on it. My interest rate is 7%. I have saved $20,000 to make a down payment.

1. What will my monthly payment be?

2. What will be the total amount that I pay the bank?

3. If I double my first payment, my loan will be paid off before the 30 years are up. How long will it take before the loan is paid off?

Suggested Time and Emphasis

1–$1\frac{1}{2}$ classes. Optional material.

Point to Stress

The concept and execution of a proof by mathematical induction.

Sample Questions

- **Text Question:** There are two main steps to a proof by mathematical induction. What is the first one?
  Answer: Any answer getting at the idea of a base case or a "proof for $n = 1$" should be accepted, even if the latter isn't technically true.

- **Drill Question:** Prove, using mathematical induction, that $1 + 2 + \cdots + n = \dfrac{n(n+1)}{2}$.
  Answer: This is Example 2 from the text.

In-Class Materials

- The main thing for induction is to give the students plenty of examples to work from, and plenty of practice.

  1. We can use induction to show that $\dfrac{(2n)!}{2^n n!}$ is an integer for all positive n. The base case is trivial. The key step in the inductive case:

  $$\frac{(2n+2)!}{2^{n+1}(n+1)!} = \frac{(2n)!}{2^n n!} \cdot \frac{(2n+1)(2n+2)}{2(n+1)}$$

  and now cancellation occurs.

  2. We can use induction to show that the sum of the cubes of three consecutive integers is divisible by 9. The base case is trivial. The key inductive step:

  $$(n+1)^3 + (n+2)^3 + (n+3)^3 = n^3 + (n+1)^3 + (n+2)^3 + 9n^2 + 27n + 27$$

  3. We can use induction to show that

  $$\frac{n^3 - n}{3} = (1 \cdot 2) + (2 \cdot 3) + \ldots + (n-1)n$$

  The base step should be $n = 2$, and the inductive step uses the fact that

  $$\frac{(n+1)^3 - (n+1)}{3} = \frac{n^3 - n}{3} + \frac{3n^2 + 3n}{3}$$

- A variant on induction can be used to prove the results of Group Work 1 in Section 9.1 ("Finding a Pattern"). The students can do these, or you can write it on the blackboard.

  1. Let $F(n)$ be the number of ways to climb n steps. We want to prove $F(n) = F(n-1) + F(n-2)$.
     Base Case: $n = 3$. It is true that $F(3) = F(2) + F(1)$.
     Inductive Step: Assume that this is true for 1 through n. Consider $F(n+1)$. The first step is either a one-step or a two-step. If the first step is a one-step, there are n steps left to climb, and the number of ways to do that is $F(n)$. If the first step is a two-step then there are $n - 2$ steps left to climb, and the number of ways to do that is $F(n-1)$. So we have $F(n) = F(n-1) + F(n-2)$.

2. Let $F(n)$ be the number of successor-free n-element sequences. We want to prove
   $F(n) = F(n-1) + F(n-2)$.
   Base Case: $n = 3$. It is true that $F(3) = F(2) + F(1)$.
   Inductive Step: Assume that this is true for 1 through n. Consider $F(n+1)$. The first number in an $n+1$ sequence will be either 0 or 1. If the first number is 0, we have n left to go. So the number of ways to finish the sequence is $F(n)$. If the first number is 1, the second must be 0, or we wouldn't be successor free. Then we have $n-2$ numbers to go, so the number of ways to finish the sequence is $F(n-1)$. So $F(n) = F(n-1) + F(n-2)$.

3. Let $F(n)$ be the number of ancestors of a female bee at stage n. In other words, $n = 1$ means the number of parents, $n = 2$ means the number of grandparents, etc. We want to prove
   $F(n) = F(n-1) + F(n-2)$.
   Base Case: $n = 3$. It is true that $F(3) = F(2) + F(1)$.
   Inductive Step: Assume that this is true for 1 through n. Consider $F(n+1)$. The worker bee has a mommy, who has $F(n-1)$ ancestors. She also has a daddy who has a mommy who has $F(n-2)$ ancestors. So, again, $F(n) = F(n-1) + F(n-2)$.

■ Examples

See above.

■ Group Work 1: A Property of Matrices

This serves as a review of Chapter 7, as well as giving the students a chance to practice induction. It is more straightforward than Group Work 2, and a little less thought-provoking. If necessary, remind the students of the definition of A^k if A is a matrix before handing out the problem. If a group finishes early, have them look at B^n, where $B = \begin{bmatrix} 1 & 1 \\ 1 & 0 \end{bmatrix}$. Notice that this is a surprisingly different problem. (It is also Exercise 33 in the text.)

Answers:

1. $A^2 = \begin{bmatrix} 1 & 2 \\ 0 & 1 \end{bmatrix}$, $A^3 = \begin{bmatrix} 1 & 3 \\ 0 & 1 \end{bmatrix}$, $A^4 = \begin{bmatrix} 1 & 4 \\ 0 & 1 \end{bmatrix}$

2. $A^{1000} = \begin{bmatrix} 1 & 1000 \\ 0 & 1 \end{bmatrix}$

3. Base Case: trivial. The inductive step boils down to

$$\begin{bmatrix} 1 & 1 \\ 0 & 1 \end{bmatrix} \begin{bmatrix} 1 & n \\ 0 & 1 \end{bmatrix} = \begin{bmatrix} 1 & n+1 \\ 0 & 1 \end{bmatrix}$$

Bonus: As stated in Exercise 33, $\begin{bmatrix} 1 & 1 \\ 1 & 0 \end{bmatrix}^n = \begin{bmatrix} F_{n+1} & F_n \\ F_n & F_{n-1} \end{bmatrix}$, where F_n is the nth Fibonacci number.

▩ Group Work 2: The Angular Triomino

This activity is a mathematical induction proof, although there are no algebraic equations involved. It helps ensure the students know what is going on in an induction proof, as opposed to learning an algebraic "hoop" to jump through.

Answer:

The base case is trivial. For the induction step, divide the $2^{n+1} \times 2^{n+1}$ checkerboard into four equal pieces as shown, then temporarily remove three squares:

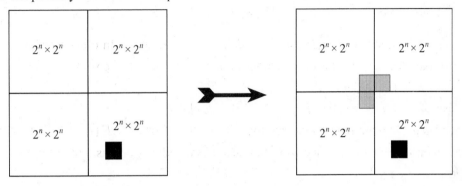

As we have four $2^n \times 2^n$ boards with one square missing in each, we can tile what is left by induction, and then we can tile the removed squares with one angular triomino.

▩ Homework Problems

Core Exercises: 3, 5, 21

Sample Assignment: 2, 3, 5, 6, 7, 10, 14, 19, 21, 27, 29, 30, 38

A Property of Matrices

Consider the matrix $A = \begin{pmatrix} 1 & 1 \\ 0 & 1 \end{pmatrix}$.

1. Compute A^2, A^3 and A^4.

2. Do you see a pattern? Compute A^{1000}.

3. Prove that your pattern is true using mathematical induction.

GROUP WORK 2, SECTION 9.5
The Angular Triomino

Meet the "angular triomino"

It is a very useful little shape. For example, suppose I had a 4×4 chessboard, with one square missing, like this:

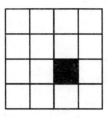

I could tile it with my friend the angular triomino, as so:

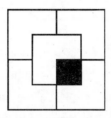

As fate would have it, I could tile the board regardless of where the missing square is. In fact, I can do it for an 8×8 chessboard, a 16×16 chessboard, etc. as long as there is one square missing. In fact, I can even *prove* that I can tile any $2^n \times 2^n$ chessboard (with one square missing) with angular triominos. But what fun would it be if *I* proved it? None, I tell you, none at all. You go ahead and prove it.

■ **Suggested Time and Emphasis**

$\frac{1}{2}$ class. Optional material.

■ **Points to Stress**

1. The expansion of $(a+b)^n$ for a, b expressions, n a positive integer.

2. The computation of $\binom{n}{r}$ using factorials and using Pascal's triangle.

■ **Sample Questions**

- **Text Question:** Compute $\binom{5}{4}$.

  Answer: 5

- **Drill Question:** Expand $(x+2y)^6$.

  Answer: $(x+2y)^6 = x^6 + 12x^5y + 60x^4y^2 + 160x^3y^3 + 240x^2y^4 + 192xy^5 + 64y^6$

■ **In-Class Materials**

- Point out that some of the formulas previously covered are just special cases of the binomial theorem, for example the formulas for $(x+y)^2$, $(x-y)^2$, $(x+y)^3$, and $(x-y)^3$.

- Pascal's Triangle is actually full of patterns. Have the students see how many they can find. They can look along the diagonals, look down "columns", find the sum of each row, etc. There are some instructors who spend an entire class on patterns visible in Pascal's triangle. As of this writing, the website `http://ptri1.tripod.com` has a good discussion of patterns to be found in Pascal's triangle.

- If every odd number in Pascal's triangle is colored black, and every even number colored white, Sierpinski's triangle is revealed. Students need only do a few rows before the recursive structure is revealed.

- The binomial theorem can be extended to the real numbers, and then some very interesting things happen. First we generalize the definition of $\binom{n}{r}$:

$$\binom{n}{r} = \frac{n(n-1)(n-2)\dots(n-r+1)}{r!}$$

Notice that this is equivalent to our former definition if n and r are positive integers, even if $r > n$ (in that case the numerator will be zero). But this new definition works even if n is an arbitrary real number. Now we can say

$$(a+b)^n = \sum_{r=0}^{\infty} \binom{n}{r} a^r b^{n-r}$$

Notice again that if n is a positive integer, then we are back to the standard binomial theorem, since $\binom{n}{r}$ is 0 for $r > n$. But now we can let $n = -1$ to obtain

$$\frac{1}{x+1} = 1 - x + x^2 - x^3 + x^4 - x^5 + \cdots$$

Similarly, we can let $n = \frac{1}{2}$ to obtain

$$\sqrt{x+1} = 1 + \tfrac{1}{2}x - \tfrac{1}{8}x^2 + \tfrac{1}{16}x^3 - \tfrac{5}{128}x^4 + \cdots$$

with the general term being $(-1)^{n-1} \dfrac{1 \cdot 3 \cdot 5 \cdot 7 \cdot \ldots \cdot (2n-3)}{2^n n!} x^n$.

▨ Examples

- $(4 - \sqrt{x})^5 = 1024 - 1280\sqrt{x} + 640x - 160\left(\sqrt{x}\right)^3 + 20x^2 - \left(\sqrt{x}\right)^5$
- $\left(x + \dfrac{1}{x}\right)^8 = x^8 + 8x^6 + 28x^4 + 56x^2 + 70 + \dfrac{56}{x^2} + \dfrac{28}{x^4} + \dfrac{8}{x^6} + \dfrac{1}{x^8}$.

▨ Group Work

Exercises *XXX*, *XXX*, and *XXX* are particularly well suited for group work.

▨ Homework Problems

Core Exercises: 5, 13, 17, 19, 25, 27, 39, 41

Sample Assignment: 4, 5, 6, 8, 13, 17, 19, 21, 23, 25, 27, 29, 39, 41, 43, 47, 48, 55

CHAPTER 10   Counting and Probability

Suggested Time and Emphasis

1 class. Optional material.

Point to Stress

The fundamental counting principle.

Sample Questions

- **Text Question:** Suppose that two events occur in order. If the first can occur in m ways, and the second in n ways (after the first has occurred) then how many ways can the two events occur together?
  Answer: mn ways

- **Drill Question:** A customer ID consists of a letter followed by a digit, such as A2, K9, B0, or Q1. How many unique customer IDs are there?
  Answer: 260

In-Class Materials

- Point out that the fundamental counting principle works only if the number of possible outcomes at each stage is independent—this is called the condition of uniformity. In other words, one cannot directly use the principle to solve the following problem: How many three-digit numbers are there such that no digit is larger than the first? In this case, there are ten ways to pick the first digit, but the number of ways to pick the second digit *depends* on that first digit. This problem would have to be solved by breaking it up into cases: $2 \cdot 2$ numbers beginning with 1 (100, 101, 110, and 111), $3 \cdot 3$ numbers beginning with 2, etc.

- If doing an example of counting by enumeration, make sure to stress that when listing a large number of objects, students should strive to do so in an organized way. This will reduce the chance of missing items.

- A major concept to get across is the difference between "with replacement" and "without replacement". These concepts are implicit in most of the exercises in the text; it is a good idea to make them explicit. Exercises 4 and 6, for example, confront the issue directly. Discuss Exercise 6: "Can a horse come in first *and* second place?" Exercise 3: "Can you answer 'B' for more than one question?" If students can distinguish clearly between the two concepts, and get into the habit of thinking about them early in the solution process, they will find this subject a lot easier to handle.

- Point out that many game companies use the fundamental counting principle to be able to give a large number of "variations" for their games. For example, when playing a game of Microprose's "Civilization III", you get to make the following choices:

World size	Barbarians	Land Mass	Water Coverage	Climate	Temperature	Age	Difficulty
Tiny	None	Pangea	$\frac{1}{4}$	Arid	Warm	3 billion	Chieftain
Small	Sedentary	Continents	$\frac{1}{2}$	Normal	Temperate	4 billion	Warlord
Standard	Roaming	Archipelago	$\frac{3}{4}$	Wet	Cool	5 billion	Regent
Large	Restless						Monarch
Huge	Raging						Emperor
							Deity

If they wanted to, Microprose could have advertised that Civilization III offers "36,450 different games!" Many game companies do make claims of that nature.

- Permutations can be foreshadowed by doing several problems of selecting objects without replacement when order counts, and having the students try to come up with a general formula. It is straightforward to come up with $nPr = n(n-1)\ldots(n-r+1)$, but with a little prompting they may be able to obtain $\frac{n!}{(n-r)!}$.

- Permutations can be foreshadowed by attempting to use the fundamental counting principle to count the ways of selecting five cards from a set of 52 (order not important), and failing. Point out that the next section will provide a method to do problems such as these.

Examples

- Counting problems that can be done with the counting principle: Numbers like 3215, 3821, 1231, 7777, and 8383 are four-digit numbers. The number 0012 is not a four-digit number, because we normally write it simply as 12. How many four-digit numbers are there? How many are there with no repeated digits?
Answer: $9 \cdot 10 \cdot 10 \cdot 10 = 9000$, $9 \cdot 9 \cdot 8 \cdot 7 = 4536$

- At the race track, you win the daily double by purchasing a ticket and selecting the winners of both of two specified races. If there are six horses running in the first race and eight horses running in the second, how many tickets must you purchase to guarantee a winning selection?
Answer: 48

- A counting problem that cannot be done with the counting principle: How many ways are there to roll a red die, then a yellow die, and then a blue die so the total of all three dice is no more than 5?
Answer: Enumeration gives 10 ways.

Red	1	1	1	1	1	1	2	2	2	3
Yellow	1	1	1	2	2	3	1	1	2	1
Blue	1	2	3	1	2	1	1	2	1	1

Group Work 1: Casting a Show

The second-to-last question does require thought. If the students are expecting to routinely apply formulas, this may take them by surprise. The last question in this activity involves combinations. At this point the students aren't expected to know how to do it, but they should be able to figure out that they don't know how to do it. The biggest danger in any educational endeavor is thinking that you know more than you do. (Of course, some students may be able to figure out how to solve the problem, and they should be duly praised.)

Answers:

1. FDSV, FVSD, SDFV, SVFD; four ways

2. Twelve ways:

$$
\begin{array}{lllll}
\text{Starting with D:} & \text{DFSV} & \text{DVSF} & & \\
\text{Starting with F:} & \text{FDSV} & \text{FDVS} & \text{FSDV} & \text{FSVD} \\
\text{Starting with S:} & \text{SFDV} & \text{SVDF} & & \\
\text{Starting with V:} & \text{VSFD} & \text{VSDF} & \text{VDFS} & \text{VDSF}
\end{array}
$$

3. $12 \cdot 11 \cdot 11 \cdot 10 \cdot 10 \cdot 9 \cdot 9 \cdots \cdots 1 \cdot 1 = 19{,}120{,}211{,}066{,}880{,}000$

4. $23 \cdot 22 = 506$

5. $23 \cdot 23 \cdot 23 \cdot 23 \cdot 23 \cdot 23 \cdot 23 = 3{,}404{,}825{,}447$

6. There are several ways to do this, but all should give the same answer. One way: There are $21 \cdot 20$ ways to finish casting the quartet, ignoring gender. But $9 \cdot 8$ of those are male-male. So the total number of "good" ways is $21 \cdot 20 - 9 \cdot 8 = 348$.

7. There would be $23 \cdot 22 \cdot 21 \cdot 20 \cdot 19$ ways to line them up, but in this case, order doesn't count. So we have overcounted by a factor of $5! = 120$. The answer is $33{,}649$.

▪ Group Work 2: A Slot Machine

If the students get really stuck, you can give them the hint to figure out each possible way to win, and then subtract it from the total number of outcomes. But don't give them hints too soon. The most common student error will be to count the same combination of dials twice. Notice: they do not yet have the knowledge to answer the third question. This activity can be revisited if expected value is to be covered.

Answers:

1. There are $6^3 = 216$ possible outcomes.

2.

Winning Outcome	Number of Possibilities
BAR BAR BAR	1
Other three of a kind	5
Two BARs	15
Cherry Cherry Blackberry	1
Cherry Cherry Orange	1
Cherry Cherry BAR	1
Cherry Anything Anything	$1 \cdot 6 \cdot 6 - 5 = 31$
All three different	$5 \cdot 5 \cdot 4 = 100$

The number of losing outcomes is thus $216 - (1 + 5 + 15 + 1 + 1 + 1 + 31 + 100) = 61$.

3. This seems a generous machine, but one would have to think of expected values to figure out the answer. In the next section we will see that the expected loss on a pull of this machine is seventy-four cents. In other words, it is fairly close.

▪ Homework Problems

Core Exercises: 3, 9, 23

Sample Assignment: 2, 3, 6, 8, 9, 11, 16, 17, 25, 29, 34, 39

GROUP WORK 1, SECTION 10.1
Casting a Show

Last year, I was directing a small show. There were four cast members; two were men (Fred and Shaggy) and two were women (Daphne and Velma). At the very end, I wanted them to take a bow, and thought it would be cute to line them up boy-girl-boy-girl.

1. List all the ways I could have arranged them. How many are there?

2. Right before opening night, Fred and Velma had a big argument. So I had to arrange them so Fred and Velma weren't standing next to each other. That was more important than alternating genders. How many ways could I have arranged them now? List them.

This year I had 12 men and 11 women in the show.

3. How many ways could I arrange them for the bow so that the genders alternated?

4. My show is going to start with an amazing solo number from a cast member, and close with a solo number from a different cast member. How many ways can I cast the solo numbers?

5. The actors aren't very well rehearsed, I'm afraid. In fact, every night they make a lot of mistakes. We have a tradition: the first person who makes a mistake in a given night has to write his or her name on the Calendar of Shame under that night's date. If the show runs for one week, in how many possible ways can the Calendar of Shame be filled out?

6. There is going to be a quartet at one point. Arthur and Steve will definitely be in the quartet. I don't care who else is in the quartet, as long as at least one of the singers is female. How many ways are there to cast the quartet?

7. At one point there will be the big Dance of the Melancholic Elves. We will need to select five cast members to do that dance. How many ways are there to select them?

A Slot Machine

A slot machine has three wheels. Every wheel in a three-wheel slot machine can show you an apple, a cherry, an orange, a lemon, a blackberry or a BAR. (They always capitalize "BAR"; I don't know why.) For the purposes of discussion, assume that it each outcome is equally likely for each wheel. (This is not the case for most real slot machines) You put four dollars in, and you get an outcome such as: "apple cherry pear", "orange BAR orange", or "cherry cherry cherry".

Here are the payouts:

Outcome			Payout
BAR	BAR	BAR	$100
Other three of a kind			$40
Two BARs			$15
Cherry	Cherry	Blackberry	$5
Cherry	Cherry	Orange	$5
Cherry	Cherry	BAR	$5
Cherry	Anything	Anything	$2
All three different			$1

You get only the single highest payout for any outcome. In other words, if you get BAR BAR BAR you get $100; you don't get $100 for the three BARs and an additional $15 for also having two. Don't be greedy!

It looks like a great slot machine! There are lots of ways to win, and even if you are very unlucky and get all three wheels different, you get a dollar back!

1. How many possible outcomes are there of a spin?

2. How many of those outcomes cause you to lose your $4 entirely?

3. Is putting a dollar into this machine a good investment?

Suggested Time and Emphasis

1 class. Optional material.

Points to Stress

1. Definitions of $P(n, r)$ and $C(n, r)$.

2. Formulas for $P(n, r)$ and $C(n, r)$.

3. The partition formula: $\dfrac{n!}{n_1! \, n_2! \, \cdots \, n_r!}$.

Sample Questions

- **Text Question:** What is the difference between a permutation and a combination?

  Answer: Order matters in a permutation, not in a combination.

- **Drill Question:** Compute $C(10, 8)$.

  Answer: 45

In-Class Materials

- Notice that there are four common possibilities for counting problems:

  1. Order counts and there is no replacement.

  2. Order does not count and there is no replacement.

  3. Order counts and there is replacement.

  4. Order does not count and there is replacement.

The first case is $P(n, r)$ and the second is $C(n, r)$. The fundamental counting principle gives us the third case: n^r. The fourth case is actually tricky: there is no simple formula that gives the answer. Have the students come up with examples to illustrate each case, such as the following:

  1. How many ways are there to assign first and second prizes to ten dogs at a dog show?

  2. How many ways are there to pick three dogs to take home at a dog show?

  3. How many ways are there to choose which family member or members walk the dogs on Monday, Tuesday and Wednesday?

  4. How many combinations of breeds are possible for the three dogs selected at the show?

In Case 4, assume there are four breeds to choose from. The twenty choices are 111, 112, 113, 114, 122, 123, 124, 133, 134, 144, 222, 223, 224, 233, 234, 244, 333, 334, 344, and 444.

Note that the above means that a "combination lock" should really be called a "permutation lock".

- If you get bored of doing examples from the standard deck of cards, you can discuss a Euchre deck. The game of Euchre is played primarily in the Midwestern United States and in Ontario. Many people believe that the Joker playing card gets its name from a mispronunciation of the German spelling of Euchre. The Euchre deck consists of the nines, tens, Jacks, Queens, Kings, and Aces. A Euchre hand consists of five cards. Lead the students in determining the number of ways to get a flush with a Euchre deck. A very good

Euchre hand will have two jacks and an Ace, all of the same color. Lead the students in figuring out how many possible very good Euchre hands there are, and how many total Euchre hands there are.

- Tie this material to the earlier discussion of binomial expansions. When multiplying out $(a+b)^2 = (a+b)(a+b) = aa + ab + ab + bb$, we are really taking all possible combinations of an item of the first term and an item of the second. So if we consider $(a+b)^{23}$ and we want to find the coefficient of $a^{10}b^{13}$, we are really asking how many ways are there to select ten as from the 23 terms. The answer is $\binom{23}{10}$, as predicted by the binomial theorem.

- Remind the students that there is often more than one correct way to solve a problem. For example, assume that a band has recorded twenty songs, and there is enough room on a CD for twelve of them. How many ways are there to arrange the CD? One way to think about this is a two step process: There are $C(20, 12)$ ways to select the songs, and then $P(12, 12)$ ways to arrange them. The other way to think about it is as a straightforward application of the fundamental counting principle: 20 ways to pick the first song, 19 ways to pick the second, and so on, giving
$$(20)(19)(18)(17)(16)(15)(14)(13)(12)(11)(10)(9) = 60{,}339{,}831{,}552{,}000$$

▪ Examples

- If there are one hundred teddy bears in a store, how many ways are there to give one to each of three children?
Answer: $100 \cdot 99 \cdot 98 = 970{,}200$

- Assume you are going to pick three bears at random, and bring them home and allow the children to fight over them as they will. How many ways are there to do that?
Answer: $C(100, 3) = 161{,}700$

▪ Group Work: The Large Lecture Class

This activity gives the students a variety of examples to work with. If a group finishes early, ask them to come up with three more questions, answer them, and pass the questions (without answer) to the next group that finishes.

Answers:

1. By one perspective, the answer is 5^{68}. But the real answer is of course 1. The students will get precisely the grades they earn.

2. $C(68, 10) = 290{,}752{,}384{,}208$

3. $\dfrac{10!}{1!4!3!2!} = 12{,}600$

4. $10 \cdot 20 \cdot 20 \cdot 10 \cdot 8 = 320{,}000$

5. There are two ways to arrange the A and F students (AF and FA) and then 4! ways to make the line, counting the A and F students as a block. The total is thus $2(4!) = 48$.

6. $\dfrac{5!}{5} = 24$

Homework Problems

Core Exercises: 23, 33, 39, 43, 47, 51, 61, 63, 65, 71, 77

Sample Assignment: 3, 4, 9, 10, 23, 33, 35, 39, 40, 41, 43, 47, 50, 51, 55, 56, 57, 61, 63, 65, 68, 71, 74, 77

GROUP WORK, SECTION 10.2
The Large Lecture Class

I am teaching a course with 68 students in it. At the end of the semester, each student will receive a grade: A, B, C, D, or F.

1. How many possible ways are there for me to assign grades to the students?

2. I was very lucky to get ten free tickets to a local production of a musical adaptation of Lord Tennyson's *Dogs*. Of course, I'm going to give them to my beloved students. How many ways are there to select which students get the tickets?

3. The ten students come to my office to get their tickets. Oh no! There are several types! There is one gold ticket that allows the bearer to get backstage. There are four red front row tickets, three blue mezzanine tickets, and two puce balcony tickets. How many ways are there for me to determine which students get which tickets?

4. At the end of the course, there were 10 As, 20 Bs, 20 Cs, 10 Ds, and 8 Fs. I wish to create a focus group of students to give me feedback about the course. The group will consist of five students, each of whom received a different grade. How many ways are there to select a focus group?

5. At the end of the focus group meeting, I line the group up to take a picture. In a touching show of solidarity, the A and the F student insist on standing next to each other in the picture. How many ways are there to line them all up, subject to that constraint?

6. Finally, we all go out for dinner. All six of us sit at a circular table. How many ways are there for us to sit? Remember, since the table is circular, these two configurations are considered to be the same:

	A B		F D	
D		C	Teacher	A
	F Teacher		C B	

■ Suggested Time and Emphasis

1–2 classes. Optional material.

■ Points to Stress

1. Computing the probability of an individual event.
2. Probability of the union of events, mutually exclusive and otherwise.
3. Probability of the intersection of independent events.

■ Sample Questions

- **Text Question:**

  (a) Give an example of two mutually exclusive events.

  (b) Give an example of two independent events.

  Answers will vary

- **Drill Question:** Assume a bag has three black balls, five green balls, and twenty white balls. If you draw one ball from the bag, what is the probability that it is green?

  Answer: $\frac{5}{28} \approx 18\%$

■ In-Class Materials

- The text presents a way to think about a statement like, "the probability is one-sixth." That statement is interpreted to mean

$$\frac{\text{Number of good outcomes}}{\text{Number of possible outcomes}} = \frac{1}{6}$$

Another way to interpret the statement is using experimental probability. In that interpretation, "the probability is one-sixth" means

$$\frac{\text{The number of good outcomes}}{\text{The total number of trials}} \to \frac{1}{6}$$

If you have a die and want to know the probability of rolling a one, the first interpretation is appropriate. If you know of a convoluted solitaire game, and it is too complex to figure out the probability of winning, you may just have a computer play one billion games and take the number of wins and divide by one billion. (Or, in the real world, to see the probability of a particular drug curing a disease, apply the drug to a large sample and see what percent of them get better, and then do it again to a control group to find the probability the disease goes away by itself.)

- An excellent example of a surprising probability result is Buffon's needle problem, named after the mathematician Georges-Louis Leclerc, Comte de Buffon (1707–1788). Take a needle and a large piece of paper with parallel lines on it. The distance between the parallel lines should be equal to the length of the needle. Ask the class what they think the probability is that, if you drop the needle, it will touch one of the lines. Perhaps do the experiment. The probability turns out to be approximately 0.64. The interesting thing is that the exact answer is $\frac{2}{\pi}$. So one can determine π by doing the experiment many times, dividing the answer by two, and taking the reciprocal. (As of this writing, an electronic demonstration of this experiment is available at http://www.angelfire.com/wa/hurben/buff.html.)

- The students can be asked to find the probability that a given randomly selected two- or three-letter "word" is actually an English word. They can try this experimentally, or they can write out all the two- and three-letter words and do this mathematically. If you have the time and the mischievousness, you may want to have them try to figure out all the two letter words by hand to solve this problem. According to the current Scrabble dictionary, there are 101 two-letter words and 1015 three-letter words, so the probabilities of randomly obtaining an English word are approximately 14.9% and 5.7%.

  In case there is interest, the two letter words are aa, ab, ad, ae, ag, ah, ai, al, am, an, ar, as, at, aw, ax, ay, ba, be, bi, bo, by, de, do, ed, ef, eh, el, em, en, er, es, et, ex, fa, fe, go, ha, he, hi, hm, ho, id, if, in, is, it, jo, ka, ki, la, li, lo, ma, me, mi, mm, mo, mu, my, na, ne, no, nu, od, oe, of, oh, oi, om, on, op, or, os, ow, ox, oy, pa, pe, pi, qi, re, sh, si, so, ta, ti, to, uh, um, un, up, us, ut, we, wo, xi, xu, ya, ye, yo, and za.

  (Aa: Rough, cindery lava. Ae: One. Ar: The letter 'R'. Ba: Eternal soul. Et: Past tense of 'to eat'. Jo: Sweetheart. Li: Chinese unit of distance. Od: Hypothetical force. Oe: Faeroe Islands whirlwind. Op: Type of abstract art from the 1960s. Os: bone. Un: One. Ut: Musical tone, now called do. Xu: Vietnamese monetary unit. Za: Ask your students.)

- Some areas are notoriously hard to compute. If, for example, the boundary of an area is a fractal or is given by a particularly messy function, even calculus will not allow us to determine the area. One method mathematicians use is the "Monte Carlo method." Take the region in question, and put it in a square. (For simplicity, say the square has side length of ten units. If the region won't fit, choose a bigger square.) Randomly select points of the square, and experimentally determine the probability that a randomly selected point is in the region. We know that this probability is equal to the area of the region divided by the area of the square, so after we have determined the probability, we can solve for the area of the region.

- In the media, probabilities are often given in the form of "odds". This is a good bit of vocabulary to share with your students:

Probability	**Odds For**	**Odds Against**
$\dfrac{\text{Good outcomes}}{\text{Total possible outcomes}}$	Good outcomes : Bad outcomes	Bad outcomes : Good outcomes

So if, for example, you were playing a game which involved drawing a card and trying to get an ace, we could express the chances in the following ways:

Probability	**Odds For**	**Odds Against**
$\frac{4}{52} = \frac{1}{13}$	$1 : 12$ for	$12 : 1$ against

Examples

- A particular game of Powerball goes as follows. There are 49 white balls of which five are chosen. There are 42 red balls of which one is chosen. If your ticket matches the chosen balls, you win the jackpot. Yay, you! What is the percent chance that a given ticket will win the Powerball?

  Answer: $\dfrac{1}{C(49,5)\,42} = \dfrac{1}{80{,}089{,}128} \approx 1.24861 \times 10^{-8}$

- My dorm floor had three positions to fill: President, Vice President, and Sergeant-at-Arms-and-Legs (don't ask). Assume there were 60 people on my floor. If the offices were filled randomly, what is the probability I would end up an officer?

Answer: $\dfrac{C(60,2)}{C(60,3)} = \dfrac{3}{58} \approx 5.2\%$

- At the race track, you win the "daily double" by purchasing a ticket and selecting the winners of both of two specified races. Assuming that all outcomes are equally likely (and many would say this is a false assumption,) if there are six horses running in the first race and eight in the second, what is the probability of winning the daily double?

Answer: $\frac{1}{48} \approx 2.1\%$

■ Group Work 1: Probability Practice

This is a straightforward activity involving the concepts from the section.

Answers:

1. $\frac{1}{8}$ **2.** $\frac{3}{8}$

3. $\frac{3}{56}$. Note that the events are not independent! So we use the Fundamental Theorem of Counting to get 3 good outcomes and $8 \cdot 7$ total outcomes.

4. $\frac{1}{8} + \frac{3}{8} - \frac{3}{56} = \frac{25}{56}$ **5.** $\frac{7}{8}$

6. Answers will vary. Sample answer: $C =$ "The first crayon I picked was violet."

7. Answers will vary. This is actually a tough problem, if the students restrict themselves to events involving the colors of chosen crayons. Sample answer: $D =$ "It rained on the day I picked the crayons."

■ Group Work 2: The Multiple-Choice Test

Students all too often spend a lot of time determining probability tables such as the one shown, rather than spending that time learning the subject in question. The last problem involves the concept of "odds". Perhaps give them this activity without first discussing the concept, to see if they can figure out the answer based on the use of the term in popular culture.

Answers:

1. 0.035 **2.** 0.5 **3.** 0.85

4. P (Parents happy) $+ P$ (Zorak happy) $- P$ (Both happy)

$$= (0.05 + 0.02 + 0.01 + 0.005) + (0.10 + 0.05) - 0.05 = 0.185$$

5. $13 : 7$ against

■ Homework Problems

Core Exercises: 5, 7, 19, 23, 25, 43, 53, 65

Sample Assignment: 3, 5, 7, 9, 10, 13, 14, 19, 23, 25, 27, 31, 34, 35, 42, 43, 51, 52, 53, 58, 59, 65, 66, 70, 73

GROUP WORK 1, SECTION 10.3
Probability Practice

I have a box of 8 new crayons: red, orange, yellow, green, blue, indigo, violet, and mauve. I pick two different ones at random. Let A be the event "the first one I picked was green" and B be the event "the color of the second one I picked ended with the letter 'e'".

Compute the following probabilities:

1. $P(A)$

2. $P(B)$

3. $P(A \text{ and } B)$

4. $P(A \text{ or } B)$

5. $P(\text{not } A)$

6. Come up with a new event C regarding the crayons. Make sure that A and C are mutually exclusive.

7. Come up with a new event D. Make sure that A and D are independent.

GROUP WORK 2, SECTION 10.3
The Multiple-Choice Test

Brak takes a multiple choice test every day, and guesses on many of the questions. So, as you can imagine, his test scores vary quite a bit, due to chance. The following table gives his probability on scoring in various ranges on a given day:

Score	P (Score)
100	0.005
95–99	0.01
90–95	0.02
85–89	0.05
75–79	0.15
70–74	0.35
65–69	0.15
60–64	0.10
Below 60	0.065

1. What is the probability that Brak will score 90 or higher?

2. What is the probability that he will score between 70 and 79?

3. What is the probability that he will not score in the 80s?

4. Brak's parents want him to score 85 or above. Brak's best friend Zorak wants him to score between 80 and 89. (He doesn't want Brak to "wreck the curve".) Nobody else really cares how he scores. What is the probability that at least one of his well-wishers will be pleased?

5. Vegas Johnny the bookmaker is taking bets on Brak's performance. What are the odds that Brak will score between 70 and 74 on the test?

10.4 | Binomial Probability

Suggested Time and Emphasis

$\frac{1}{2}$ class. Optional material.

Point to Stress

The derivation and use of the binomial probability formula.

Sample Questions

- **Text Question:** In the context of this section, if the probability of a "success" is p, is it possible to determine the probability of a failure? If so, what is it?
  Answer: Yes, $1 - p$
- **Drill Question:** On a given night, the probability that my cat will wake me up by vomiting on the bed is $\frac{2}{7}$. What is the probability that he will so wake me on exactly 3 days of a given week?
  Answer: $C(7,3)\left(\frac{2}{7}\right)^3\left(\frac{5}{7}\right)^4 \approx 0.2125$

In-Class Materials

- The derivation of the binomial probability formula is very straightforward and should not be skipped. The text has a nice, quick explanation that can be discussed, perhaps using a die instead of a coin for variety.
- Point out a very non-intuitive aspect of Example 2. With a sample size of only ten, we are able to make a strong conclusion about the probability of a drug's effectiveness. Note that sample sizes used by statisticians are often surprisingly small to the layperson. In the year 2002, for example, there were only 5000 "Nielsen families" that determined the national ratings for television shows in the United States. (For local ratings, each of only 210 local markets has an additional 500 Nielsen households.)
- If your local lottery was discussed (in Section 9.4 we discussed the Powerball, for example) you can point out that some people play every week, hoping to win "one of these days". If you have not already done so, compute the probability of winning the lottery on a given day. Then compute the probability of winning at least once if you play every week (or every day, depending on the frequency of the game).
- Many people misunderstand the role of skill in games where skill and chance combine. For example, consider the game of Cribbage. Assume that Tracy is so much better than Paul that she wins three times as much as he does. (Given that cribbage is played with cards, and has some degree of luck to it, she must be very much better to overcome the vagaries of chance.) Assume they play once a day for a week. Have the students guess the chance that she will win every game. Repeat for two weeks. Then compute the chance that Paul wins two or fewer games.

Examples

- When I play the "throw a dart" game at the carnival, I have a five percent chance of winning a doll.
  1. What is the probability I will win at least one doll if I play ten times?
     Answer: $1 - C(10,0)\left(\frac{1}{20}\right)^0\left(\frac{19}{20}\right)^{10} \approx 40\%$
  2. I have two children! What is the probability I will win at least two dolls if I play twenty times?
     Answer: $1 - C(10,0)\left(\frac{1}{20}\right)^0\left(\frac{19}{20}\right)^{10} - C(10,1)\left(\frac{1}{20}\right)^1\left(\frac{19}{20}\right)^9 \approx 8.6\%$

3. How many times do I have to play in order to have a 75% chance of winning at least two dolls?

Answer: 36 times

■ Group Work 1: Who Will Catch More Fish?

Students may think that there is a quick one-line way to answer this question. There is not—there are several cases to compute. The students should use the fact that they are in a group to their advantage, and divide up the work. This activity can be made a bit harder by asking the questions in a different order.

Answers:

For clarity we make the following computations, (not all of which are used in solving this problem)

$$P\,(\text{Doug catches }0) \approx 73.5\% \qquad P\,(\text{Laurel catches }0) \approx 37.7\%$$
$$P\,(\text{Doug catches }1) \approx 23.2\% \qquad P\,(\text{Laurel catches }1) \approx 39.9\%$$
$$P\,(\text{Doug catches }2) \approx 3.05\% \qquad P\,(\text{Laurel catches }2) \approx 17.6\%$$
$$P\,(\text{Doug catches }3) \approx 0.21\% \qquad P\,(\text{Laurel catches }3) \approx 4.15\%$$
$$P\,(\text{Doug catches }4) \text{ is negligible} \qquad P\,(\text{Laurel catches }4) \approx 0.55\%$$
$$P\,(\text{Doug catches }5) \text{ is negligible} \qquad P\,(\text{Laurel catches }5) \text{ is negligible}$$
$$P\,(\text{Doug catches }6) \text{ is negligible} \qquad P\,(\text{Laurel catches }6) \text{ is negligible}$$

1. $P\,(\text{Doug catches }0 \text{ and Laurel catches }0) \approx 0.735 \cdot 0.377 = 0.277095 \approx 27.7\%$

2. $P\,(\text{Doug catches }1 \text{ and Laurel catches fewer than }2)$

$$+\, P\,(\text{Doug catches }2 \text{ and Laurel catches fewer than }4)$$

$$+\, P\,(\text{Doug catches }3 \text{ and Laurel catches fewer than }6)$$

$$\approx 0.232\,(0.377 + 0.399) + 0.0305\,(0.377 + 0.399 + 0.176 + 0.0415)$$

$$+\, 0.0021\,(0.377 + 0.399 + 0.176 + 0.0415 + 0.0055 + 0)$$

$$\approx 0.21243165 \approx 21.2\%$$

3. $1 - 0.277095 - 0.21243165 = 0.51047335 \approx 51\%$

■ Group Work 2: Is It Due to Chance?

Students may need a bit of help in getting started, because the problem never states the probability that Gordon will win a particular backgammon tournament. In fact, that is the very fact they are disputing. Prompt the students to assume that the percent chance of a win for Gordon is 50%, and then figure out the probability that this tournament outcome is due to chance. Students may make the mistake of just computing the probability that Gordon wins exactly nine games. The pertinent question is the probability he will win nine *or more*.

If a group finishes early, ask them to take it a step further, and try assuming that Gordon's probability was 60%, and then that his probability was 40%. Another interesting way to extend the problem is to ask the students to redo the problem assuming that Gordon won 11 games while Bruce won only 4.

Answer:

If Gordon and Bruce were equally good, then the probability of this outcome happening by chance is 30%, which isn't all that unreasonable. It is not yet valid to conclude that Gordon is the better player. After another 15 years, if the outcomes are similar, Gordon's case will become stronger.

▣ Group Work 3: The Bingo Problem

There are many places where Bingo is legal, either at casinos or as fund-raisers. This activity is based on a true story. This was designed with a solution sheet to hand out, so this can be used as an out-of-class group activity with an answer sheet. In Bingo, there are 75 numbers that are drawn. The Ns are between 31 and 45, and there is a free space in the N column.

▣ Homework Problems

Core Exercises: 21, 35

Sample Assignment: 2, 3, 5, 6, 12, 17, 20, 21, 25, 29, 31, 33, 35

GROUP WORK 1, SECTION 10.4
Who Will Catch More Fish?

Laurel and Douglas go fishing at her mother's house in the woods. Laurel has been fishing all her life, and is rather good at it. In fact, every time she casts her line, she has a 15% chance of catching a fish. Douglas has never fished before. The first time Laurel handed him a worm, he named it "Fabian" and refused to impale it on a hook. He eventually consents to using a lure, and has only a 5% chance of catching a fish every time he casts his line. Laurel boasts that she can catch twice as many fish as he can. He takes exception to this, and they decide to have a contest. Each will cast six times. If Laurel catches twice as many fish as Douglas, then Douglas has to clean all the fish. If she does not, she has to take Fabian home with her and keep him as a pet. They agree that if neither catches any fish, the bet is off. (Laurel points out that if neither catches any fish, then technically she has caught twice as many, but agrees to be a good sport about it.)

1. What is the probability that the bet is called off because neither of them catches a fish?

2. What is the probability that Douglas will win the bet?

3. What is the probability that Laurel will win the bet?

GROUP WORK 2, SECTION 10.4
Is It Due to Chance?

Gordon and Bruce are brothers who like to play backgammon. Every Thanksgiving when they get together at their parent's house, they have a backgammon tournament. Here are the outcomes for the past fifteen years:

Year	Tournament winner
1990	Gordon
1991	Bruce
1992	Gordon
1993	Gordon
1994	Bruce
1995	Gordon
1996	Gordon
1997	Bruce
1998	Gordon
1999	Bruce
2000	Bruce
2001	Gordon
2002	Gordon
2003	Bruce
2004	Gordon

Gordon maintains that he is better at backgammon than Bruce. Bruce disagrees, and says that they are equally good, but Gordon tends to be lucky. Use the science of probability to analyze their dispute. Who do you think is right, and why?

GROUP WORK 3, SECTION 10.4
The Bingo Problem

Last Friday, my friend Laurel and I were due to go to the St. Paul Winter Carnival. We were in the car, and we suddenly got this... urge. "BINGO!" we yelled, and off to Shakopee we went, to play BINGO at Mystic Lake.

We lost our money, but had a good time. The pace of the game surprised us. The number to be called would be shown on a large television screen, there would be a pause, and then the number would be called. So, if someone was going to BINGO on, say, B7, the B7 would come up on the screen, there would be a pause, the caller would call "B7!" and then the winner would call "BINGO!"

Observation 1: It is hard to cover all the numbers in time, because you have to play at least 12 cards to be allowed in the BINGO room.

Observation 2: Some of those people move *fast*! They could cover their 12 cards while still making sure that Laurel and I didn't miss any.

Observation 3: Before BINGO was called, the more experienced people would tear their cards up. In other words, they *knew* that BINGO was going to be called before they had any apparent way of knowing.

This latter observation really annoyed Laurel and me. How did these people psychically know that BINGO was going to be called?

Laurel and I were at a friendly table, so at one point we asked our neighbor, "How did you know to tear your sheet up before the number was called?"

He replied, "They called four Ns. You know that someone is going to BINGO after four Ns."

I couldn't believe that. He had no way of *knowing*. So I wondered, what is the probability that there is at least one BINGO after the fourth N?

GROUP WORK 3, SECTION 10.4
Solution and Postscript to the Bingo Problem

The number of possible combinations of numbers that can appear in the N column is

$$\binom{15}{4} = \frac{15!}{11!\,4!} = \frac{15 \cdot 14 \cdot 13 \cdot 12}{4 \cdot 3 \cdot 2} = 15 \cdot 7 \cdot 13 = 1365$$

Therefore, if four Ns are called, the chances of winning on a particular card are $\frac{1}{1365}$.

Assume that there are P people playing BINGO. There are (at least) 12 cards per person, by house rules. So say there are $12P$ cards. We want to compute the probability of at least one winner. It turns out that this is a hard computation (You would have to add up the probability of one winner, plus the probability of two winners, plus the probability of three winners, all the way up to the probability of $12P$ winning cards.) A much easier way is to find out the probability of *no* winner, and subtract from 100%.

The probability of a given card not winning is $1 - \frac{1}{1365} = \frac{1364}{1365}$.

The probability of no winners is then $\left(\frac{1364}{1365}\right)^{12P}$ and the probability of at least one winner is $1 - \left(\frac{1364}{1365}\right)^{12P}$ (multiplied by 100 to get a percentage, if you like).

There were about 300 people playing BINGO. So the probability that at least one person was going to call "BINGO!" and hence the probability that my BINGO colleagues weren't being premature in their paper perforation, was about 93%. So it turns out that they would be wrong roughly one in fourteen times. Ho ho! They *were* being silly!

I have since called the Mystic Lake BINGO manager and found out three interesting facts.

Fact 1: He said that 300 players would be a "slow night". He was nice enough to ask around and find out that there were about 450 people playing BINGO on the night in question.

Fact 2: He said that a significant number of people play more than the 12 cards that they get for admission, but didn't know what the average was. Let's assume that the average person plays 13.5 cards. (You buy the "extra" cards in threes, and I'm conservatively assuming that, on average, every other person has bought one.) Combining this estimate with Fact 1 gives us the revised figure of 98.8%, making my BINGO mentors correct 85 out of 86 times, if not more. Wow.

Fact 3: Being, at core, a pleasant enough fellow, I told the Mystic Lake BINGO manager about my reasons for wanting to know this stuff, and my preliminary results. He listened patiently to my 93% figure, then I gave him my revised 98.8% figure. And he responded thusly:

"Well, that's a very interesting fact. But, y'know, the reason they're tearing their cards isn't because four Ns were called. When yer experienced players get BINGO, they'll wave to their floor attendant before the number's called on the speaker, so she's there as soon as it's called, so they speed up their payoff. So when a BINGO is possible, yer experienced players look around for someone waving their hand, and then once several people are tearing their sheets up, everyone hears it and tears up their own, figurin' that most people basically know what they're doin'."

I think I'll stick to the Winter Carnival next year.

▪ Suggested Time and Emphasis

$\frac{1}{2}$ class. Optional material.

▪ Point to Stress

Definition and applications of expected value.

▪ Sample Questions

- **Text Question:** I'm going to roll a die. I'll pay you a dollar if I roll a 1, and three dollars if I roll an even number. What is the expected value of this game?
  Answer: $\frac{5}{3} \approx \$1.67$

- **Drill Question:** Is it possible for the expected value of a game to be $3.50 if you can only win a whole number of dollars at the game? Why or why not?
  Answer: Sure. If you flip a coin and get $4 for heads and $3 for tails, the expected value is $3.50.

▪ In-Class Materials

- Describe the law of large numbers. If you play a game long enough, your average winnings will approach your expectation. But there are no guarantees for the short term. If you have a 99.9% chance of losing a dollar and a 0.1% chance of winning $10,000, the game has a highly positive expected value, but it would be a bad idea to play without a dollar in your pocket.

- Several of the suggested problems from earlier sections can be reformulated as expected value questions. For example, if you have computed the probability of winning a lottery, it isn't hard to compute the expected value of a lottery ticket. See the In-Class Materials in Section 9.4 of this guide for the rules and payouts of a sample Powerball lottery.

- The concept of expected value can be used to foreshadow the idea of standard deviation. Consider these two deals:
  Game 1: You pay one hundred dollars to play. There is a one in a thousand chance of winning $101,000.
  Game 2: I give you a dollar, no questions asked.
  Ask your students which game they would rather play. Let them discuss and debate (fostering debate if necessary). Point out that both games have the same expected value, but they are qualitatively different. The fact that people have preferences one way or another shows that they are different. Now you can discuss the idea of standard deviation.

▪ Examples

- I had a garage sale. 50% of the people didn't buy anything, 30% of the people spent $5, and 20% spent $10. What is the expected value of a sale?
  Answer: $3.50

- Pick a number at random between 1 and 333. If the number is divisible by 3, I give you $10. If not, you give me $10. What is the expected value of this game for you?
  Answer: $-\frac{10}{3} = -\$3.33$, unless of course you know the rules in advance, in which case it is $10.

- The Illinois State Lottery used to have a Daily Game. You would pick a three-digit number. They would pick one at random, and if they matched, they would give you $500. A ticket cost $1. What was the expected value of the Daily Game?
  Answer: $-\$0.50$

■ Group Work 1: The Wheel of Fate

Don't overexplain this one. Perhaps, before handing out the activity, remind the students that the area of a circular sector is $\frac{1}{2}\theta r^2$ where θ is measured in radians. You can allow them to assume that the radius of the circle is 1; it turns out not to matter.

There are two ways to look at Problems 1(b) and 2(b). The students can make a decision based on the chance of having to pay over $1, or they can think about the expected value of a sundae (or a grade). Discuss both approaches at the end.

Answers:

1. (a) 54% (b) 94.6 cents   (c) See instructions; the answer is controversial.

2. (a) $\theta \geq 150$

     (b) If $\theta = 100$, there is a 39% chance of getting less than 80% on the test. The expected value is 80.97%. The students can discuss whether or not the risk is worth it.

■ Group Work 2: The Frequency Table

This activity requires the students to figure out how to compute probabilities from a frequency table

Answer: $\frac{400}{706}(-10) + \frac{195}{706}(0) + \frac{75}{706}(10) + \frac{30}{706}(20) + \frac{5}{706}(90) + \frac{1}{706}(240) \approx -\$2.78$

■ Group Work 2: The One-Turn Board Game

Feel free to change this game around in any way to make it more fun for your particular class. The students will have to apply a bit of the lessons they've learned from the previous sections.

Answer: $\frac{209}{36} \approx 5.81$

■ Homework Problems

Core Exercises: 3, 13

Sample Assignment: 2, 3, 4, 6, 13, 14, 15, 17, 21

The Wheel of Fate

1. In Westbury, New York, there used to be an ice-cream store that offered its young customers a special deal. They could buy a hot-fudge sundae for $1.00, or spin the Sundae Wheel and pay the price upon which the spinner stopped. The Sundae Wheel (and the store that housed it) no longer exist, but the author remembers it as looking something like this:

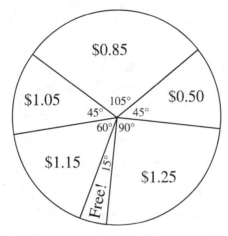

(a) What is the probability of a sundae costing over $1.00?

(b) What is the expected value for the cost of a sundae?

(c) In light of parts (a) and (b), would you rather pay a dollar for the sundae, or choose to spin the wheel? Why?

2. One young person who loved eating sundaes at the store grew up and became a math professor. He had the idea of allowing students to take a certain quiz, or (instead) opt to spin...

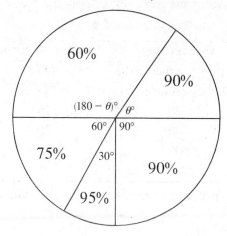

(While this idea was still in its planning stages, it was vetoed by the department head.)

Now, assume that you think you can score 80% on the quiz.

(a) What angle would θ have to be in order to give you at least a 75% chance of spinning a grade of at least 80%?

(b) If θ was $100°$, would you take the quiz or spin? Why? Which would give you the best score, on average?